'John Yandell's remarkable book will be an inspiration for teachers of literature at every level. Here are children reading and discussing texts together with confidence and pleasure, not as recipients of the culture, but as makers of it. Yandell writes with passion, knowledge and rare intellectual energy. His book should certainly be read as a challenge to much government policy. It should also fill us with optimism.'

Jane Miller, Professor Emeritus, Institute of Education, University of London

'This is an optimistic book, imbued with a vision of social democracy that provides a powerful counterpoint to the reform agenda of neoliberal governments around the world in their attempts to subordinate schooling to the interests of a corporate economy. ... [It] provides a model of rigorous scholarship and sustained inquiry into classrooms. Yet it is not written from outside the scenes it describes, but from the standpoint of someone who is deeply respectful of what these English teachers do. ... Because of its congruence with the richness and complexity of the semiotic exchanges that occur within classroom settings, [*The Social Construction of Meaning*] is a far more persuasive account of teaching and learning than the standardized tests that neoliberal governments privilege in their attempts to make schools and teachers accountable.'

Brenton Doecke, Professor of Education, Deakin University, Melbourne, Australia

'*The Social Construction of Meaning* shows the energy, thoughtfulness and commitment of students and teachers in English classrooms. Its generosity of vision offers a way out of the present miasma of educational "reforms". It shows how we may recognize the resourcefulness and potential of the young as our one great social resource for an optimistic future.'

Gunther Kress, Professor of Semiotics and Education, Institute of Education, University of London

The Social Construction of Meaning

This book takes a fresh look at secondary urban English classrooms and at what happens when students and their teachers explore literature collaboratively. By closely examining what happens in English lessons, minute by minute, it reveals how literary texts function not as a valorised heritage to be transmitted, but as a resource for the students' work of cultural production and contestation.

The reading that is undertaken in classrooms has tended to be construed as either a poor substitute or merely a preparation for other reading, particularly for that paradigmatic literacy event, the absorbed and simultaneously discriminating consumption of the literary text by the independent, private reader. This book argues for a different understanding of what constitutes reading, an understanding that is informed by historical and ethnographic perspectives and by psychological and semiotic theory. It presents the case for a conception of reading as an active, collaborative process of meaning-making and for a fully social model of learning. Drawing extensively on data gathered through classroom observation and filming of English lessons taught over the course of a year by two teachers in a London secondary school, the book explores students' engagement with literary texts and the pedagogy that facilitates this engagement.

The book offers new insights into reading, and reading literature in particular. It challenges the paradigm of reading that is offered in government policy and the assumption, common to much work within the field of 'new literacies', that 'schooled literacy' is the already-known, the default, against which the alternative literacy practices of homes and communities can be defined. It will be valuable reading for researchers, teachers, teacher educators and postgraduate students, and will have particular appeal for those with an interest in the fields of English studies and literacy.

John Yandell taught in inner London secondary schools for 20 years before moving to the Institute of Education, University of London, UK. He is the editor of *Changing English: Studies in Culture and Education*.

Routledge Research in Education

The Social Construction of Meaning

Reading literature in urban English classrooms

John Yandell

Routledge
Taylor & Francis Group

LONDON AND NEW YORK

First published 2014
by Routledge
2 Park Square, Milton Park, Abingdon, Oxon OX14 4RN

and by Routledge
711 Third Avenue, New York, NY 10017

Routledge is an imprint of the Taylor & Francis Group, an informa business

© 2014 John Yandell

British Library Cataloguing in Publication Data
A catalogue record for this book is available from the British Library

Library of Congress Cataloging in Publication Data
A catalog record for this book has been requested

ISBN: 978-0-415-85599-0 (hbk)
ISBN: 978-0-203-72833-8 (ebk)

Typeset in Galliard
by RefineCatch Ltd, Bungay, Suffolk

To the students at Wharfside School, whose meaning-making is at the heart of this book, and to Monica and Neville, their teachers.

Contents

Acknowledgements

Given that what follows is, *inter alia*, an attempt to construct an argument for a social model of learning, it is to be expected that a complete account of my indebtedness would be interminable. Of necessity, then, I will make do with a mention only of my largest and most generous creditors.

Tony Burgess and Jane Miller, my PGCE tutors at the London Institute of Education in 1984, opened my eyes to the complexities and the endless fascination of classrooms and what goes on in them. They taught me to attend to the histories of the learners I would encounter in such places.

I am grateful to all the colleagues with whom I have worked at the Institute of Education: to Gill Anderson, Richard Andrews, Jeff Bezemer, Theo Bryer, Caroline Daly, Deirdre Diffley-Pierce, Anton Franks, John Hardcastle, Carey Jewitt, Gunther Kress, Morlette Lindsay, Di Mavers, Anne Turvey and Cathie Wallace. I am also grateful to Ken Jones, of Goldsmiths, University of London, and to Brenton Doecke, of Deakin University, Melbourne, both of whom have been kind enough to read drafts of this book. My life has been the richer for the conversations about English and learning, about meaning-making and development, that I have been lucky enough to have had with all of them.

Without the consent of the headteacher at Wharfside School, and without the amused forbearance of its students, none of this research would have been possible. To Neville Gomes and Monica Brady I owe a huge debt, not only for their generosity in allowing me to haunt the classrooms where they taught, but also for their willingness to engage in dialogue with me about their students and my observations of them. They have been full and active participants in this research.

Last, but by no means least, I want to put on record my appreciation of the support that my family has given me, for longer even than it has taken me to produce this book. Arthur and Rosa, my children who are no longer children, have tolerated the presence of Vygotsky and Vološinov, or at least my clumsy attempts to explain their ideas, at the kitchen table. And Claire, my beloved partner, from whom I have learnt more about the craft of writing than I would want to admit, has maintained a confidence in me that I have often found bewildering.

* * *

I would also like to thank Pearson Education for their kind permission to reproduce the front and back covers of *Young Warriors* (Reid 1967, see Chapter 6) and two different front covers of *A View from the Bridge* (see Chapter 7). For their permission to reproduce the photograph of Brooklyn Bridge in one of these front covers, I would like to thank Getty Images; for his permission to reproduce his design, used in the other *View from the Bridge* cover (and for his warmly enthusiastic response to my request for this permission) I would like to thank Keith Pointing.

* * *

The publishers have made every effort to contact authors/copyright holders of works reprinted in *The Social Construction of Meaning*. If we have been unable to trace any copyright holder then we welcome correspondence from those individuals/companies.

Chapter 1

Introduction

What happens when literature is read in urban English classrooms? What processes and activities are involved? How is meaning made? What is the value of such reading? Is it merely a poor substitute for the private reading of individual, independent readers? And how should students' reading of literature be assessed?

In what follows, I attempt to address these questions. Drawing on data gathered through classroom observation, I explore the meanings that are made collaboratively by students and teachers in interaction with literary texts. I make the claim that there are, in the urban English classrooms that I have observed, literacy practices that merit attention because of what they reveal about the possibilities of learning through an engagement with literature.

In this opening chapter, I set out the parameters of my research and indicate something of the history of my interest in the subject. Before doing so, though, it might be helpful to clarify some of the terms employed to describe this interest. I use 'urban' as shorthand for a series of interlocking characteristics of schools in inner-city areas: their comprehensive (non-selective) intake; the multicultural, multilingual student population; the predominance of children from working-class families; high levels of poverty (see also Anderson and Summerfield 2004; Hill 2004; Kress *et al.* 2005).

In focusing attention on the reading of 'literary texts' I do not intend to signal that I regard the category of the literary, or literature, as unproblematic: what constitutes the text, and how it might be thus constituted, are questions that continue to exercise me. To some extent, my interest is in the reading of literary texts because those are still the texts most widely and most often read within secondary English classrooms. My argument, though, is that literary texts are read in these classrooms in ways that open up distinct possibilities for the readers – possibilities of learning and development, possibilities of social semiotic work. The argument is not, however, that these possibilities are inherent in the texts themselves – in their literary qualities, say – but rather that the possibilities arise out of the kinds of engagement with the text, out of ways of reading that are deeply historied.

To suggest that these ways of reading might be construed as a 'literacy practice' is, in part, to acknowledge that what I describe is susceptible to a kind of ethnographic analysis: it is to make the claim that there are regularities in the phenomena that I observe, and that these regularities amount to an identifiable practice (or set of practices) involving a group of participants (students and teachers). Implicit in this claim is another, more fundamental, one, that there are different ways of reading, different ways of doing things with texts: that, in other words, there is not a single, universal form of literacy but rather a variety of different, and differently situated, literacy practices.

The autobiography of the question[1]

My interest in reading, or rather readings, predates my experience of London classrooms. In what really does seem like a former life, I spent several years puzzling about the audiences that populated the London theatres in the years leading up to the English Revolution. These audiences were constituted in difference; they were representative, particularly in the 'public', open theatres such as the Globe, of a broad cross-section of the population of London; they were sophisticated, knowing consumers of the multimodal texts that were performed for their benefit (and the sharers' profit). A play like John Ford's *'Tis Pity She's a Whore*, a self-conscious reworking of *Romeo and Juliet* in which the lovers are reconfigured as brother and sister, depends for its effect on the existence of an audience that recognises it as such – an audience that is capable of reading its representation of incest within the context of an established theatrical tradition – not a canon, but certainly a repertoire of familiar dramatic texts. The extent to which the experience of theatre had become, as it were, both common culture and common representational currency can be gauged, with the closure of the theatres in 1642 and the removal of close state censorship of the printing presses, by the astonishing frequency with which theatre reappears as a structuring metaphor in the political and religious pamphlets of the 1640s (Butler 1984; Gurr 1987; Heinemann 1980).

I was interested, then, in the theatres of early seventeenth-century London as places of cultural and political activity and transformation. I wanted to understand more about the relationship between the worlds represented by the plays (particularly the city comedies of Jonson, Dekker, Middleton and Brome) and the lifeworlds of their audiences. So what seemed important to me was less the texts in and of themselves than the effect that the texts (in performance) had on their audiences – and what their audiences made of them.

When, in the mid-1980s, I started work as a teacher in an inner London school, it was the unmissable fact of the diversity of the student body that interested me – and it was precisely this diversity which refocused my earlier preoccupation with the meanings that readers (or audiences) make of texts. In the multicultural environment of a London classroom, the consideration of what readers bring to texts, of the interface between textual and extratextual reality, and of the complex play of intertextuality, was no longer a fraught and frustrating exercise in theatrical archaeology but rather an everyday part of teaching and learning (Burgess 1984, 1988; Burgess and Hardcastle 1991). One of my first experiences as a newly-qualified teacher, working at a boys' school in East London, was of teaching a unit of work on storytelling to a class of 30 12- and 13-year-old students, all but two of whom were of Bangladeshi heritage. Underprepared and casting around for a story to tell, I chose *King Lear*. I had got no further than 'Once there was an old king who had three daughters' when I was interrupted. 'We know this story,' the boys informed me, as one, 'it's Bengali.' Graciously, they allowed me to continue, only occasionally pointing out where I had got my facts wrong.

Throughout the 20 years I spent as a teacher in inner London secondary schools, I continued to be fascinated by the ways in which students would illuminate and make sense of the literature that they encountered in the classroom, making meanings that were informed by their subjectivities, lives, cultures and histories. For the young women of Turkish and Kurdish heritage with whom I read *Romeo and Juliet* at a school in Hackney, East London, Juliet's attempts to negotiate the contradictions in her relationships with her family and her lover were often all too recognisable, all too close to their own lifeworlds (Yandell 1995). In other cases, with other texts, the correspondences were less obvious, less direct: I have written elsewhere about teaching *The Merchant of Venice* in the same Hackney school, and about one student in particular, Hong Hai, whose writing in role as Shylock, reflecting on his daughter's elopement with a Christian, seemed to me to be simultaneously drawing on her own experiences to shed light on the Shakespearean character and using the distancing perspective of the role to explore her own feelings, her complex cultural positioning (Yandell 1997a).

As a student teacher, I had encountered the Bullock Report's exhortation regarding the relationship between schools and their communities, between students' identities in school and in the outside world, between the learning that happens within and beyond the school gates (DES 1975, and see Chapter 6). At the time, I had welcomed this commitment to a principle, a view of the place of schooling in the wider society that I shared, and the report's attempt to address questions of what would constitute appropriate provision for 'Children from Families of Overseas Origin' (DES 1975: Chapter 20). Almost at the same time as I started teaching, however, a very different conception of the relationship of the curriculum to the cultures of school students was being articulated. It was expressed most clearly in the consultation document that preceded the imposition of the National Curriculum in England and Wales, which announced that the National Curriculum was intended to ensure 'access to broadly the same good and relevant curriculum and programmes of study' (DES 1987: 4). In this paradigm, the school curriculum derives its validity not from its responsiveness to local interests but from its universality. Equality of opportunity is to be delivered through access to a homogenous, preformed entity, the already-specified curriculum.

The centralised model of the curriculum, promoted by the 1987 consultation document and by the earlier HMI *Curriculum Matters* publications (DES 1984), has maintained a hegemonic position in policy throughout the following three decades, and has been a vital constituent in the standards-based reforms throughout that time (Apple 1996, 2001, 2004; Barber 1996; Darling-Hammond 2004; Hatcher and Jones 1996; Jones 1989, 2003; Lawton and Chitty 1988; Plaskow 2004). It continues to underpin more recent policy pronouncements around the theme of 'personalisation', to the extent that personalisation has been carefully defined as a set of increasingly individualised interventions to ensure access to the same pre-specified curricular goals (Boston 2007).

Implicit in the 1987 consultation document's notion of 'access' is a particular pedagogy, one that was rendered more explicit in the increasingly frequent appearance of the phrase 'pupils should be taught to . . .' in subsequent versions of the National Curriculum (DES/Welsh Office 1990; DfE/Welsh Office 1995; DfEE 1999a, 1999b). The assumption is that what is learnt is equivalent to what is taught, that knowledge can be transmitted, and that, in effect, a curriculum can be delivered (like a sack of potatoes). Learning is conceptualised as linear, measurable and the property of the individual learner.

I worry about approaches to teaching and learning that fail to take sufficient account of the subjectivities of the learner, that fail, therefore, to conceptualise teaching and learning as relational, socioculturally situated practices. I want to explore approaches to pedagogy that are more conscious of the agency of the learners and I want to suggest that there is a pressing need to look closely (and critically) at the ways in which the current discipline-based curriculum is negotiated and instantiated in urban classrooms.

Part of what seems to me deeply problematic about curriculum policy post-Bullock is that it does not reflect my experience in the (multicultural, urban) classroom. What attracted me, more than 20 years ago, to Bullock's advice that students should not be 'expected to cast off the language and culture of the home' was that it gestured at a more inclusive, pluralist conception of schooling. In other words, my initial reaction was an ideological one, supportive of what appeared to me to be a move in the direction of a more socially just education system. What I did not appreciate then, I think, was the force of Bullock's words in relation to pedagogy: students do not simply cast off their out-of-school identities and histories as they enter the classroom. I make this claim on the basis of experience, but also because of what seem to me to be centrally important philosophical arguments about the resources that people use to make sense of things; these arguments, traceable to the Bakhtin/Vološinov circle of cultural and linguistic theorists, insist that the act of interpretation is never abstract but must always, necessarily, stand in a specific historical relationship to the text. I develop this point in Chapters 2 and 3. The question is, therefore, what opportunities are there for students to draw on these cultural resources in their learning within the classroom? The danger of that one word, 'regardless', deployed in 1987 in the preparation for the National Curriculum and since reiterated in hundreds of school mission statements, is that it encourages an approach to curriculum and pedagogy that is inattentive to such cultural resources.

I referred above to the ways in which my school students had read (and responded to) *King Lear*, *Romeo and Juliet* and *The Merchant of Venice*. It is because of such experiences that I want to argue for the importance of approaches to curriculum and pedagogy, specifically within the field of English, that are properly attentive to the cultural resources that students bring with them to the classroom. I want to argue for a conception of the classroom as a dialogic, multi-accented space, within which the activity of reading literature is not neatly separable from a complex web of sociocultural relationships, not separable from issues of power and the contestation of power. And I want to argue for a conceptualisation of the activity of reading as fully, irreducibly social.[2]

Of course, the position that I seek to occupy and defend is not in any simple sense the product of experience. Experience – the 20 years I have spent as a classroom teacher in London schools, or the time that I now spend visiting my PGCE students as they begin to grapple with the complexities of urban classrooms – might be a great teacher, but what it teaches depends on how it is framed, on the theoretical and political lenses through which it is viewed. I have already gestured at a commitment to social justice – a commitment that preceded and partly motivated my move into teaching in London – as well as a prior interest in reading positions and in approaches to reading that tend to destabilise the text. Such interests and commitments were nourished, deepened and concretised by my experience as a teacher and as an active trade unionist, by my participation over two decades in the work of the National Union of Teachers, by my involvement in a series of campaigns on educational questions, by my editorship, for much of this time, of *Socialist Teacher*, the journal of the Socialist Teachers' Alliance. My analysis, then, comes from a particular perspective.

When training to be a teacher, I also read Shirley Brice Heath's *Ways with Words* (1983). Its careful analysis of the diversity of literacy practices within distinct communities helped me to look at literacy differently in the classrooms where I worked. It provided me with an alternative to the model of a single, universal, linear scale of literacy development, the model which has had, within the past two or three decades, hegemonic status within public and policy discourse around the field of literacy.

The theoretical field

My interest in the ways in which literary texts are read in urban classrooms places my work at the intersection of separable but related theoretical fields. I draw upon work in these fields in order to address the question of how such reading might be described and theorised.

The first field is sometimes referred to as the New Literacy Studies. Investigating the plurality of (local, domain-specific) literacies, its practitioners have tended to focus on sites outside mainstream schooling; often, indeed, the literacies explored have been explicitly counterposed to the paradigm of mainstream/dominant/ schooled literacy (Barton and Hamilton 1998; Barton *et al.* 2000; Baynham

1995; Boyarin 1993; Brice Heath 1983; Cope and Kalantzis 2000; Gee 2004; Gee *et al.* 1996; Gregory 1996, 2004; Gregory and Williams 2000a, 2000b; Prinsloo and Breier 1996; Street 1984, 1995, 2001). The insights derived from these studies, their insistence on the situated – and ideological – nature of all literacies, together with their use of ethnographic approaches, inform the approach I have taken to my research and provided me with a fresh way of thinking about literacy practices in the classroom.

More recently, there has been a particularly significant development from literacy studies, a broadening of focus to include a much wider range of semiotic resources and practices. Gunther Kress and others have developed multimodal social semiotics both as a theory of semiotic activity and also as, in effect, a research methodology. Unlike most researchers associated with the New Literacy Studies, Kress and his collaborators have focused attention on schools and classrooms as sites of semiotic activity, though largely concentrating on the role of the teacher (Kress 1997, 2003; Kress and Van Leeuwen 2001; Kress *et al.* 2001, 2005). My research makes use of multimodality as a research tool, but devotes as much attention to the activity of the school students as it does to the teachers involved.

The second theoretical strand of my analysis, as indicated above, draws on aspects of literary and broader semiotic theory. Any account of developments over the past century must, necessarily, greatly simplify the bewildering variety of strands that have emerged. For my purposes here, however, it is important to note that the dominant trajectory of literary theory since New Criticism has been away from the model of the text as stable, isolable, knowable and the proper object of critical attention and towards an emphasis on the role of the reader. To a greater or lesser degree, post-structuralist and post-colonialist schools have all tended to focus on readers, and reading positions, through which texts may be (re-)/(de-)constructed. Whereas in an earlier dispensation the place of literature in the curriculum might be construed as reading the great tradition, these theoretical movements allow for the possibility of disruption, of re-reading, and of a plurality of readings. These ideas are discussed further in Chapter 3.

There is not, historically, any sharp divide between social semiotics and the terrain of literary theory. The latter has borrowed heavily from linguistics and from other disciplines (such as psychology and anthropology), while Bakhtin, whose work is of particular significance in what follows, moved between literary and more general semiotic analysis and theory. Bakhtin and Vološinov's insistence on the contested, dialogic, multiaccented and irreducibly historical nature of the sign, which marks a radical departure from the Saussurean model of language as abstract system, provides part of the theoretical framework within which my analysis of classroom interaction is conducted. Theories of the sign are addressed in the first part of Chapter 2.

In the second part of Chapter 2, I address the third, interlocking, theoretical field, that of Vygotskian psychology. In addressing the question of how and why literary texts are read in the urban classroom, I am interested not merely in the semiotic work that is done in the classroom but also in the effects of this work: in other words, I am interested in the learning and development that happen. What Vygotskian psychology provides is a fully sociocultural model that situates learning in the social interactions between people, not merely in the mind of the learner. To the extent that Vygotsky emphasises the crucial significance of the semiotic in the processes of learning, there are clear points of contact between this theoretical field and that of social semiotics; to the extent that Vygotsky emphasises the dialectical relationship between everyday and scientific concepts, there is a connection, too, between this field and literary theory's interest in what readers bring to the texts that they read. These emphases come together in Vygotsky's picture of development, a picture in which the concept of the evolution of word meaning, of the sign, is critically important.

The empirical field

To explore my research interest empirically, I collected data from two English classes, taught by two different teachers, in a mixed secondary comprehensive school in the East End of London. The data, collected between April 2005 and July 2006, consist of lesson observations (just under 40 one-hour lessons, 27 of which were videotaped), together with samples of students' written work, interviews with groups of students and with the teachers. I discuss methodological questions in detail in Chapter 4. Here, though, it might be helpful to provide a theoretical frame for the empirical research.

At best, my data offer snapshots at a particular moment in development. To state this is also to suggest that the snapshots need to be read, to be interpreted: their meaning is not fixed, but depends, significantly, on the interests of the observer/interpreter. I am conscious, too, that, when I return to the data, my interpretation changes as my interests shift and develop. Researchers, like other readers, do not read the same text twice: each reading is historically situated, historically determined.

I should also make it clear that the data were collected in a school that I already knew well, that the classes were taught by teachers whom I already knew, a former colleague and a former student. I explore the complexities of these relationships, and of the impact of these pre-existing relationships on my role as a researcher, in Chapter 4. For now, though, I should make it clear that the research was situated in particular ways, in a particular nexus of relationships and identities.

Weis and Fine (2004: xxi) write of their commitment as researchers to documenting 'those spaces, relations, and/or practices in which possibility flourishes':

> Our commitment to revealing sites for possibility derives not only from a theoretical desire to re-view 'what is' and 'what could be,' but also from an ethical belief that critical researchers have an obligation not simply to

dislodge the dominant discourse, but to help readers and audiences imagine where the spaces for resistance, agency, and possibility lie.

It is, precisely, this sense of 'revealing sites for possibility' that motivated my choice of empirical site for my data collection. Through the description and analysis of the lessons which I observed and of some of the work that was produced in the context of these lessons, I address two further questions:

- What pedagogy is implicated in these reading practices?
- What kinds of learning are accomplished in and through engagement with literary texts in these classrooms?

Chapters 5–11 are devoted to the presentation and discussion of my data. These chapters are organised, to a large extent, around individual observed lessons, or sequences of lessons, which exemplify particular aspects of classroom engagement with literary texts.

Chapter 5 focuses on Monica's class, then in Year 8, working on *Julius Caesar*. Through observation data derived from a single lesson, I explore how literacy is constituted in the classroom, and how Bakhtinian and Vygotskian theories of the social can enable us to make sense of these literacy events.

Chapters 6 and 7, both of which focus on lessons involving Neville's Year 10 class, examine the relationship between texts, teachers and school students. Attention is directed towards the concept of 'multicultural literature', in policy and in practice, and towards the significance of the students' reading positions.

Chapters 8 and 9 develop the multimodal social semiotic analysis of classroom-based literacy practices. Chapter 8 focuses particularly on the physical instantiation of such practices and makes an argument for the need to attend to the embodied quality of students' engagement with the text. In Chapter 9, observational data from different lessons are brought together in an exploration of social learning over time.

Chapters 10 and 11 draw on different kinds of data, principally students' written work, both on paper and on screen, as evidence of their learning. These chapters also begin to problematise the assessment of students' reading and the assumptions which underpin the dominant, externally-imposed, forms of assessment.

The final chapter draws together the analysis conducted through Chapters 5–11. It focuses on two strands that emerge in the course of the analysis of moments of classroom engagement with literature. The first of these, returning to the contested Vygotskian concept of the Zone of Proximal Development, explores the significance of play, and particularly role-play, in these moments. The second concerns the methodological value of re-reading.

Notes

1 I borrow the phrase, and also the invitation to attend to the particularity of the researcher's history of interest in a field, from Jane Miller (1995).

2 My sense of the shape of this argument, of the ways in which encounters with literature in urban classrooms might be theorised, was sharpened by the research I conducted into my own practice and that of my colleagues in the English department at Kingsland School, Hackney. This TTA-sponsored research, conducted in the mid-1990s, was published in two articles in *Changing English* (Yandell 1997a, 1997b).

Chapter 2

Social theories of the sign and of learning

In this chapter, I attempt to provide a theoretical foundation for the exploration of the reading of literary texts. I address two questions:

1   What theory of the sign might be helpful in understanding what is involved in reading in classrooms?
2   What theory of learning might be similarly helpful?

That these questions are in any sense separable, or even that they might seem so, is a product of the disciplinary specialisation that occurred across the twentieth century. Earlier Enlightenment interest in epistemological questions recognised no such disciplinary boundaries. As Hans Aarsleff (1982: 109) has argued, for philosophers from Locke onwards: 'The progress of the mind becomes a question of the progress of language. The history of thought – in the characteristic, 18th century sense – can be pursued in the origin of language.'

Locke's *Essay Concerning Human Understanding* ([1690] 2004), devoting an entire book to 'language and words in general', 'placed the problem of language at the center of his epistemology' (Aarsleff 1982: 284). What Locke had to say about language is worth attending to. He recognised the complexity of the relationship between words and thoughts, and the developmental significance of that relationship. Thus, for example, he acknowledges that abstract concepts ('compound ideas', in his terms) are often first encountered as mere words, only later to be filled out with meaning. And he notes the imperfection, the sheer slipperiness, of both words and ideas:

> Hence it comes to pass that men's names of compound ideas, such as for the most part are moral words, have seldom in two different men the same precise signification, since one man's complex idea seldom agrees with another's, and often differs from his own, from that which he had yesterday, or will have to-morrow.
>
> (Locke [1690] 2004: 426)

Locke places language within the broader frame of the semiotic. These ideas were developed further by, among others, de Condillac ([1798] 2001), who wrote persuasively about the origins of language in gesture, about the complex interaction between cognitive and linguistic development and about the shaping influence of context on both: 'In our examination of the progress of languages, we have seen that usage fixes the meaning of words only by means of the circumstances in which we speak . . .' (Condillac [1798] 2001: 200).

What was central to both Locke and Condillac's picture of humanity was the commitment to an idea of semiotically-mediated development.[1]

Towards a theory of the sign

In *The German Ideology*, Marx and Engels, inheritors of the Enlightenment legacy of Locke and Condillac, make a series of claims about language and consciousness:

> Language is as old as consciousness, language *is* practical consciousness that exists also for other men, and for that reason alone it really exists for me personally as well; language, like consciousness, only arises from the need, the necessity of intercourse with other men . . . Consciousness is, therefore, from the very beginning a social product, and remains so as long as men exist at all.
>
> (Marx and Engels 1970: 51)

The first claim is that language and consciousness (or thought) are inextricably linked; the second, and perhaps more challenging, claim is that both language and consciousness have their origins in the social, in the interaction between people. The third claim, conveyed here in the phrase 'social product' and explored more fully elsewhere in *The German Ideology*, is that both language and consciousness (or rather, given the claim that 'language *is* practical consciousness', language-and-consciousness) are *produced*, that they are products of work or activity – and thus that they cannot be seen outside history. These claims, of course, have a history (gestured at above and explored more fully in Aarsleff 1982, 1983; Hardcastle 2009; van der Veer and Valsiner 1991); they have also been generative of subsequent theoretical work, and it is to some of this work that I now turn.

The first substantial attempt to flesh out a Marxist theory of the sign was Vološinov's *Marxism and the Philosophy of Language* ([1929] 1986).[2] Saussurean linguistics, which quickly became established as the dominant approach to the study of language, sought to focus attention on language structure and system (de Saussure [1915] 1986: 9, 77). Vološinov ([1929] 1986: 21), writing in polemical opposition to the abstractions of Saussurean linguistics, insisted on an attentiveness to language in use:

> Every sign, as we know, is a construct between socially organized persons in the process of their interaction. Therefore, the forms of signs are conditioned above all by the social organization of the participants involved and also by

the immediate conditions of their interaction. When these forms change, so does the sign. And it should be one of the tasks of the study of ideologies to trace this social life of the verbal sign.

As Lecercle has observed, the break with Saussure entails a conception of language not as a structure but as a process, a 'system of variations' (Lecercle 2005: 11). It is worth noting, too, Vološinov's emphasis on the sign as a construct – as something that is made (and remade) in social interaction. For Vološinov, it is not simply that there is a problem with any theory of the sign, such as Saussure's, that tends to abstract the sign from the concrete particulars of the social interaction in which the sign is used; it is that there is a problem with the concept of *sign use* itself. Vološinov makes a clear distinction between *signs* and *signals*: only the latter, a much more limited category, have stability, fixity; signs, on the other hand, are unstable, 'always changeable and adaptable' (Vološinov [1929] 1986: 68). Where this distinction really matters is in its implications for the role of the listener or reader. Confronted with a fixed signal, the receiver merely recognises, or fails to recognise, the signal; in relation to the sign, the listener has a much more active, agentive role – the task of 'understanding it in a particular, concrete context . . . understanding its meaning in a particular utterance . . . understanding its novelty and . . . recognizing its identity' (Vološinov [1929] 1986: 68; see also Williams 1977; Hodge and Kress 1988).

For Vološinov, then, the sign is constantly being remade, in particular contexts, in the interests of those who make and remake it. These interests differ, and these different interests, all of which leave their mark on the sign, are what make the sign unstable, complex, 'multiaccented':

> The social *multiaccentuality* of the ideological sign is a very crucial aspect. By and large, it is thanks to this intersecting of accents that a sign maintains its vitality and dynamism and the capacity for further development.
>
> (Vološinov [1929] 1986: 23)[3]

In the work of Bakhtin, who was, at the very least, closely associated with Vološinov, the concept of *multiaccentuality* is developed into *heteroglossia* and *dialogism*. Meanings constantly interact with each other, since any act of meaning-making is in dialogue with already-existing (and competing) meanings: 'all utterances are heteroglot in that they are functions of a matrix of forces practically impossible to recoup, and therefore impossible to resolve' (Bakhtin [1975] 1981: 428; see also Holquist 2002: 69). Bakhtin ([1975] 1981: 293–294) captures well the complexity of the individual entry into sign-making, an entry that is inextricably dialogic:

> As a living, socio-ideological concrete thing, as heteroglot opinion, language, for the individual consciousness, lies on the borderline between oneself and the other. The word in language is half someone else's. It becomes 'one's

own' only when the speaker populates it with his own intention, his own accent, when he appropriates the word, adapting it to his own semantic and expressive intention. Prior to this moment of appropriation, the word does not exist in a neutral and impersonal language (it is not, after all, out of a dictionary that the speaker gets his words!), but rather it exists in other people's mouths, in other people's contexts, serving other people's intentions: it is from there that one must take the word, and make it one's own . . . Language is not a neutral medium that passes freely and easily into the private property of the speaker's intentions; it is populated – overpopulated – with the intentions of others. Expropriating it, forcing it to submit to one's own intentions and accents, is a difficult and complicated process.

Bakhtin's representation of the complexity – and the struggle – that is involved in sign-making, including the violence of the appropriation that this (sometimes) entails, informs the analysis of the Year 10 students' argument over 'Half Caste' in Chapter 6, and also the exploration of the same class's reading(s) of *A View from the Bridge* in Chapter 7.

In this account of the sign, it is no longer helpful, or valid, to construe the context of sign-making as merely a set of background variables. Context is all, and is inseparable from the production of meaning. The point has been made very forcefully by Roy Harris, whose integrationist linguistics owe much to Vološinov:

> Texts are extrapolations from contexts . . . this makes texts context-dependent. Texts are communicational products, not communicational 'data'. They have no existence except by courtesy of contextualization. As soon as we are persuaded to treat the 'text' as having an independent existence of its own (by reference to which its 'context' is defined) we have already fallen into the subtle trap of *decontextualization*.
>
> (Harris 2006: 22)

As Lecercle observes, 'There is, therefore, no separation between language and the rest of human action' (Lecercle 2005: 70). If that is the case, then clearly any attempt to treat texts, or a particular category of text such as literature, as isolable objects of study, detached from the concrete circumstances of history and culture in which they are made and re-made with each reading, is based on false premises. This understanding was central to the attack, mounted by members of the Vološinov/Bakhtin circle, on the formalists' approach to literary criticism. To treat the literary work as 'a datum external to consciousness' was to 'sever it from the objective fact of social intercourse' (Bakhtin and Medvedev [1928] 1991: 151). The distinction that the formalists sought to make between the literary work and other texts, other uses of language, was equally unsustainable: 'Every utterance, including the artistic work, is a communication, a message, and is completely inseparable from intercourse. At the same time, the work is never a ready message given once and for all' (Bakhtin and Medvedev [1928] 1991: 151).

There are clear connections between the Vološinov/Bakhtin circle's insistence on the sign's contingency, its embeddedness in the specificity of culture and history, and Jauss's version of reception theory, to be explored in the following chapter.[4]

From the title of *Marxism and the Philosophy of Language* as well as from his use of the term 'verbal sign', it is clear that Vološinov's interest is primarily linguistic. He is careful, however, to show that his theory of the sign has much wider applicability:

> *Outside objectification, outside embodiment in some particular material* (the material of gesture, inner word, outcry), *consciousness is a fiction.* It is an improper ideological construct created by way of abstraction from the concrete facts of social expression. But consciousness as organized, material expression (in the ideological material of word, a sign, drawing, colors, musical sound, etc.) – consciousness, so conceived, is an objective fact and a tremendous social force.
>
> (Vološinov [1929] 1986: 90; original emphasis)

Like Marx and Engels before him, Vološinov rejects the separation of consciousness and semiosis. Vološinov emphasises, moreover, the materiality of the sign: it is the stuff, the matter, that is worked on by the sign-makers, using the resources that are available, and it is this materiality of the sign that enforces the contingency and specificity of sign-making.

Kress's insistence on the importance of a multimodal, rather than a purely linguistic, theory of social semiotics thus might seem to be less a radical departure from existing theory than a development and codification of the theoretical framework already present in Vološinov:

> [Social semiotics] rests on several fundamental assumptions: signs are always newly *made* in social interaction; signs are *motivated*, not *arbitrary* relations of meaning and form; the motivated relation of a *form* and a *meaning* is based on and arises out of the *interest* of makers of signs; the forms/signifiers which are used in the making of signs are made in social interaction and become part of the semiotic resources of a culture.
>
> (Kress 2010: 54–55, original emphasis)[5]

The implications of this approach to sign-making are explored in later chapters: in Chapters 6 and 8, particular emphasis is placed on the materiality of the sign-making in which school students engage, while in Chapter 10 attention is focused on the interests of the two students as they are revealed in the PowerPoint presentation they create.

This might be an apt place to draw attention to an implication of the view of the sign that is being proposed here. To conceptualise people in general, or readers in particular, not as 'users' of pre-existing signs but rather as sign-*makers* is to suggest that what is going on in such activity is a form of work. Marx, who described work as 'the eternal natural condition of human existence' (Marx [1867] 1976: 998) was careful to present purposiveness as a defining characteristic of labour: 'Man not only effects a change of form in the materials of nature; he also realizes . . . his own purpose in these materials. And this is a purpose he is conscious of, it determines the mode of his activity'. Part of what is significant about this is the emphasis on the irreducibly intellectual nature of work. Wage labour under capitalism thus becomes only one – deformed – instance of work (see also Marx 1973: 110). In *The Long Revolution*, Raymond Williams develops this broader conception of work. The passage comes in the course of an argument for socialism as not just a new political and economic order but a new social order. Williams insists on the central place of cultural activity within this alternative conception:

> It is of course necessary to see the facts of power and property as obstacles to this order, but the alternative society that is proposed must be in wider terms, if it is to generate the full energies necessary for its creation . . . A good particular example of this general problem is the question of the definition of work, which has been discussed and then neglected in the socialist tradition. Our common meaning of work has become 'effort rewarded by money': comparable effort, either of a 'private' or 'public' kind, may be as much work, but is described as 'leisure-time activity' or, curiously, 'good works' . . . The integration of work and life, and the inclusion of activities we call cultural in the ordinary social organization, are the basic terms of an alternative form of society.
>
> (Williams [1961] 1965: 131–132)

This was not, however, a project that could simply be consigned to some imagined future: Williams' argument is that the everyday work of cultural production needs to be acknowledged (and valued) in contemporary society. His conception of culture as everyday activity, of everyday activity as the making and remaking of culture, and his insistence that such activity should be taken seriously, inform my argument about reading in Chapter 3 and throughout this thesis: that reading needs to be conceptualised as a complex set of motivated, historied processes, not merely as the acquisition of a set of skills or as a preparation for something else.

Towards a theory of learning

The quotation from *The German Ideology* that was my starting-point for the previous section offers more than a theory of the sign; it also asserts an absolutely fundamental connection between language (or sign-making) and consciousness (or thought) – and it is to the implications of this that I will now turn. My main focus in this section will be on the body of research and scholarship within a Vygotskian sociocultural tradition.

Lev Vygotsky, the Soviet psychologist whose work from the 1920s and early 1930s has become increasingly widely known over the past half century, provides us with a set of insights into learning that are immensely powerful.[6] Of central importance to the current argument are three aspects of Vygotskian theory. First, there is the understanding that the relationship between thought and semiotic activity is a complicated one: language enables the development of thought, gives learners access to resources beyond their immediate experience, but the process whereby learners develop a full sense of a word is a lengthy one. To be given a dictionary definition – the meaning – of a word is not enough; learners need time to explore the connotative dimensions that have accreted around the sign as it is used, and has been used, and to fill out for themselves the semiotic potential of that sign (see Bakhtin, above; Vygotsky 1987: 276; Gregory 1996: 16–18; Kellogg 2009: 94–95).

The second aspect, closely related to the complexity of the relationship between thought and sign, is the complexity of the process whereby 'scientific concepts' are acquired. What Vygotsky meant by scientific concepts was, very loosely, disciplinary knowledge – the kind of codified, abstract ways of understanding the world that are, at least to some extent, represented in school subjects.[7] What Vygotsky insisted on was the necessity of a dialectical relationship between scientific and everyday concepts: the latter, the concepts that learners bring with them from their lives outside school, are the intellectual resources that enable them to make sense of the scientific concepts they are presented with in the school curriculum, the ideas that will be reorganised and transformed through the processes of schooling. To suggest that there is a dialectical relationship between everyday and scientific concepts, however, is to make a further claim, namely, that the everyday knowledge that the students bring may also transform and reorganise the curricularised knowledge of schooling.[8] As Vygotsky was at pains to emphasise, these theoretical insights are confirmed by teachers' practical experiences:

> No less than experimental research, pedagogical experience demonstrates that *direct instruction in concepts is impossible*. It is pedagogically fruitless. The teacher who attempts to use this approach achieves nothing but a mindless learning of words, an empty verbalism that simulates or imitates the presence of concepts in the child. Under these conditions, the child learns not the concept but the word, and this word is taken over by the child through memory rather than thought. Such knowledge turns out to be inadequate in any meaningful application. This mode of instruction is the basic defect of the purely scholastic verbal modes of teaching which have been universally condemned. *It substitutes the learning of dead and empty verbal schemes for the mastery of living knowledge.*
>
> (Vygotsky 1987: 170, emphasis added)

To suggest this means having to reconceptualise the notion of access. No longer is it enough to throw open the school gates and allow the students to enter. As the authors of the Bullock Report acknowledged:

> No child should be expected to cast off the language and culture of the home as he crosses the school threshold, nor to live and act as though school and home represent two totally separate and different cultures which have to be kept firmly apart.
>
> (DES 1975: 286)

In part, this argument is about the practicalities of pedagogy. School students will, whether one likes it or not, arrive in the classroom with all sorts of other experiences, with histories that will inform their school identities and the sense that they make of school knowledge. They will have particular interests in the knowledge that the school has to offer.

In part, this argument is about the ethical implications for teachers' practice. Following the line taken by the Bullock Report, I am suggesting that part of the respect that teachers owe to their students is to attend to their lives, cultures, histories and experiences beyond the school gates, to see these out-of-school identities as integral to the students' identities within the classroom. And this does mean that teachers might usefully make it their business to find out about their students, to find out about their other languages and literacies, to find out about the 'funds of knowledge' (Moll 1994, 2000; Gonzalez *et al.* 2005) that are valorised within their communities.

In part, however, this argument is about the construction of knowledge itself – not merely about pedagogic strategy or about ethical obligations but about the day-to-day remaking of knowledge in the classroom. The argument emerges most clearly in Chapter 6 of *Thinking and Speech*, where Vygotksy proposes a radically different understanding of the relationship between everyday and scientific concepts than that put forward by Piaget. For Piaget, scientific concepts replace – drive out – the everyday or 'spontaneous' concepts that children have when they arrive at school. For Vygotsky, however, the everyday concepts continue to develop in a dialectical relationship with the scientific knowledge that is structured in the school curriculum. He recognises, too, that this dialectical process is variable and contingent, that different concepts are encountered differently, are differently situated in culture and history. As Michael Young (2008: 61)[9] has suggested,

> to the extent to which Vygotsky was a Marxist, epistemological questions about knowledge as a separate category distinct from practice did not exist: they were always resolved in practice, in the course of history. It follows that Vygotsky's distinction between scientific and common-sense concepts was a contingent one, to be overcome in practice and through learning.

A concept such as that expressed in 'Archimedes' law', Vygotsky says, develops differently from a concept such as 'brother': the former is likely to be encountered only in schooling, whereas the latter: 'did not begin with a teacher's explanation or with a scientific formulation. This concept is saturated with the child's own rich personal experience' (Vygotsky 1987: 178). Such experience, of course, is not merely of the world – of the child's own family, or other families – but of other texts – of the brothers that figure so prominently in folktale and fairy story, for instance.

In the chapters that follow, attention is directed towards those moments when school students' out-of-school knowledge is brought into productive – dialectical – relationship with school knowledge. This can be seen, for example, in Chapter 5, in the Year 8 class's exploration of *Julius Caesar*, as well as in Chapters 6 and 7, in the Year 10 class's work on a range of texts. What we see in these classrooms, I argue, is not the encapsulation of school knowledge (Engeström 1996), the production and reproduction of some limited form of curricularised knowledge that bears scant relation to the disciplinary knowledge that it is supposed to reflect, or provide access to; what we get is the thing itself – a full intellectual engagement with texts and with meaning-making in which disciplinary knowledge is being remade and in which there are no absolute divisions between such disciplinary knowledge and the participants' everyday knowledge, their knowledge of the world.

The third aspect of Vygotskian theory that I want to foreground is the emphasis on the social, on learning happening in the interaction between people and on that learning being mediated through culture and history. Learning, in other words, is not something that occurs in isolated individuals, or, to put it more polemically, 'The "isolated individual" is a myth':

> We cannot imagine any intellectual function that does not have a sociocultural character. Perception, memory, and thinking all develop as part of the general socialization of a child and are inseparably bound up with the patterns of activity, communication and social relations into which he enters.
>
> (Cole and Scribner 1974: 8)

One way of exploring this idea, and its implications for learning in general and schooling in particular, is through the Zone of Proximal Development (or ZPD).[10] Whether or not the concept should properly be attributed to Vygotsky (van der Veer and Valsiner 1991: 331), the ZPD has become firmly established as part of the Soviet psychologist's contribution to learning theory. In its appearance in *Mind in Society* (Vygotsky 1978), the idea of the ZPD emerges in the context of a discussion of assessment, and specifically as a challenge to already dominant ideas about IQ testing and ability as a fixed individual attribute from which subsequent attainment can be extrapolated (Kozulin 1998: 69).[11] In *Thinking and Speech*, on the other hand, the ZPD becomes centrally implicated in Vygotsky's probing of the role of instruction in the development of scientific concepts: the assertion that 'what the child is able to do in collaboration today he will be able to do independently tomorrow' (Vygotsky 1987: 211) opens up the possibility of social models of learning. The ZPD is thus directly relevant to questions of pedagogy: what Vygotsky was grappling with was the issue of intervention – of the ways in which an individual's development can be assisted (Wells 1999, 2000). What, in other words, is the role of instruction – and hence what is the teacher's role? How is the ZPD construed, and how is it relevant to the consideration of teachers' construction of English as a school subject?

Within the discursive field of recent government policy on literacy in the UK, one version of the ZPD has attained an influential space. In a metaphor borrowed from Wood *et al.* (1976), the teacher's role is to provide 'scaffolding' for the learner's linguistic development in general and, more particularly, the move to writing.[12] 'Scaffolding' is presented as one of a range of 'effective teaching styles' intended 'to support pupils' early efforts and build security and confidence' (DfEE 2001b: 16; see also DfEE 2001c). Government-sponsored in-service training materials provide information as to what the scaffolding might look like:

> Scaffold the writing. Pupils could:
>
> • Use a writing frame which provides overall structure and typical language
> • Use a word bank
> • Add written sections to a semi-complete version of the text
> • Use an existing writing template on computer
>
> (DfEE 2001a: 44)

The term is used both as a shorthand for a variety of tools that can be provided to assist the emergent writer, as above, and also as a way of conceptualising the sequence of learning activities:

> The teaching sequence is designed to scaffold success for all, and the steps between the learning activities are small enough to allow little mistakes to be picked up so naturally and quickly that no one needs to make a big mistake. This means intervening early to correct errors, not allowing them to become embedded.
>
> (DfEE 2001d: ix)

The connection between the concept of scaffolding and its Vygotskian origins is made explicit in a research report on the Literacy Strategy (Harrison 2002: 17) and in Beard's echo of Vygotsky in his definition: ' "Scaffolding" refers to a process that enables pupils to solve a problem or carry out a task which would be beyond their unassisted efforts' (Beard 1998: 39).

What unites all these forms of scaffolding is the way in which they position the learner and the teacher, the assumptions that are made about agency, knowledge and pedagogy. The learner is presented as incapable: without sufficient scaffolding, her first attempts would, presumably, collapse; she is prone to 'little mistakes'; she is defined, in effect, by her inability. The teacherly other, in contrast, is the one who knows, who 'correct[s] errors' and whose shaping of texts (through the use of writing frames and the provision of 'semi-complete' versions) ensures the acceptability – and hence success – of the learner's attempts at writing. Wray and Lewis, whose work on the development of literacy was hugely influential in determining the content and orientation of the Literacy Strategy as the UK government's intervention in pedagogy, make the claim that Vygotsky 'put forward the notion that pupils first experience a particular cognitive activity in collaboration with expert practitioners' (Wray and Lewis 2000: 26). They proceed to redefine the ZPD as a four-stage process whereby expertise is transferred from expert to learner:

1   Demonstration
2   Joint activity
3   Supported activity
4   Individual activity

(Wray and Lewis 2000: 26–27;
see also Wray and Lewis 1997: 21–22)

It is worth noting that the end-product is both the acquisition of expertise (knowledge or skill) and autonomy. The process is fleshed out by another contributor to the same volume:

> Teaching is about scaffolding: the model of teaching demonstrated here is very complex, but is based on the belief that teaching is not simply about the transfer of a body of knowledge. More importantly the teacher is one mechanism through which children are given the structure and pathway in which the subject content becomes the vehicle for other skills. This role as an 'expert facilitator' is one where children's learning is 'scaffolded' rather than 'constructed' . . . The outcomes of learning are in some ways modelled by the teacher, and the students then apply this 'expert' view to their own understanding. The eventual aim under this model is that the students should become equipped to carry out the work and learning for themselves, so that the expert facilitator can withdraw.
>
> (Greig 2000: 88–89)

Though Greig is at pains to emphasise that what is being advocated here is not (old-fashioned) transmission, it would seem that the difference is that what is being transferred from expert to novice is both content and skills: it is, in other words, still a transmission process, but one in which more is delivered. Learners, it is acknowledged, are different from each other, but only in their 'levels of ability.' What is not at issue in this model is the direction of transfer. At the end of the process, the reason that the expert is able to withdraw is because the learners have become like the expert. In essence, then, this is a technicist version of the ZPD, from which all questions of subjectivity, of culture, of power relations and possible conflict have been removed. It positions the teacher as expert and the process of learning as one that enables the replication of the teacher's expertise. As Searle (1984) asked, 'Who's scaffolding whose building?'

A radically different conception of the ZPD has been developed by those for whom the significance of Vygotskian thought lies in its attention to what might be termed sociocultural perspectives. It is to this interpretation that I will now turn.[13] Vygotsky's ideas about the ZPD were still evolving at the time of his death (Wells 1999, 2000). As Daniels (2001) observes, a richer version of the ZPD has been produced by reading Vygotsky in conjunction with his contemporary, Bakhtin, and in particular the latter's 'emphasis on multiple voices engaged in the construction of . . . meaning which is not necessarily located within the individual' (Daniels 2001: 67; see also Moll and Whitmore 1993; Tolman 1999). Bakhtinian heteroglossia renders problematic the dyadic simplicity of the expert-novice relationship, and hence:

> This speculation on the nature of support with the ZPD raises questions about broader social influences. Multiple and possibly conflicting discourses with different sociocultural historical origins may be in play within the ZPD. This view of the ZPD as the nexus of social, cultural, historical influences takes us far beyond the image of the lone learner with the directive and determining tutor. It provides a much expanded view of the 'social' and the possibility of a dialectical conception of interaction within the ZPD.
>
> (Daniels 2001: 67)

What would be the consequences of such a view of the ZPD for classroom practice? What forms of pedagogy would be implicated in the ZPD as a fully sociocultural space? And, more specifically, what literacy practices might be accommodated, developed and promoted within a classroom where the ZPD could be conceptualised in this way?

Daniels' emphasis on 'a dialectical conception of interaction' returns us to the issue of knowledge and power, of scientific and everyday concepts. The attempts by Daniels and Wertsch to synthesise Vygotskian and Bakhtinian perspectives have been challenged by Wegerif (2008). Wegerif argues that there are fundamental, ontological differences between Vygotskian dialectic and Bakhtinian dialogic, between Vygotsky's commitment to modernist, Enlightenment values and Bakhtin's suspicion of such values. There may well be real tensions here, but I am inclined to the view that Wegerif overstates them through a selective reading of both Vygotsky and Bakhtin. Emphasising Vygotsky's links with Hegelian dialectic, Wegerif tends to underestimate Vygotsky's materialism, his insistence on the concrete and on the specificity of historical experience. Thus, for example, where Wegerif quotes Vygotsky on the 'monologous' quality of written language, what Wegerif neglects is the context in which this occurs: the comment is made as part of a discussion about the difficulty of beginning to write – a discussion that is fundamentally pedagogic in orientation, as is clear from Vygotsky's description of writing as 'a conversation with a white sheet of paper' (Vygotsky 1987: 202): still a conversation then, and thus still less than entirely monologic.

Vygotsky, like Bakhtin and Vološinov, understood that 'concepts or word meanings develop, and . . . this developmental process is complex and delicate' (1987: 171). Later in the same chapter, Vygotsky, having just quoted Marx on the reason why scientific concepts are necessary ('if the form in which a thing is manifested and its essence were in direct correspondence, science would be unnecessary'), makes the point that any scientific concept has to be understood in relation to a system of concepts (1987: 193). Wegerif's reading of Vygotsky tends to treat scientific concepts – the authoritative bodies of disciplinary knowledge – as the fixed point, as the monologic goal of instruction, but this is to ignore Vygotsky's emphasis on the dialectical relationship between the two kinds of concept – a point which is further complicated by his later admission that spontaneous concepts might also be the product of instruction outside the context of schooling (1987: 238).

This last suggestion by Vygotsky is significant, to the extent that it once again foregrounds the social: concepts, whether scientific or 'spontaneous', are developed in interaction with others. Recent research by Hobson (2002; Hobson *et al.* 2006; see also Hasan 2005: 130–156; Tomasello 1999) is worth mentioning in this context. Investigation of the very early stages of development in children has led Hobson to posit three key influences: symbolic play, the growing awareness of self and others, and language all work together, interacting with each other in the development of thought. For Hobson and for Tomasello, just as for Marx and Engels, the social and the semiotic are inextricably linked in human development, with each other and with the achievement of consciousness:

> The symbolic representations that children learn in their social interactions with other persons are special because they are (a) intersubjective, in the sense that a symbol is socially 'shared' with other persons; and (b) perspectival, in the sense that each symbol picks out a particular way of viewing some phenomenon (categorization being a special case of this process). The central theoretical point is that linguistic symbols embody the myriad ways of construing the world intersubjectively that have accumulated in a culture over historical time, and the process of acquiring the conventional use of these symbolic artifacts, and so internalizing these construals, fundamentally transforms the nature of children's cognitive representations.
>
> (Tomasello 1999: 95–96)

Tomasello's picture of development as always simultaneously social and semiotic, his representation of the social as the site where meanings are made and re-made, on the 'intersubjective' and 'perspectival' character of the semiotic work that transforms children's minds, returns us to the insight from Marx and Engels with which this chapter began.

This chapter has emphasised the primacy of the social. Rejecting what Ilyenkov refers to as 'a Robinson Crusoe model of epistemology' (Ilyenkov [1960] 2008: 40), it has insisted on the social and historical nature of consciousness, and on the need to see readers as historically situated agents. The following chapter explores strands in a social model of reading, while the fourth chapter sketches out some aspects of a research methodology consonant with the theoretical positions that have been suggested here.

Notes

1 The role of language in development is perhaps not quite sufficiently acknowledged in Roy Porter's summary of Locke's pivotal contribution to Enlightenment thought; but what Porter does capture, wonderfully well, is the Lockean commitment to the process of education and hence to the idea of human progress. See Porter (2000: 60–71).

2 I refer to Vološinov as the author for ease of reference: the works which I cite are published in his name. I am aware of the controversy over the attribution of authorship (see Vološinov 1929/1986, translator's preface; Vološinov [1927] 1976, translator's introduction; Brandist 2002); I remain unconvinced of the importance of the ascription of individual authorship, particularly to work produced in a period such as the 1920s in the Soviet Union.

3 Stalin had different ideas. He presented a view of language as existing outside struggle and, to all intents and purposes, outside history:

> Language . . . was created not by some one class, but by the entire society, by all the classes of the society, by the efforts of hundreds of generations. It was created for the satisfaction of the needs not of one particular class, but of the entire society, of all the classes of the society. Precisely for this reason it was created as a single language for the society, common to all members of that society, as the common language of the whole people. Hence the functional role of language . . . as a means of intercourse between people.
>
> (Stalin 1954: 5; see also Lecercle 2005: 74–83)

4 There is, too, a broader connection between the interest in the Vološinov/Bakhtin circle's work that was shown in the West in the 1970s and 1980s and the movement beyond structuralism in cultural studies and literary criticism. Central to this development was the recognition, across a spectrum of writers working in a more or less Marxist paradigm, of the significance of difference in reading positions, about which I will say more in Chapter 3 (see also Holquist 2002; Todorov 1984). At times, though, it seems that the (re-)discovery of Vološinov/Bakhtin was more simply fortuitous: Higgins (1999: 196) reveals that Raymond Williams happened upon Vološinov's *Marxism and the Philosophy of Language* by accident – he came upon it on the open shelves of Cambridge University Library.

5 Kress's emphasis on the non-arbitrary relation of form and meaning, of signifier and signified, does indeed mark a breach with dominant theories of the sign from Locke onwards. But, as Vološinov or Bakhtin would argue, this difference needs to be understood contextually. For Locke, the arbitrariness of the sign was an important (rationalist) bulwark against contemporary beliefs in the god-given power of words to reveal essential truths about the things to which the words referred (see Aarsleff 1982). For Kress, the contrary position – that there is a motivated relation of signifier and signified – is also a means of asserting (human) agency in semiotic processes.

6 This is, of course, an oversimplification. Vygotsky did not work alone and his work took place in a particular context – the aftermath of the Russian Revolution of 1917. His exploration of problems in relation to how children learn was given an urgency by the revolutionary context of his work: the aim was to make a new society, and education had a key role to play in its construction. Equally, Vygotsky's ideas have a history that extends back over centuries of western thought. For a more detailed account of this intellectual history, see van der Veer and Valsiner (1991); Bakhurst (1990, 1991); Hardcastle (2009); and Rey (2011).

7 The relationship between school subjects and academic disciplines is, of course, not quite so straightforward – a point that has been made by Engeström (1996) and by Lave and Wenger (1991).

8 Since the 'rediscovery' of Vygotksy in the 1960s, his intellectual legacy has remained a subject of fierce contestation. It is clear that his ideas were developing, and there are internal tensions and contradictions in what is available to us. What I am presenting here is a necessarily simplified account. It is also one that contests a number of readings of Vygotsky that I find somewhat reductive. For a fuller account of these debates, see Britton (1987); Bakhurst (1990, 1991); Daniels (2001); Gillen (2000); and Kozulin *et al.* (2003).

9 For Young (2008), Vygotsky's failure to recognise knowledge – and specifically the 'powerful knowledge' of the disciplines – as a separate category, is a problem. For me, Vygotsky's insistence on dialectical contingency, on learning as situated practice and process, is a strength, offering a persuasive theoretical perspective on what happens in the classroom.

10 A version of the following discussion of the ZPD appeared in Yandell (2007).

11 The main discussion of the ZPD in *Mind in Society* occurs in Chapter 6, 'Interaction between learning and development' (Vygotsky 1978: 84–91). It is also mentioned, in a very different context, in the following chapter ('The role of play in development'): I consider this later reference in Chapter 12.

12 Stone (1998) and Harrison (2002) ascribe the first use of 'scaffolding' to Wood *et al.* (1976). However, in an earlier contribution, Bruner (1975) uses the term to refer to the interaction between a mother and her child:

> In such instances, mothers most often see their role as supporting the child in achieving an intended outcome, entering only to assist or reciprocate or 'scaffold' the action. 'Scaffolding' refers to the mother's effort to limit, so to speak, those degrees of freedom in the task that the child is not able to control – holding an object steady while the child tries to extract something from it, screening the child from distraction, etc.
>
> (Bruner 1975: 12)

What is noteworthy about this earlier coinage is that the activity thus described is one initiated by the child – not part of a planned intervention by the mother.

13 Lave and Wenger (1991; Wenger 1998) counterpose the view of the ZPD as scaffolding with cultural, societal and collectivist interpretations: their model of situated learning as legitimate peripheral participation in communities of practice can be construed as a sociocultural investigation of the ZPD. However, though Lave and Wenger admit the possibility of conflict and change within the community of practice, the central relationship within their model remains the dyad of newcomer and oldtimer – a dyad which may not seem entirely at variance with Wray and Lewis's expert-novice relationship. On the limitations of Lave and Wenger's dyadic model, see, for example, Fuller *et al.* (2005).

Chapter 3

Literacies and literature

The dominant paradigm of reading is vividly represented in the opening scene of Charlotte Brontë's *Jane Eyre* (1847). We first meet the 10-year-old Jane as she escapes from the obnoxious Mrs Reed and her equally obnoxious three children by hiding in a window seat, where she settles down to read Bewick's *History of British Birds*. What is paradigmatic about this moment is Jane's solitariness, her absorption in the world of the book and the extent to which her communion with the book is a means of escaping from the unpleasant reality of the world around her into the richer, more satisfying realm of her own imagination. Jane's reading *within* the novel is paralleled in Virginia Woolf's reading *of* the novel 80 years later:

> So intense is our absorption that if someone moves in the room the movement seems to take place not there but up in Yorkshire. The writer has us by the hand, forces us along her road, makes us see what she sees, never leaves us for a moment or allows us to forget her. At the end we are steeped through and through with the genius, the vehemence, the indignation of Charlotte Bronte.
> (Woolf 1925: 155)

Woolf's use of the first person plural to describe the reading experience enforces the sense that the experience is generalisable – that it is, indeed, the experience of the 'common reader', common to all (proficient) readers. We, Woolf insists, are lost in the world of the book, willingly surrendering ourselves to the 'genius' of the authorial consciousness.

This conception of what it is to read, and of the rewards that are attendant on such ways of reading, particularly when the object of such reading is a literary text, have come to seem mere common sense. This common sense is firmly embedded in policy. The English National Curriculum, for example, presents the development of competence in reading as a movement towards greater independence, greater ability to cope unaided with more demanding texts:

> Reading: during Key Stage 2 pupils read enthusiastically a range of materials and use their knowledge of words, sentences and texts to understand and

> respond to the meaning. They increase their ability to read challenging and
> lengthy texts *independently*.
>
> (DfE 2011: 8, emphasis added)[1]

One might want to remark, in passing, on the curiously limited perspective on the resources that readers might employ: the implication here is that what counts is knowledge of the word, but not of the world. There is also an assumption here that meaning is in the text: the reader's role is merely to 'understand and respond' to this already-existing meaning. (There may be a parallel here with the premise of synthetic phonics – that the sounds are somehow *there* in the letters, waiting to be correctly identified, and voiced, by the reader.)

We will return to Jane Eyre and her reading habits. Before we do so, though, I want to suggest that the dominant assumptions about reading are far from universally applicable; on the contrary, they are the product of a particular history – and a fairly recent one at that.

Historical and ethnographic accounts of reading

In July 2001, the President of the United States met a group of children from a primary school in Hackney, East London. Mr Bush listened while his wife read a story. He then commented on the importance of literacy: 'You teach a child to read, and he or her will be able to pass a literacy test' (as reported in the *Times Educational Supplement*, 24 August 2001). It is intriguing that the leader of the most powerful nation on earth had such a circular view of literacy, what it is and what it is for. Children are taught to read so that they can pass a test which, presumably, is designed to assess whether they can read.

George W. Bush's model – that learning to read is important because one is thereby enabled to pass a literacy test – would have made perfect sense to criminals in Tudor or Stuart England. From mediaeval times, a member of the clergy could not be condemned to death for his first capital offence. Instead, he was branded on the hand or thumb — M for murder, T for theft. (He could, however, be executed if convicted of a second offence.) This 'benefit of clergy' was extended to anyone who could read. The courts determined whether the accused was literate or not by giving him a reading test. The test passage was usually the first verse of Psalm 51:

> Have mercy upon me, O God, according to thy loving kindness; according
> unto the multitude of thy tender mercies, blot out my transgressions.

This was known as the 'neck verse'. Many criminals learned the passage by heart while in jail and were able to read it when on trial. Often references to this practice suggest that the condemned men were not actually reading, that the act of committing the verse to memory was, in effect, cheating. Not having undergone the prescribed course in phonics, they were pretending to read (but not actually reading). But, as George W. Bush understands, these men had indeed learned to read – they were functionally literate. (Functional illiteracy, for them, would have had a simple consequence: hanging.)

For many Muslim people today, literacy in Arabic constitutes a different kind of literacy from literacy in other languages. It is about recognising grapho-phonic correspondences, and so being able to produce the right sounds, when reading the Qu'ran aloud (see Goody 1987: 215). Such literacy is, of course, not confined to Islam: Latin has occupied an equivalent place within the rituals and liturgy of the Roman Catholic Church.

What reading was – how reading was understood – in other periods and societies helps to illuminate the specific and partial nature of our society's assumptions about reading. Thus, for example, as Daniel Boyarin has argued, 'Reading in ancient Jewish culture signifies an act which is oral, social and collective' (Boyarin 1993: 11). Boyarin cites the biblical description of reading in 2 Kings 22, where the scribe reads the Torah aloud in the presence of the king and the king is then said to have read the scroll. He goes on to argue that, within the Hebrew culture of the biblical and Talmudic periods:

> there was simply no word in that language at all which meant what we mean by 'reading a book,' that is, the essentially private, individual consumption of narrative with the effect of and for the purpose of 'pleasure.'
>
> (Boyarin 1993: 18)

Similarly, Howe (1993) presents a view of reading within Anglo-Saxon society as an inescapably social practice. On the Old English words *raed* and *raedan*, Howe points out that 'these words and their cognate forms in other Indo-European languages first denoted the act of giving counsel through speech' (Howe 1993: 60; see also Stock 1983, 1990). He describes the 'medieval textual community' as:

> a group bound together by the reading aloud of texts to listeners for the purpose of interpretation. In a culture unaccustomed to the written text, the act of reading would have seemed remarkably like solving a riddle. For it meant translating meaningless but somehow magical squiggles on a leaf of vellum into significant discourse.
>
> (Howe 1993: 62–63)

Overlapping but nonetheless distinguishable from the concept of what counts as proper reading is the issue of who counts as a proper reader. In the Renaissance, argues Kevin Sharpe (2000: 40), the relation of text to reader was determined by the power relationship existing between writers and their patrons:

> Patronage, for example, the tradition not only of dedicating to patrons but writing as if for them primarily, implicitly placed the reader in a position of

greater authority (as he or she usually was) than the author. The dedicatee not only provided the livelihood that was the most basic precondition of writing, but also facilitated publication, authorized the work and at times used influence to bypass the censor. The patronage system placed the reader, chronologically and hierarchically, before the author of the text; and arguably the decline of aristocratic patronage was necessary for the emerging prominence of the author by the early eighteenth century.

Central to Sharpe's argument is the historically specific, autonomous position of Renaissance readers (or at least some readers, given that patrons and readers were not coterminous groups). For him the Protestant Reformation entails a reconfiguration of the reader:

> Experience, not least the bitter quarrels over the interpretation of biblical passages during the English reformation, had instructed that, like it or not, textual meaning was not absolute, that individuals read – and even chose to read — differently.
>
> (Sharpe 2000: 42)

And yet Sharpe accepts as unproblematic the common-sense notion that reading occurs, as it were, in the communion of the individual reader with the text; that it is, necessarily, an individual act rather than a group activity. Sharpe's perspective on reading from the Renaissance on might be regarded as the mainstream one. In this version, some combination of the printing press, the Protestant Reformation and the development of capitalism led to the privatisation of reading and the construction of the individual bourgeois reader for whom the novel was to be the perfect form (see e.g. Watt [1957] 1979; Eisenstein 1983; Olson 1994; Baron 2000). Such assumptions are open to challenge. They run counter to Robert Darnton's claim that 'for the common people in early modern Europe, reading was a social activity. It took place in workshops, barns and taverns. It was almost always oral' (Darnton [1991] 2001: 166).

Darnton's more ecumenical definition of reading allows him to make connections between early modern practices and contemporary ones:

> In the nineteenth century groups of artisans, especially cigar makers and tailors, took turns reading or hired a reader to keep themselves entertained while they worked. Even today many people get their news by being read to by a telecaster. Television may be less of a break with the past than is generally assumed. In any case, for most people throughout most of history, books had audiences rather than readers. They were better heard than seen.
>
> (Darnton [1991] 2001: 168)

Just how inadequate the model of literacy as individual practice might be, for scholars as well as for the masses, is suggested by Adrian Johns' account of the epistemological issues that confronted Robert Boyle and his colleagues at the Royal Society in the late seventeenth century. As experimental philosophers, they were developing the notion of replicability that has become 'central to the authority of modern science' (Johns 1998: 44). One might have imagined, then, that the dissemination through print of their accounts of experiments would have achieved the repetition of the procedures described (and thus have furnished further proof of the original experiments' validity). This does not appear to have been the case:

> Extensive social contact between practitioners was needed in order to reproduce cultural skills and settings in a new site. A skilled practitioner might even have to travel in person between the two locations in order for the attempted replication to succeed – or, for that matter, for it definitively to fail. It thus seems that nobody in 1660s Europe built an air-pump successfully by relying on Boyle's textual description of the engine. Some, we know, tried; all, we think, failed.
>
> (Johns 1998: 44)

What is at stake here is the issue of the autonomy or self-sufficiency of the written text. Informing this problem is the issue of the relationship between orality and literacy. The research of Howe and Johns, referred to above, stands in opposition to the notion, long associated with the work of Walter Ong (1982), that literacy in some sense displaces oracy – that societies are marked by, and hence organised through, communication in one mode or another. There is plenty of historical evidence – of the kind provided by Howe and Johns – that this is simply not the case. Literacy does not supersede orality: new technologies, new modes and media, complicate the existing communicational landscape, allow new forms to develop alongside and in combination with older resources for meaning-making. And the meanings that are made, differently in different times and places, are made in the social, in people's interactions with each other.

The approach to literacy as social practice has been developed by ethnographers (and others) in the past three decades. Careful attention has been paid to the diverse ways in which literacy is used, and to what indeed constitutes literacy, in different parts of the world and in a wide range of sites beyond the school, often in communities that are marginalised by and in official discourses (Barton and Hamilton 1998; Barton et al. 2000; Gallego and Hollingsworth 2000; Gee 2003, 2004; Gee et al. 1996; Gregory 1996; Gregory and Williams 2000a, 2000b, 2004; Li 2008; Prinsloo and Breier 1996; Richardson 2003; Rogoff 2003; Rogoff et al. 2001; Street 1984, 1995, 2001; see also Szwed 1981).

Shirley Brice Heath's *Ways with Words* (1983) presents the findings of a 10-year ethnographic study of the literacy practices of different communities in the Piedmont area of the Carolinas. The two working-class communities at the centre of her study, Trackton, a black community, and Roadville, a white community, are shown to have different ways with words, to do literacy differently, both from each other and from the ways that literacy is done (and is expected to be done) in school, whereas the middle-class inhabitants of Maintown have a culture that is similar to the school culture.

Brice Heath's ethnography provides a fundamental challenge to the model of literacy development as a matter of the acquisition of a set of value-free, context-independent skills. She shows that there is more than one answer to the question of what literacy is or what it is for. But there is more to *Ways with Words* than this: the different literacy practices of the different communities are used to explain the problems that the children of Roadville and Trackton, the two working-class communities, experience with the literacy of school – problems that are to do both with the difficulties faced by children who are, in effect, socialised into two incompatible literacies and with teachers' ignorance of the very existence of community literacy practices that are at variance with the school's institutionalised ways with words.

Ethnographic work of describing what people do with literacy in their homes and in community settings beyond formal schooling has, following Brice Heath, often been used as a way of problematising the assumptions of what Street (1984) has termed the 'autonomous model' of literacy – literacy as a set of skills, as cognitive, individual, context-free – and to associate this model with schooling and with the pedagogies and technologies of 'schooled' literacy. In opposition to the autonomous model, Street proposes an 'ideological' model of literacy, where particular literacy practices are always to be seen within specific social and cultural contexts and power relations.

While acknowledging the huge gains that this challenge to the autonomous model has brought to our understanding of the real diversity of literacy practices, and of the necessarily ideological character of all such practices, I want to draw attention to two areas of difficulty within this ethnographic tradition. First, there has been a tendency to present communities and their practices as homogenous. As Solsken (1993: 121) and Moss (2007: 48–50) have argued in relation to Brice Heath's work, such accounts may understate both the diversity of practice *within* a single community and the extent to which community members are involved in the *negotiation of different practices and values,* even when that community is relatively stable, with relatively clear boundaries separating it from other communities. (Moss points to an example within Brice Heath's own account, where two girls from Roadville are, in their conversation on the school bus, actively negotiating the different values of school and home.)

The danger of a kind of essentialist fallacy becomes all the greater in settings where communities are less stable, less homogenous, where boundaries are porous and where processes of cross-cultural negotiation are an inevitable feature of everyday life.[2] This is, it seems to me, an issue in Gregory's representation of the literacy practices of the Bangladeshi community in Tower Hamlets (Gregory 1996), despite the fact that in her more recent work she has acknowledged the development of what she terms 'syncretic literacies' – practices emerging as the hybridisation of school and home literacies (Gregory and Williams 2000a, 2000b;

Kelly *et al.* 2001; Gregory 2004).[3] In contrast, Jones (2004) focuses directly on the experiences of bicultural and bilingual negotiation that she has observed in adolescent readers. (It is possible, too, that the age group is significant here – that such processes are more characteristic, or more prominent, in teenagers than in younger children.)

Second, there has been a tendency to treat the literacy practice(s) of schooling as a constant, as the already-known against which the practices of communities can be compared and contrasted. This tendency is evident in Gee (2003, 2004), for whom 'traditional schooling' functions largely as a convenient construct, against which can be opposed the cognitive and affective advantages of informal, out-of-school sites of learning and literacy, such as video-gaming. Li's account draws on much more detailed knowledge of schooling; what emerges, though, is a picture of school literacy as a single, known entity, experienced within a 'scripted, one-size-fits-all curriculum' (Li 2008: 186) to be contrasted with the richness and diversity of wider cultural practices of the home – whether the home in question is that of white, Vietnamese or Sudanese families. For Li, as for Brice Heath, this contrast speaks of the ignorance of teachers about the home literacy practices of the students whom they teach. For Collins and Blot, on the other hand, the ideological function of schooled literacy is to be located precisely in its supersession, and hence suppression, of such heterodox alternative practices:

> The advent of universal schooling did not simply replace prior nonliteracy with literacy. Instead, schooled literacy emerged out of and in response to a complex, multifaceted commonplace literacy – of workplace, church, family and politics. But schooling and schooled literacy became the norm, against which other practices and capacities are either invisible or seen and judged deficient.
>
> (Collins and Blot 2003: 95)

Their argument is a valuable corrective to accounts that fail to acknowledge the tensions and contradictions involved in the history of schooling and of schooled literacy. And yet there are dangers in an overemphasis on structure, on the larger ideological interests at play, if what is thus neglected is the specificity of the experience of literacy acts – and the agency of those involved. It is worth bearing in mind here Linda Flower's representation of literate acts as:

> sites of construction, tension, divergence, and conflict. They happen at the intersection of diverse goals, values and assumptions, where social roles interact with personal images of one's self and one's situation, where individual rhetorical agendas mix with highly conventional practices . . . literate acts are often sites of negotiation where the meaning that emerges may reflect resolution, abiding contradiction, or perhaps just a temporary stay against uncertainty.
>
> (Flower 1994: 19)

Within the New Literacy Studies, relatively little attention has been paid to the literacy practice(s) to be found within mainstream schooling. The tendency has been to assume that these practices are already known, and indeed part of the point of the focus of New Literacy Studies on other sites of literacy had been to insist on the inadequacy of a view of literacy that treats it as coterminous with schooling. There are, however, significant exceptions to this general neglect. In the United States, Anne Haas Dyson (1997, 2003) has written extensively on classrooms where literacy is conceptualised – and practised – as dialogic, social, inextricably related to the out-of-school cultures of the students. In the UK, Gemma Moss (2007) has used ethnographic approaches to demonstrate the variability of literacy practices in different primary classrooms.

I first read Brice Heath's work when I was doing my PGCE (1984–1985); I returned to it when I started to write about teaching Shakespeare in a London comprehensive school (Yandell 1997a). What impressed me was, in part, the 'thick description' (Ryle cited in Geertz 1973) of literacy events, the attention that Brice Heath paid to what people actually did with texts. It mattered, too, that the ethnography was presented as an intervention in a debate about pedagogy: what were the implications of these observable differences in literacy practice for any teacher, and particularly for teachers working in schools where students were likely to occupy different positions in relation to culture, literacy and learning?

I suspect, though, that there was an aspect of my reading of *Ways with Words* that was against the grain. Brice Heath's account of the literacy practices of Trackton excited me because, for all its specificity, it articulated something about my own practice, and about my sense of how literacy was done in other London classrooms: it made it possible for me to begin thinking about those aspects of school literacy that tended to remain unnoticed, unexplored, untheorised. In Trackton, literacy is seldom a solitary pursuit. Meanings are negotiated socially, in dialogue around the text: no one assumes that meanings are self-evident, or that texts speak for themselves:

> For Trackton adults, reading is a social activity; when something is read in Trackton, it almost always provokes narratives, jokes, sidetracking talk, and active negotiation of the meaning of written texts among the listeners. Authority in the written word does not rest in the words themselves, but in the meanings which are negotiated through the experiences of the group.
>
> (Brice Heath 1983: 196)

Reading is, to all intents and purposes, inseparable from talk. Reading in Trackton thus looks a lot like reading in ancient Jewish culture (Boyarin 1993, above) and it has much in common with the meaning of the Old English words *raed* and *raedan* (Howe 1993, above). And it looks rather like the reading that I have observed and participated in over the past three decades in secondary English classrooms in London schools – the reading which is explored in Chapters 5 to 11.

Such a paradigm of reading also takes us back to John Milton and his denial of a neat separation of production and consumption, of writer and reader or of the activities of writing and reading. I want to turn now to how literacy practices are represented in the more limited field of literature and the reading of literature.

Different readers, different reading: from Milton to Wordsworth

At more or less the same time that Boyle and his colleagues were writing *and* talking to one another, John Milton was at work on a rather different kind of text. In the magnificent opening of Book VII of *Paradise Lost*, Milton positions himself combatively in relation to classical literary traditions and conventions:

> Descend from heaven, Urania, by that name
> If rightly thou art called, whose voice divine
> Following, above the Olympian hill I soar,
> Above the flight of Pegasean wing.
> The meaning, not the name I call: for thou
> Nor of the Muses nine, nor on the top
> Of old Olympus dwell'st, but heavenly born,
> Before the hills appeared, or fountain flowed,
> Thou with eternal Wisdom didst converse,
> Wisdom thy sister, and with her didst play
> In presence of the almighty Father, pleased
> With thy celestial song.
>
> (Milton [1674] 1971: 356–357)

Milton simultaneously draws on Graeco-Roman classical traditions and rejects them. His Muse is named as Urania, and yet he is at pains to explain that this name is, in effect, provisional ('If rightly thou art called'), and that he certainly does not mean the same thing by this as might have been meant by classical poets. Here, as elsewhere, he uses both the forms of classical poetry and the web of allusions that the tradition has given him, but insists on a different – explicitly Christian – perspective. Milton's 'heavenly born' Urania is not to be confused with one of the nine muses who hung out 'on the top/Of old Olympus.'

But Milton also positions himself within a specific political (and deeply personal) history. As he moves to the terrestrial second half of his epic, he refers to the moment at which he is writing, to the defeat of the revolution of which he had been the foremost propagandist, to the threat of persecution that he faces, and also to his own blindness:

> More safe I sing with mortal voice, unchanged
> To hoarse or mute, though fallen on evil days,

> On evil days though fallen, and evil tongues;
> In darkness, and with dangers compassed round,
> And solitude.
>
> (Milton [1674] 1971: 358–359)

Milton's invocation of his muse is no mere imitation of a classical trope, and certainly no indication of a retreat, either literary or spiritual, from present realities; rather it is central to the political project of *Paradise Lost*, a project that insists on the intersection of the particular and the universal. In the lines quoted above, Milton offers an image of the writer as lonely seer – a model of writing and the writer which is powerfully embedded in western cultural assumptions about the nature of literary production – but then emphatically rejects this notion of the writer's isolation:

> And solitude; yet not alone, while thou
> Visit'st my slumbers nightly, or when morn
> Purples the east: still govern thou my song,
> Urania, and fit audience find, though few.
>
> (Milton [1674] 1971: 359)

The significance of this is not that the poet is saved from loneliness by the visitations of his muse. What Milton insists on here is a direct link between the act of writing and the audience for whom he writes, while the terms in which he conceptualises both his poetry ('song') and his readership ('audience') simply do not entertain any absolute separation of oral and written language, nor do they imply a model of reading as private, solitary or individual. And if Urania is responsible both for the production of the epic and for its consumption – not only the source of inspiration but also charged with the task of finding the 'fit audience . . . though few' – this opening section of Book VII serves not only to reconstruct the project of the epic but also to indicate the attitudes and attributes expected of the audience. Milton is thus not only positioning himself but also constructing his readers. What he demands of them is not merely knowledge of classical literary tradition (the 'old Olympus'), nor even a shared set of religious beliefs (Urania's 'celestial song'), but also a shared understanding of and orientation towards contemporary political experiences (these 'evil days'). For Milton, as for Boyle, reading becomes meaningful in the social, in interactions that are necessarily located in specific times and places.

I want to compare Milton's construction of his readers with the reader who is constituted by Wordsworth in his Preface to the *Lyrical Ballads*. The comparison is not entirely arbitrary. Wordsworth, as Hazlitt observed, should be read in the context of the French Revolution: his poetry was 'carried along with . . . the revolutionary movement of [the] age: the political changes of the day were the model on which he formed and conducted his poetical experiments' (Hazlitt 1825). Throughout the Preface, Wordsworth is at pains to emphasise a radicalism that is simultaneously aesthetic and political. He announces that his work is 'a selection of the real language of men,' and he defines himself, the poet, as 'a man speaking to men'. As with Milton, there is no hint of subservience to a patron: the relationship of reader and writer is a democratic, egalitarian one. But what has changed, fundamentally, is the sense of how his work will be read, what the act of reading looks like:

> I have one request to make of my Reader, which is, that in judging these Poems he would decide by his own feelings genuinely, and not by reflection upon what will probably be the judgment of others. How common is it to hear a person say, 'I myself do not object to this style of composition or this or that expression, but to such and such classes of people it will appear mean or ludicrous.' This mode of criticism so destructive of all sound unadulterated judgment is almost universal: I have therefore to request that the Reader would abide independently by his own feelings, and that if he finds himself affected he would not suffer such conjectures to interfere with his pleasure.
>
> (Wordsworth and Coleridge 1800: xli–xlii)

In little over a hundred years, the relationship between text and reader has changed beyond recognition. Here, explicitly and unmistakably, the reader is configured as singular: sound judgements are made by individual readers, reading alone. When their views are influenced by others, this is a process of adulteration; when others' opinions are considered, even when they become a matter of speculation, this impedes the proper process of judgement – and hence, presumably, of reading itself. The clear demand on the reader is to 'abide independently by his own feelings': response is located in the individual, and authentic responses, given the emphasis on 'feelings', are visceral rather than noetic.

What is presented here is a model of reading that is entirely compatible with what I described above as the dominant paradigm. Independence is prized as a primary attribute of the reader, and pleasure is both an appropriate purpose and a desirable outcome. For Milton, the question of value does not arise, at least not explicitly: what validates *Paradise Lost* is not, in any recognisable sense, a matter of literary quality – and that is the whole point of the dismissive rejection of 'old Olympus'. For Wordsworth, on the other hand, what is being produced and offered to individual consumers – buyers as well as readers, indeed readers because they are buyers – has to assert its value in the marketplace. This leads, inevitably, into a consideration of the criteria that should underpin the judgements of literary value:

> From what has been said, and from a perusal of the Poems, the Reader will be able clearly to perceive the object which I have proposed to myself: he will determine how far I have attained this object; and, what is a much more

important question, whether it be worth attaining; and upon the decision of these two questions will rest my claim to the approbation of the public.

(Wordsworth and Coleridge 1800: xlvi)

If the reader is to be discriminating, what is the basis of his discrimination? Wordsworth's answer to this shows an awareness of the contradictions entailed in his emphasis on the individuality of the reader, since if all readers are to judge what they read on the basis of their own feelings, without reference to the views of others, can any more objective criteria be adduced? Yes, says Wordsworth:

> for an *accurate* taste in Poetry and in all the other arts, as Sir Joshua Reynolds has observed, is an *acquired* talent, which can only be produced by thought and a long continued intercourse with the best models of composition.
>
> (Wordsworth and Coleridge 1800: xlii–xliii)

In itself, then, the 'foul rag-and-bone shop of the heart' is not up to the job. For the reader to gain the capacity to judge, to discriminate, requires practice: taste is acquired by reading other texts, and in particular other texts that are themselves of high quality. The answer may beg other questions (who is to determine which other texts afford 'the best models of composition'?) but it is precisely the answer that lies behind the National Curriculum's attachment to 'reading a wide range of texts' and to the promulgation of a canon.

Wordsworth's model of development in reading is also echoed in the National Curriculum. If accurate judgement is to be acquired through long acquaintance with the best models:

> This is mentioned not with so ridiculous a purpose as to prevent the most inexperienced Reader from judging for himself (I have already said that I wish him to judge for himself) but merely to temper the rashness of decision, and to suggest that if Poetry be a subject on which much time has not been bestowed, the judgment may be erroneous, and that in many cases it necessarily will be so.
>
> (Wordsworth and Coleridge 1800: xliii)

One can see in this a foreshadowing of the National Curriculum's prescription that, even within Key Stage 1, children should read texts and 'say why they like them or do not like them'. On the face of it, such a practice appears to cede to the reader the power of judgement: in the open market of texts, the reader-as-customer is king. Below the surface, though, lurks the question of taste. Some opinions are more valid than others. In emphasising the dangers of erroneous judgements, and the importance of the acquisition of (the right kind of) reading experience, Wordsworth foreshadows the paradigm of reading and reading development that has remained dominant for the past two centuries. As Ian Reid (2004: 95) has argued, 'much Romantic literature was itself already articulating a quasi-pedagogical strategy and prefiguring the conditions for its own reading'. Reid draws specific attention to the abiding influence of Wordsworth's 'Immortality Ode' in 'picturing children as full of innate brilliance which fades when they become socialized' (Reid 2004: 96). There are, thus, in this Romantic version of what reading is and what it is for, the seeds of the Arnoldian project, in which literature (culture) is counterposed to material existence and in which the function of literature is the inculcation of value in the individual.

This view of the function of literature is also inseparable from issues of taste, of judgement or discrimination. Reading (literature) is the means whereby taste or judgement is acquired, and also how reading – and hence the reader – is to be assessed. Good readers, discriminating readers, are able to judge the value of a text, and are able to talk (and write) about a text in ways that demonstrate their worth by showing their knowledge of the text's worth. On current examination papers, questions that invite candidates to write about the success of a text and about how the writer has achieved particular effects are traceable back through Leavis and Arnold to Wordsworth. A jaundiced observer of this process might wonder if it, like synthetic phonics, might amount to little more than making the right noises, learning to gasp in awe and wonder at the canonical literature which Michael Gove describes as 'the best in the world . . . every child's birthright' (Gove 2010).

What might be suggested by the contrast between Milton and Wordsworth, and more generally by the recognition that reading has been done differently, and can be differently understood, is that it might be helpful to reconceptualise literacy not in terms of competency or ability but rather as 'a set of cultural practices that people engage in' (Resnick 2000: 28). For teachers, one of the problems that is posed by the Wordsworthian or Woolfian model of reading is that it does not have much connection with the reading that is accomplished in the classroom. Perhaps such reading, the reading enacted among school students and their teachers, might usefully be explored neither as a poor substitute nor as a preparation for something else (the independence of the solitary, private reader) but as a practice in its own right – or rather as an array of interwoven but markedly different practices.

This pluralist view of reading brings me back to Jane Eyre in her window seat. Despite what I suggested above, Jane's absorption in the world of the book is really rather different from the experience described by Virginia Woolf. Indeed, from the perspective of the devotees of synthetic phonics, what Jane is doing isn't really reading at all. The book that she is (not) reading, Bewick's *History of British Birds*, is organised into short chapters, each dealing with a different species. Each chapter opens with a line drawing of the bird, followed by a couple of pages of print, devoted to the bird's physical appearance, habitat, feeding and mating habits, and so on. These drawings, precise, minutely observed and beautiful, marked a breakthrough in the technology of wood engraving, and hence in the dissemination of high quality images to a mass market.[4] It is easy to see in Bewick's *Birds* the direct ancestry of Dorling Kindersley, the book as vehicle for a project of popular scientific education. But what interests Jane Eyre is not primarily the birds, either the images or the words. Wherever there is space at the end of a chapter, this space is filled with another engraving, and another kind of image entirely – categorically not the sort one would encounter in a Dorling Kindersley book. It is these vignettes that attract Jane's attention:

> The two ships becalmed on a torpid sea, I believed to be marine phantoms.
> The fiend pinning down the thief's pack behind him, I passed over quickly: it was an object of terror.
> So was the black horned thing seated aloof on a rock, surveying a distant crowd surrounding a gallows.
> Each picture told a story; mysterious often to my undeveloped understanding and imperfect feelings, yet ever profoundly interesting: as interesting as the tales Bessie sometimes narrated on winter evenings . . .
> With Bewick on my knee, I was then happy: happy at least in my way. I feared nothing but interruption, and that came too soon.
>
> (Brontë [1847] 1948: 3)

Looking at the thief with the devil pinning his pack (see Figure 3.1), one can quite see why Jane might have been drawn to it, yet reluctant to dwell on it.

Bewick's vignettes are hugely varied in tone and content, representing the everyday and the macabre – country cottages and corpses swinging from gibbets – with equal relish. Wordsworth was among Bewick's earliest and most emphatic admirers. He represented Bewick as someone whose skill rendered language superfluous and who was able to bring art to the masses:

> Oh! now that the boxwood and graver were mine,
> Of the Poet who lives on the banks of the Tyne,
> Who has plied his rude tools with more fortunate toil
> Than Reynolds e'er brought to his canvas and oil.
>
> (Uglow 2006: 311)

The stanza appears in a manuscript version of 'The Two Thieves; or, the Last Stage of Avarice', one of the poems to appear in the second (1800) edition of the *Lyrical Ballads*. Something of the unresolved tensions in Wordsworth's own political and aesthetic position is evident in the contrast between this dismissive reference to Reynolds and the respect Wordsworth affords him in the Preface (quoted above): Reynolds represents an attachment to aesthetic judgement, but also the social exclusivity that is attendant on, and enacted through, such regimes of value; Bewick represents popular art, a category to which Wordsworth aspired, at least in his more radical early years.

So is Jane reading, or just looking at pictures? Both, of course – the binary opposition is absurd. She makes meaning, follows her own interests, uses Bewick's vignettes as the rich semiotic resource that they are. The pity is not that she is failing to follow an approved course of systematic instruction in synthetic phonics,

Figure 3.1 Illustration from Bewick ([1797] 1847: 232)

but that she has no one with whom to share her pleasure in reading. (When she shows Bewick's *Birds* to nasty John Reed, he throws the book at her. Literally.)

Virginia Woolf was more fortunate. At a much younger age, Bewick's *Birds* was a book she read with her father, sitting on his knee while they read the pictures together (Uglow 2006: 402). And that's also what reading looks like.

Literary theory, canonical texts and classrooms

Running alongside arguments about literacy (or literacies) have been debates more specifically concerned with literary texts. As the exploration of Milton and Wordsworth indicates, these debates have been both about how texts are to be read and about what texts are to be read – about values and about canons. What I want to focus on here is not some potted history of literary theory but rather an account of the ways in which literary theories have constructed different accounts of reading and readers.

With Wolfgang Iser and the development of reception theory in the 1970s, it is possible to see a significant shift in the focus of literary theory, an acknowledgement that meaning does not simply reside in texts. What Iser does, first and foremost, is to insist that it is worth focusing on the reader's role. Iser represents the reading process as an interaction between text and reader, and hence arrives at the conclusion that 'The meaning of a literary text is not a definable entity but . . . a dynamic happening' (1978: 22). What is most helpful here is the emphasis on reading as a process. But Iser conceptualises the act of reading as 'basically a kind of dyadic interaction' (Iser 1978: 66). This positions reading as the interaction of a (single) text with a (single) reader, and thus remains closer to the New Critical approach than might at first appear. Light is to be shed on the reading process by an examination of the individual text and the (imagined?) reader. What gets left out of this account is any notion of the contexts within which reading occurs – contexts which shape, inform and inflect the reading. (Extratextual reality is allowed in – but only to the extent that it is referred to or immanent in the text.) And reading as a collaborative or collective act is not entertained.

Moreover, in so far as Iser conceptualises readers as different, it would appear that these differences are to be imagined as points on a linear scale, or perhaps on several different linear scales – more or less approximating to maximal/ideal performance:

> The degree to which the retaining mind will implement the perspective connections inherent in the text depends on a large number of subjective factors: memory, interest, attention, and mental capacity all affect the extent to which past contexts become present. There is no doubt that this extent will vary considerably from reader to reader.
>
> (Iser 1978: 118)

For Iser, the proper province of literary theory, which he takes to be the theory of literary effect produced through 'the intersubjective structure of meaning-production', is, in effect, the text; on the other hand, he sees an interest in readers, and hence a theory of reception (the significance ascribed to meaning) as 'more sociological than literary' (Iser 1978: 151).

Though there is much common ground between Iser and Jauss, the latter makes a crucial move in insisting on the historical specificity of the act of reading. Because he theorises reading as necessarily happening in history, his understanding of literature is also historicised:

> A literary work is not an object that stands by itself and that offers the same view to each reader in each period. It is not a monument that monologically reveals its timeless essence. It is much more like an orchestration that strikes ever new resonances among its readers and that frees the text from the material of the words and brings it to a contemporary existence.
>
> (Jauss 1982: 21)

By placing texts and readers in history, Jauss makes two decisive breaks with Iser. First, texts are no longer to be understood in themselves but intertextually, in relation to other texts. Second, the historicity of the reading position means that different readings are not, as Iser would have it, better or worse, approximations to some Platonic ideal, but rather interpretations made in, and appropriate to, the historical circumstances of the reader.

As Nelms observes, there is a sense in which (school-) teachers 'have always had to be reader-response critics' (Nelms 1988: 3): we have always been interested in what our students made of the texts we read with them, always interested in the active construction of meanings in and around the reading process. Louise Rosenblatt's work ([1938] 1995, 1978) is testimony to the longevity of this interest, at the same time that her emphasis has tended to be on the interaction of text and individual reader. This approach, typified by her assertion that 'The reader brings to the work personality traits, memories of past events, present needs and preoccupations, a particular mood of the moment, and a particular physical condition' (Rosenblatt [1938] 1995: 30), is informed by an unresolved tension in her model of the relationship between the individual and society. 'Language,' she asserts, 'is socially evolved, but it is always constituted by individuals, with their particular histories' (p. 25). Agency, in this model, lies with individuals, who remain oddly abstracted from the social: Rosenblatt's theory, for all its acknowledgement of history and of wider social forces, does not challenge the paradigm of the individual reader, whose transactions with the text are too personal, too idiosyncratic, to be easily related to larger cultural movements. This individualistic tendency in the dominant strand of reader-response theory is often expressed as the goal towards which the reading experiences of the classroom should lead. In the NCTE-published collection of essays from which I quoted at the start of this paragraph, the orientation is made explicit in the conclusion to Early and Ericson's paper: 'For all students, the ultimate goal must be: "I can read it myself – and I will!"' (Early and Ericson 1988: 42).

In direct contrast to Rosenblatt's individualist paradigm is Stanley Fish's notion of a community of readers that limits the free play of interpretation (Fish 1980). What Fish means by an interpretive community, however, is a very particular subsection of society: those readers within the academy. And when one sees Fish putting reception theory to work in his readings of real texts, it becomes apparent that the interpretive community is even smaller and more select than one might have imagined – closer to Iser's ideal reader and, by a happy coincidence, closely aligned with Fish himself (see e.g. Fish 1967, 1972 and also Eagleton 1996). The historical contingency of such readings remains largely unacknowledged; where it is mentioned, its significance is diminished (Fish 1995).

What is missing from such accounts is any systematic attention to readers as historically situated – and to the otherness of other readers (Eagleton 1996). My early years as a teacher coincided with a period of fundamental change in the English curriculum, particularly in relation to the teaching of literature and particularly in London, where I worked.[5] Whereas the past two decades have been a time of centrally-imposed change from above, the preceding decades saw change from below, change that was responsive to social movements and to school students themselves: change that was motivated, primarily, by taking seriously questions of representation. In the classrooms such as those where I worked, classrooms that were constituted in diversity, both the senses of representation teased out by Spivak (1988), the cultural and the political, were centrally and inextricably implicated: this was both about acts of *sign-making* (re-presentation) and about *speaking for*. So we chose writers whose work represented something of working-class experience (Barry Hines, Alan Sillitoe,

Alan Bleasdale, Shelagh Delaney); we chose African and Caribbean (Chinua Achebe, Sam Selvon, V.S. Reid, Buchi Emecheta), and Black American (Angela Walker, Maya Angelou, Rosa Guy, Mildred Taylor) writers; we chose writers who were attempting to speak to the experiences of contemporary British urban youth (Farukh Dhondy, Jan Needle, Geraldine Kaye). What was at stake here was more than a rebalancing of the canon, to make it less male or more up-to-date, to give it a postcolonial or a proletarian flavour. The category of literature itself was problematised, in two important ways. First, our work as English teachers took seriously Raymond Williams' insistence that 'culture is ordinary' (Williams 1958). The 1970s and 1980s was a period in which community publishing flourished and its fruits, largely in the form of autobiography and poetry, figured prominently in English classrooms. Allied to this was the tradition of publication of school students' own work, from Chris Searle's editions of *Stepney Words* (1971) to the steady stream of anthologies produced by the Inner London Education Authority's English Centre, such as *Our Lives* (Ashton and Simons 1979), *City Lines* (Simons *et al.* 1982) and *Say What You Think* (Moger and Richmond 1985). The presence of such collections and community publications in the classroom had the effect of blurring the boundaries of literature; it also acted as a powerful reminder of the cultural productivity of school students and the communities from which they came.

Second, there was an overtly political dimension to some of the texts that we chose to read with our classes: the selection of Beverley Naidoo's (1985) *Journey to Jo'burg*, for example, could not be seen as entirely separable from a shared set of commitments to the struggle against apartheid (see Chapter 6, below).

To some extent, these changes in what was read reflected teachers' shifting conceptions of the processes and purposes of reading. There was a widespread recognition of the significance of students' interests – of what they brought to the reading that happened in classrooms – and, perhaps, of the validity of diverse reading positions. There was, too, a shared understanding that literacy involved reading the world as well as the word (Freire and Macedo 1987), and hence that encounters with literature were never simply a matter of induction into an academic discourse. But it might be legitimate to ask whether the arguments about which text to read left unexamined how these texts were read, or whose readings (really) counted.

Thus far, I have drawn on historical, ethnographic and literary perspectives in an attempt to problematise the paradigm of reading as an activity that somehow lies outside the social. In the next chapter, I explore the methodological issues involved in observing and analysing reading in particular urban English classrooms.

Notes

1 Similar emphases on independence in reading are to be found in curriculum policy documents across the globe. See, for example, *English in the New Zealand Curriculum* (Ministry of

Education 1994: 31), the Singaporean *English Language Syllabus* (Ministry of Education, Singapore 2001: 7), the *Massachusetts English Language Arts Curriculum Framework* (Massachusetts Department of Education 2001: 2) and the New South Wales *English K-6 Syllabus* (Board of Studies, New South Wales 2007: *passim*).

2 The epilogue of the second edition of *Ways with Words* acknowledges that the effect of new technologies has been to complicate the picture of literacy practices even in the Piedmont communities where Brice Heath had conducted her research (Brice Heath 1996: 370–376).

3 Chapters from Gregory (1996) and Gregory and Williams (2000a) are prescribed reading on the PGCE course on which I teach. In recent years, there have been several occasions when student teachers of Bangladeshi heritage who grew up in Tower Hamlets have contested the claim (Gregory and Williams 2000a: 175) that reading for pleasure played no part in their family literacy practices, citing memories of listening to fairy stories read to them by their parents.

4 Jenny Uglow's (2006) biography of Thomas Bewick provides a fascinating account of these processes.

5 The following brief sketch of the recent history of literature teaching in secondary schools first appeared in Turvey and Yandell (2011: 152–154).

Chapter 4

Reading classrooms
Towards a methodology

This book is simultaneously an argument about what reading looks like in secondary classrooms and a report of a specific research project. In this chapter, I discuss the methodological issues that confronted me in the course of my research. In what follows, I attempt to represent my methodological choices and decisions as a process, and a rather messy one at that. I explore at some length my role as researcher and my relationship with Monica and Neville, the two teachers whose classrooms provided the site of my research. The negotiation of these roles and relationships was not something that was accomplished prior to the collection of data, but a struggle with issues of research identities, ethics and orientations that continued through every stage of the research, including successive drafts of this chapter. My research has been an irreducibly social process, as fully implicated in the specificity of history, culture and identity as the reading that is its focus. Over time, too, I have come to recognise that my research is itself a form of reading, an active making of meaning, an interpretation of the complex multimodal text of the classrooms.

Social science research – research that involves looking at what people do and worries away at the meanings of what they do – has long been recognised as a problematic activity, one in which the researcher is, necessarily, deeply and personally implicated:

> Sociology is often bedevilled by a somewhat naïve view of 'objectivity'. As human beings studying human groups, all sociologists cannot but experience many complex forms of involvement. The very choice of any research project in sociology inevitably presumes an act of judgement in which personal values and personal history play their own – perhaps deep-hidden – role. The true science lies in recognising this, not in avoiding the terrain where involvement is most perceptible. We jumped in at the deep end, tried to be methodical, tried to be honest, and tried to leave the reader free to redeploy the evidence.
> (Jackson and Marsden 1966: 17)

I started with the idea that my research might be seen as a case study (Yin 2003); I am no longer sure that applying this somewhat capacious term to my work offers as much clarity as I had originally imagined. I have drawn on ethnographic perspectives (Brice Heath 1983, 1996; Gregory 1996, 2004; Street 1984, 1995, 2001; Szwed 1981), but this research is not an ethnography. I have made use of multimodal approaches to data collection and analysis (Jewitt and Kress 2003; Kress and van Leeuwen 2001; Kress *et al.* 2001, 2005; Lomax and Casey 1998; van Leeuwen and Jewitt 2001), but I am not convinced that my research can be seen as sitting neatly within a multimodal methodological paradigm. I draw on Vygotsky (1987) and others working in a Vygotskian tradition (Bakhurst 1991; Tolman 1999) to construct an argument for my research as the socially and historically situated reading (and re-reading) of the complexity and specificity of what goes on in urban English classrooms. My research, then, *is* reading as well as being *into* reading.

The school, the classes, the teachers

My 'sample' consisted of two English classes in the same school, Wharfside,[1] and the two teachers who taught these classes during the academic year 2005–6. The selection of these two classes was largely a function of the school timetable, since this was what determined which classes I could observe fairly regularly throughout the year. It would be possible to perceive the two teachers as representative, in their differences, of a broad spectrum of possibilities: one had 30 years' experience as a secondary school teacher, the other was in his first year of teaching; one is white and female, the other is male and from an ethnic minority. But this representativeness was not the criterion by which the teachers were chosen: what marked them out, and what made me want to ground my research in their practice, was my prior knowledge of them as teachers and hence my expectation that I would be able to observe in their classrooms particular pedagogies, particular forms of teaching and learning, particular ways of reading literary texts. My sample, then, was arrived at by a process of 'purposive sampling' (Denscombe 1998: 15–16) or 'theoretical sampling' (Brown and Dowling 1998: 30–31): these were envisaged as critical cases, chosen to be representative of particular approaches to teaching and learning in urban secondary English classrooms.

I have known Monica for over 20 years. I met her in my first year as a secondary school teacher, when I was working at a school in Tower Hamlets. Monica, already an experienced teacher, was working at a different school in the same borough; she was also, at the time, the secretary of the local branch of the National Union of Teachers, and it was in that capacity that I, becoming active in teacher trade unionism, first got to know her. In 1989, when I became editor of *Socialist Teacher*, the journal of the Socialist Teachers' Alliance, Monica was on the editorial board and a regular contributor to the magazine. Writing at that time about the imposition of the National Curriculum, she produced an analysis that emphasised the inevitably contested nature of the curriculum and the importance of paying attention to the agency of the learners (Brady 1989). In the late 1990s, Monica and I worked at the same school in the inner London borough of Hackney, where she was Head of Humanities and I was Head of English.

We collaborated in drafting a language policy for the school, and on a project that sought to make connections between the English and Humanities curriculum. In the course of this project, we team-taught lessons in English and Humanities, and we spent time planning lessons together and reflecting on the linguistic and cognitive development of the students whom we both taught. I thus knew a great deal about Monica, and particularly about her deep commitment to work in mixed ability classrooms in which all students would be expected, encouraged and enabled to develop and express their ideas.

After moving to Wharfside in 2001, Monica started to teach English. The English class which I planned to observe was one that Monica had taught since their arrival at the school at the start of Year 7. I met them first towards the end of Year 8 (the summer of 2005) and continued to observe them until late in Year 9 (the summer of 2006).

The second teacher, Neville, joined Wharfside as a newly-qualified teacher in September 2005, shortly after he had completed his PGCE at the Institute of Education. At the Institute, he had been in my tutor group, and I had visited him on his first practicum at Wharfside School. Neville's commitment to what might be conceptualised as a Vygotskian tradition was evident in the subject studies assignment which he wrote at the end of the course; inextricably linked with this was his commitment to the agency of school students and to the teacher's obligation to remain respectfully attentive to the complex histories and subjectivities of the students. His decision to work at Wharfside was motivated by a recognition that the approach to teaching that he valued was one shared by members of the English department at the school.

My sample was thus chosen because I wanted to research particular forms of practice within the English curriculum and because I was confident that I would be able to do this by observing classes taught by Monica and Neville. Also implicit, I think, in the way that I have characterised the two teachers is that I hoped that Monica and Neville would be active participants in the research, engaging me in dialogue about what went on in the classroom and about my analysis of the data that I gathered.

Negotiating roles

Those were my reasons for wanting to work with Monica and Neville; but I also want to trace something of their sense of what might be involved in this research, what their expectations might have been, both of my role and of their own, and how the relationships developed over time.

The possibility of my conducting research in Monica's classroom had arisen in a face-to-face conversation early in 2005. In a subsequent email, I attempted to provide Monica with some sense of what I hoped would be the focus of my research:

> I would like to talk to you more about my research. I'm actually quite enthusiastic about it, and I can see a way of using the data that I hope

will emerge from your class to make an almost coherent argument about teaching, as well as about reading Shakespeare. I'm attaching two pieces to this: one is something I've written for *Changing English* (this version is not quite the final version), but it begins to sketch out some of the territory, in a very anecdotal and fragmentary way, that I would wish to explore more systematically through your class; the other is a very rough piece that begins to address some issues of methodology, but descends into incoherence.

And I really would like to come in next term to begin to get to know the class and to work out more detailed methodological questions with you. I do hope you've not gone off the idea completely – I confess that I am relying on you.

(JY to MB, 14 March 2005)

The article to which I refer (Yandell 2005) is one in which I had used an 'opportunity sample' (Brown and Dowling 1998: 29) – collected during visits to schools as part of my work as a PGCE tutor – to begin to explore some of the ways in which secondary students were reading literary texts in London classrooms. Two aspects of the email seem noteworthy: first, that there is an attempt to construct Monica as an active, informed participant in the research – not just as a convenient source of data; second, the pressure that I was applying on her, particularly in the final sentence, to allow me to use her classroom as a site of my research.

Monica's response refers forward to the unit of work around *Julius Caesar* that she was planning to start with her class after the Easter holiday; it also refers back to the reading she had done when on sabbatical in Australia:

Of course I am happy to do this. Perhaps not about the filming aspect of it but apart from that very excited I'd say. One thing sort of worries me and that is that I am not an English teacher. This doesn't concern me any more in terms of the deal that the class get because they seem to be making progress the same as everyone else and what they lose in my expertise in English they gain in my expertise as a teacher so I'm comfortable with that. It is just where you refer in the first page about a 'tradition of English teaching'. Some days I think I am still a sort of humanities teacher. Does it matter?

. . . The class . . . are really looking forward to doing the Shakespeare. M— [a colleague] did a lot of work last year on it but only used Brutus' speech in the original. I read the play yesterday and thought I could use quite a lot of it. I'd like to talk to you about it.

I wondered if you had access to an article I liked very much in Australia and would like to re-read. It is . . . called 'Is October Brown Chinese?' [Lee 2001].

(MB to JY, 19 March 2005)

When Monica talks about her sense of her own professional identity – 'I am still a sort of humanities teacher' – she makes explicit an anxiety about her position in relation to subject English that was to re-surface much later on in the research project. This anxiety, as she indicates, arises here out of her sense of what is entailed in my research. If I am to look at English teaching, and traditions of English teaching, is she suitable to be included in the sample? My response was intended to allay Monica's fears about her status as an English teacher – but what the exchange does is also to force me to clarify (for my benefit as well as hers) what I mean by a tradition of English teaching:

> As for whether it matters that you're not an English teacher: absolutely not at all! . . . What I think I mean is by this tradition is not so much the content or even the methodology of 'English studies' but rather a pedagogical tradition: by this I mean a set of ideas (about how students learn, about the relationship of language to learning, and even about the relationship between students' experiences and identities within and beyond the classroom) and a set of practices (what students and teachers do in the classroom, how language is involved and addressed in these activities, how resources of all kinds are deployed).
>
> (JY to MB, 31 March 2005)

What is happening within the exchange of emails is much more than sorting out the details of a school visit. As indicated above, Monica had been a professional and political colleague for 20 years or so before the research project began. The emails function as a means whereby, in explaining my research interests and questions to someone else, I was also clarifying my ideas for myself. At the same time, there is an attempt to convince Monica that she is the right person to participate in the research project. What is happening, then, in this exchange, is a definition not merely of the research project but of Monica's role within it: and hence our relationship is also being redefined within this new and different domain of 'doing research.' And yet this domain is not really new, but rather a reframing of existing – longstanding – shared interests and commitments, pedagogic and political.

Email became the vehicle whereby Monica could update me on the work she had been doing with the class:

> I started on JC yesterday with 8P. We looked at some pictures of JC/death of JC and did a sort of inference grid. We had quite a good discussion. I then did a background sheet that M— did last year.
>
> (MB to JY, 7 April 2005)

> Had a crap lesson with 9P this morning. Realised that I didn't know what I wanted them to get out of the *Looking for Richard* film so it was all a bit unsatisfactory.
>
> (MB to JY, 18 November 2005)

Had another great lesson with 9P today! We read the first part of the play and I just questioned them . . . Then we talked a bit about the history and tried to sort out the family tree and which Edward was which.

(MB to JY, 24 November 2005)

We watched a bit of film today and did the work on the characters, looking at the pictures and annotating them.

. . . Kirsty said Richard doesn't have a conscience but she couldn't say what a conscience was so Caroline helped define it by saying, 'he knows what he should do but he doesn't do it'.

(MB to JY, 9 December 2005)

In these emails, it is clear that my interest in the class – and therefore Monica's desire to keep me informed about what has been happening – has an effect. Monica uses email to reflect on the lessons – thereby both informing me and reflecting on her own practice and on her students' contributions. But I must be careful not to exaggerate the effect; this is not something new for Monica: of all the colleagues I have worked with as a teacher, Monica was always one of the most acute observers of students' learning, one of the most systematically and rigorously reflective about her practice.

In these accounts, too, there is little sense of particular research identities: I am constructed more as an interested colleague, familiar with the class and with the work that the students are doing, rather than as a researcher. In the early stages of the research project, though, there were occasions when the question of my role had been more directly addressed. After the second lesson that I observed (12 May 2005), Monica and I spent an hour discussing what had occurred. The conversation continued in an exchange of emails the same evening:

I was thinking about the things you said today and have several sort of unconnected thoughts.

Firstly I am not afraid of criticism from you. Nobody challenges me now and I sometimes feel the lack of combat.

Secondly . . . sometimes I lose confidence in what I am doing and worry that I am not doing the best for the class. That if I was a different sort of teacher they might do better in their SATs exams and that I don't have a right to deny them that. That if I was a different sort of teacher Kirsty would be able to spell properly by now . . . At the same time I know that when I talk to the kids I am making them think so I also feel confident that they are doing OK with me . . . And if I do try to be that different kind of teacher now (as I sometimes do), someone like Foyzur will relentlessly draw me back with questions.

Thirdly, I wonder if it is OK for me to get something from you in the lessons. Whether you could have for example suggested, that I draw them together and focus them on the why and the who. Or whether this would in some way distort your evidence.

(MB to JY, 12 May 2005)

Monica's sense of herself as a teacher, and as an English teacher, is subtle, layered, self-conscious, complex. Acutely aware of the fact that she is, in a sense, new to English, she nonetheless maintains a confidence in the pedagogical values and practices that have long informed her teaching: 'when I talk to the kids I know that I am making them think'. There is, too, a consciousness of herself as historically situated: her relationship with this group of students has been built up over time, and the kind of teacher she is is implicated in these relationships (see also Chapter 5, which explores these relationships and their effects).

But my relationship with Monica is also historied. What she has to say about herself as an English teacher in this email is not neatly separable from her sense of me, her addressee, as an experienced English teacher and as a former colleague. In an earlier version of this chapter, I suggested that this relationship 'inevitably complicated' Monica's sense of me as a researcher. It is an interesting phrase, revealing, perhaps, my desire (at the time) for a more straightforward research identity.

In my reply, I tried to dispel the notion that my role as researcher meant that I must remain a detached observer of Monica's lessons – as if the classroom were a crime scene and I the forensic scientist, clad in protective overalls and ready to bag up whatever evidence came to light.

> First, thank you for writing this: it is really important, I think, that we preserve/create/maintain this kind of openness. And thank you, too, for making it OK for me to be critical.
>
> I want to come back to the second thing (about your role as an English teacher). But the third thing – about my role – I think I can answer easily. There is no problem with me intervening (if you don't think there's a problem). The more I think about (and find out about) research, the less I believe in notions of a researcher's detachment.
>
> (And in any case, I was intervening by being there, by talking to the kids and listening to them – and, inevitably, my presence in a lesson is going to make you, or M—, or anyone else, behave in slightly different ways from if I wasn't there. I was conscious of the extent to which this was true for me at Kingsland, when you and I were both involved in your tutor group's English lessons: there, I think, it was pretty straightforward – your presence made me a better teacher, in lots of ways, some easily identifiable, others not. And yes, of course, that was a different context – but you get the point.)
>
> There was, though, a powerful reason why I couldn't have intervened in the way you suggest in the lesson today – and that's because it wasn't till I had talked it through with you that I had even begun to work out why the shift in focus mattered, and thus was able to start to think about ways in

which it might be achieved. So in the lesson I wasn't sitting there thinking, oh, what Monica should do now is . . . (This sounds like a caricature to me – because I can't imagine the situation arising like that. But if it did, if I had a thought in mid-lesson, about how things could go, I would definitely suggest it to you.)

(JY to MB, 12 May 2005)

This exchange is also an opportunity for me to clarify and develop my thinking, about planning and pedagogy, in dialogue with Monica. The email continues:

But your second point opens up a more complicated area, I think. Not because you might be selling the kids short because you're not a proper English teacher – I do just think that that's laughable. No, what I was beginning, very clumsily, to think about after the lesson was what the lesson revealed about the complexity of using someone else's SoW [Scheme of Work] . . . But that's not the only thing, I think, that was at issue today. I think I was being a bit lazy when I started to pose it as if it is (simply) a difference in subject specialisms (English/History) that explains the tension between what you were doing with the assassination idea. It's got far more to do with what you say about making them think (Vygotskian problem-solving, as I put it a fortnight ago). But . . . something that might appear to be (just) a kind of theoretical difference actually really does inform a different set of practices, to the extent that you intervene in the lesson to pull the activity in different directions – and thus the activity becomes a different activity: it's no longer an information retrieval exercise, linked thematically to the play but actually adding precious little to students' understanding of it; instead, it opens up the possibility that students will, in thinking about assassinations as political acts, involving not just isolated individuals but much wider movements and forces, perhaps begin to think about what is going on in the play, and about how Shakespeare represents these political acts, these social processes. One version is, as it were, Assassinations through the Ages – hitting a range of NC English buttons, good fun, and maybe boosting everyone's store of general knowledge; the other version is using all of this to . . . return again to the central problem posed by the play: what is going on here, how is it represented, and how can we begin to make sense of it . . .? What are these characters doing when they kill Caesar, and what do we think of it?

(JY to MB, 12 May 2005, continued)

Some of the issues raised in Monica's email and taken up by me in my response to her – about planning, pedagogy and professional identity as they are instantiated in teaching a scheme of work around *Julius Caesar* are explored again in later chapters (Chapter 10 focuses on some of the work produced by students in these lessons in particular). Here, though, I want to emphasise something which now, nearly eight years on, seems much clearer to me than it did at the time: there is no neat division in these exchanges between teacher and researcher identities. That research and pedagogic interests coalesced in this way no longer seems to me to require an apology: it was, rather, a defining characteristic of this research.

Inevitably, my research in Neville's classroom entailed different negotiations and revealed different tensions and anxieties. The relationship had a different starting point: my suggestion to Neville that he might be prepared to allow me to conduct research in his classroom appeared in some ways to promise continuity with our previous relationship, where, as his tutor, I had visited Neville on teaching practice.

In mid-October, I emailed Neville a draft of the letter that I intended to give to each of the students in his class. What follows is part of his response:

> I like the letter about your research. Though it's hard to reconcile what goes on in my classroom with the phrase 'good practice', I like the idea that there's a lack of description and theorisation of whatever it is I am trying to do. On Monday, I set 10.6 the task of debating which character is to blame for the tragic events of *Romeo and Juliet*. (This reminded me of my argument with L— D— the day you were at K—: this outcome was never part of any scheme of work, and occurred to me only because of the students' [lack of] response so far.) In the event, about ten students blamed more than half a dozen different characters; they showed an understanding of the play's events which they'd spent weeks insisting they didn't have; and (I thought) some of the readings were entirely their own. A couple of girls were very cross with Capulet for not supporting his daughter ('She hasn't been shown any love in her life, it's not surprising she wants to be with Romeo'); another blamed Friar Lawrence and his harebrained schemes; and one boy blamed the Nurse, who, apparently, should just have told Capulet about the tryst, so that he could give Juliet a slap, and all the silliness would have been over and done with.
>
> (NG to JY, 21 October 2005)

There is in his account of the *Romeo and Juliet* lesson an acknowledgement of our shared history – of my visit to the school where he had been placed for his second teaching practice, and in this reference, too, an allusion to shared values, shared understandings about teaching and learning and a shared scepticism about objective-led teaching. Alongside Neville's self-deprecating presentation of his part in the lesson, there is a real interest in what the students bring to the lesson, a pleasure in their engagement in talk about the text, in their readiness to offer opinions. There are, here, indications of the attentiveness to student voices that is common to Neville and Monica's practice.

I suspect, too, that my presence as a researcher in Neville's classroom may have seemed relatively unproblematic to him because of the extent to which it was not readily distinguishable from the observer role of the PGCE tutor, lurking in the classroom, making notes, occasionally contributing something to the lesson. He welcomed the kind of observation that I offered because it differed from that conducted by senior staff at the school: my focus was on learning, on longer trajectories of development, rather than on the effectiveness of his behaviour management. And I remained someone with whom he could discuss lesson plans, coursework requirements and problematic students – and all the other difficulties that confront any newly-qualified teacher in a challenging urban school.

Between Neville's acceptance of a job at Wharfside and his taking up the post, his Head of Department had taken his own life. Mark, a deeply principled man and an experienced, thoughtful and caring teacher, had been a significant reason for Neville choosing to work at Wharfside. His death left a gaping absence. When I remember my visits to Neville's classroom during his newly-qualified teacher (NQT) year, I am struck again by my sense of how isolated he seemed. I hope that my occasional presence helped to alleviate this situation.

Did this mean that my role as researcher was insufficiently clearly defined?

The answer to this question depends on the extent to which one subscribes to the view that the researcher, and the research itself, should remain detached from the object of analysis. As time has passed, I have become readier to discount this view and to accept that my research was simultaneously a pedagogic intervention.

My role: from teacher to researcher?

A moment from an early visit to Monica's class, in the summer of 2005. The class was reading *Julius Caesar*, and had been working on the funeral orations. Students had been asked to present speeches. Monica was videoing each performance. I had brought a camera: I thought that some images of the students would be an interesting, useful extension of the data that I was just beginning to collect. So I took photographs of the students as they delivered their speeches.

What I had not anticipated was how disruptive my intervention in the lesson would be. It was not, I am sure, the taking of photographs: this act was a frequent occurrence in Monica's lessons. It was because I was taking the pictures – and I was an outsider, an unknown. It felt uncomfortable to me at the time, but I persevered. Reflecting on the lesson afterwards, with the teaching assistant (TA) who had been present, and who also knew the class well, Monica confirmed my fears:

Hi John,
Today was another odd lesson – as you said, interesting things . . .
    Z— (the TA) commented that the pupils felt pressured by photographs and videos . . . And perhaps they wondered why you were taking photos? I think I/we need to talk to them a bit more about why you are there. Z— thought they might feel like they are being inspected, and if this is happening over many lessons it is too hard to keep up their best behaviour!

Also, I think we need to talk a bit about what happens if the best laid plans go wrong. Today, I might have changed the lesson when so few had their HW [homework] done . . . but I sort of felt that I had to persevere with the plan. I suppose I'm saying that not all lessons will have the outcomes we expect and perhaps that is fine with you but I need to know that . . .

(MB to JY, 6 June 2005)

Hi Monica

I'm sure that Z— is absolutely right, and actually it felt intrusive, or at least inadequately explained, to me . . . it certainly was making some of them feel uneasy. I should have stopped, I think. In any case, I do need to explain to them what I'm doing there. I'd be happy to come in and talk to 8P some time soon, if we could arrange this, though it might all seem a bit pointlessly retrospective; it might be better to leave it until next term, before we launch into *Richard III* . . .

The second point – and again I am really glad that you raise it. It's obviously no use saying things like 'pretend I'm not there', because I am there, and that's bound to affect things. But as much as you possibly can you should go with your instincts, change things when it seems right, and so on. As far as the point of me being there is to collect evidence, that is:

(a) subordinate to the lesson – i.e. it would be wholly unethical for the research to interfere with what you feel you should be doing/want to be doing

(b) my problem, not yours.

Whatever happens in the lesson is useful to me – it's all real material, and in any case, what I am interested in is a sociocultural model of reading, teaching and learning – so it would be a bit strange if life didn't intervene . . . So as far as is humanly possible, you shouldn't feel in any way constrained by me.

(JY to MB, 6 June 2005)

Clandinin and Connelly (2000) emphasise the central importance of relational factors in the negotiation and conduct of research. In my work with Monica and Neville and their classes, the issue for me was not how to construct working relationships but how to manage a research relationship that intersected with and overlaid other, longer-standing roles and relationships.

With Monica, I agreed that it would be helpful if I were to teach a couple of lessons so that her class could get to know me – in effect, so that I could establish a relationship with them. And so, in October 2005, I introduced the class to *Richard III*, using the *Developing Tray* software about which I have written elsewhere (Yandell 1997a; see also Moore 1999: 131–143). In the next English lesson, I introduced my research to the class. Thereafter, I found it much easier to inhabit a role within 9P's classroom – a role that involved observation but also some (limited) involvement in partnership teaching. The students thus were able to see me as someone whose primary purpose might have been something different (research) but whose presence in their classroom could be accommodated within a spectrum of teacherly roles. What this also achieved, I think, was a way that I could be in Monica's lessons that was least disruptive, least unnerving, least undermining of her teaching. In Neville's lessons, too, and for more or less the same reasons, I became a peripheral participant, an occasional contributor to class.[2]

It is fatuous to pretend to a kind of invisibility as an observer in a classroom – because any observation is inevitably an intervention; it is also not the case that the least disruptive intervention is the most self-effacing. For many teachers, indeed, the most unnerving presence is that of the silent, detached Ofsted inspector.

Earlier, in my mention of the forensic scientist, I gestured at a particular model of detached research, a particular orientation towards data collection. In this account of the two teachers who participated with me in this research, I have located the research inquiry in a nexus of specific histories and relationships. In constructing this text, I am conscious of a way of reading it that would dismiss any findings produced by such methods as hopelessly contaminated. How, after all, could one hope to claim any kind of objectivity when the whole business of data collection is, by the researcher's own admission, so thoroughly enmeshed in particularity?

Or could this particularity be a strength of the research? And is the attention to roles and relationships an inevitable constituent of any account of qualitative research? My approach is premised on the understanding that the researcher is inevitably part of the social world being studied (Hammersley and Atkinson 1983). My presence, even without the presence of a video camera, changed the empirical setting – the classrooms in which the data were gathered. Neither full participant nor wholly-detached observer, my position within the empirical setting remained necessarily problematic. But what research position is not?

What I would want to argue is that my history – as a teacher, and as a teacher with already-existing relationships with Monica and Neville – shaped this research in centrally important ways: it enabled me to participate in the lessons; it enabled me to enter into particular forms of dialogue with Monica, with Neville and with their students; it enabled me to observe the lessons from a particular perspective and thus to make the meanings that I have made – the meanings that are explored in the following chapters. Thus, also, there are places in the second part of this book where I examine my empirical data (Chapters 5–11), when I return to my experiences as a teacher. My history as a teacher, and hence my engagement with questions of pedagogy and policy, frames and informs these empirical data and my readings of them (see Chapter 6, in particular).

Another manifestation of my difficulties with my role as a researcher and my relationship with the participants in the research arose over the question of names. The standard answer to this question is provided by Sanchez-Jankowski (2002: 153):

> Even in those cases where the subjects say they don't care about either, or they request that their names be made public in the report, both anonymity and confidentiality must not be compromised. If they are compromised, then there exists the potential for increased feelings of internal conflict about what the 'proper' position of responsibility should be. Such conflict can lead only to confusing issues regarding loyalty to informants for aiding them in their research with loyalty to the data themselves.

I take the point that, in some sense, my commitment as a researcher must be to the data that I present. I certainly take responsibility for the interpretation of those data presented in this book. But I cannot accept that Monica and Neville were my informants, let alone that they were 'subjects.' They weren't: they were participants, and for their participation I remain very grateful. In this respect, therefore, I would want to place my research within the paradigm that 'positions teachers as collaborators rather than as objects of inquiry' (Doecke *et al.* 2007: 12; see also Lunenberg *et al.* 2007).

The fundamental principle of research, that no harm should be caused to participants by their involvement in it, informed the negotiation of roles outlined above, to the extent that decisions about my positioning, physically and figuratively, in the class were informed by a desire not to disrupt the education of the students. As I have already indicated, though, being minimally disruptive did not mean being minimally visible or maximally passive.

To preserve confidentiality, students' names have been replaced with culturally appropriate pseudonyms, and the name of the school that was the site of this research has also been changed. Such decisions may seem entirely straightforward: they reflect the procedure that is normally adopted in reporting on social science research. I have adopted this approach because, in relation to the school students, I could not be confident that they were in a position to give informed consent to be identified by name. And yet I confess that I regret this decision, because I would have liked to acknowledge more directly the students as participants in this research.

Data collection

Thirty-seven one-hour lessons were observed, 16 of which involved Neville and his Year 10 English group, 20 involved Monica and her Year 9 English group (including two in the summer term preceding their arrival in Year 9) and 1 involved the same Year 9 group in a History lesson. Of the Year 10 lessons, 10 were videotaped; 16 of the Year 9 English lessons were videotaped, as well as the Year 9 History lesson.

Room questions

Wharfside School was designated as a Training School, equipped with a special observation room – a classroom kitted out with a two-way mirror, and video cameras mounted on the ceiling. The room is designed to facilitate the observation and digital video recording of teaching. When I was planning the programme of classroom observations to be carried out during 2005–2006 I had originally envisaged that we would use the observation room. I knew that I wanted to collect digital video data, and the existence (and availability) of this room seemed to simplify my task.

But I became less sure that the benefits of the observation room outweighed its disadvantages. Filming might have been made easier, but at the cost of a disruption to the normal routines of the classes I wished to observe. To use the observation room felt wrong – because it would have been imposing an element of artificiality on the data: abstracting the teachers and their classes from their regular, timetabled classrooms would have produced different – less representative – lessons. Of course, my presence, and the presence of the video camera, would in any case alter the lessons. But I wanted to minimise this element of disruption – not to create a kind of laboratory lesson.

Neville's class was, therefore, observed in his regular teaching room throughout.

Monica's story is somewhat more complex. Monica, as a teacher who worked part-time in the English department, had not been assigned her 'own' classroom, and her class was timetabled in at least three different classrooms. In addition to the fact that students often arrived late because they had forgotten which of the rooms the English lesson was in, this situation created problems of continuity. Monica makes extensive use of displays of students' collaborative work: ideas shared in groups and presented on large pieces of sugar paper are mounted on the walls and referred to in subsequent lessons. Because this way of working was not possible when successive lessons were held in a series of different classrooms, Monica made the decision to use the observation room as the only consistently free (unoccupied) classroom. And so, for part of the time that I observed and filmed the Year 9 group, I did so in the observation room – but not because of the recording equipment available therein.

Monica's students, moreover, made it clear that they did not like the observation room. They felt uncomfortable in it – unsettled by the two-way mirror, which some of them associated with the presence, behind the mirror, of a member of the school's senior management – an authority figure.

Decisions and choices about filming

As I indicated above, I had decided, before beginning to gather data, that I wanted to use the resources of digital video. I wanted to be able to explore the possibility of multimodal analyses of the interactions that took place in the classroom. I wished to analyse 'the systematic practices used by participants in interaction to achieve courses of collaborative action with each other' (Goodwin 2001: 160). Such analysis, Goodwin asserts (p. 160):

> requires data of a particular type, specifically a record that maintains as much information as possible about the setting, embodied displays and spatial organization of all relevant participants, their talk, and how events change through time. In practice, no record is completely adequate. Every camera position excludes other views of what is happening. The choice of where to place the camera is but the first in a long series of crucial analytical decisions.

But I had not worked out – or even considered – the issues about where to place the camera: indeed, I didn't realise that this was an issue.

As Lomax and Casey (1998: 4.3) argue:

> the researcher, by doing 'being a researcher', reflexively contributes to the videoed definition of the encounter. This is not least because she must make choices within the context of interaction about when and how to film the event and when it is more felicitous not to film. These actions are influenced, in part, by what is 'appropriate' behaviour in the field.

What follows is an account of those choices.

With both classes, I felt that I had to get to know the class – and to become known to the students – before I could introduce a video camera into the lesson. This was something that had emerged from my experience with a (still) camera (see above). I felt that the camera would be less intrusive if I were already a known and trusted presence. I also felt that I needed to explain to the students what I was doing (and why) before beginning to film them.

What I found was that a camera mounted on a tripod in the corner of a classroom becomes unobtrusive, forgotten about, very quickly. This was, therefore, the way I filmed most of the lessons; the only exception to this was when, in Monica's class, students were performing role-plays or making presentations to the rest of the class. In these moments, the performance element in the task seemed to justify – encourage – a different approach: where I could, I filmed these sections of lessons holding the camera, tracking the students who were performing.

What is clear from my experience is that there is not one single effect of this method of data collection, but several. To talk as I have done in the previous paragraph of minimising the disruption caused by the presence of the camera is not to pretend that there was no effect. But the experience of the early lesson with Monica's class, when I took still photos, demonstrated to me the need to address these issues explicitly – and to minimise any such disruption as far as was possible.

My strong impression was that there were different effects, at different times and in relation to different participants. There was some self-consciousness on the part of Monica – a self-consciousness that I was aware of because of her declared (though low-key) reluctance to be filmed. For the students, part of the variability lay in their proximity to the camera – but it also varied according to the activity. To some extent, this is what Heider (1976: 53–54) talks about in terms of 'relative energy level' – more consciousness of the camera when there is, as it were, less going on. But it also varied according to the activity: for example, in the presentation of role-plays, students seemed to accept a much more intrusive camera role – hand-held, with me moving to get a clearer/closer shot. There is, thus, not a single variable but several, including: the position of the camera; the nature of the activity; the students' relationship to the lesson and their relationship with the researcher: this last is the point made by Heider (1976: 99) about the participants' familiarity with the filmmaker.

What was at issue, in practice, was not the validity of Lomax and Casey's insistence (1998: 4.3) that all participants necessarily display an orientation towards the research process, but rather the extent to which this awareness was a source of distraction – the extent to which the awareness ran counter to the explicit purposes of the lessons in which they were (meant to be) engaged.

In Neville's class, there were more explicit references to the presence of the video camera, a more obvious awareness of it. This was manifested in a variety of ways: most common were questions, mid-lesson, about whether the camera was on.

Some of Monica's lessons in the observation room – lessons where I was not present – were filmed using the video cameras attached to the ceiling. I watched this footage. One of the most striking things about it is how great a difference the camera angle makes. With the camera mounted on a tripod, the digital video footage is shot from a point of view slightly higher than students' heads as they are sitting at the tables. What is presented is thus a view of the classroom fairly closely equivalent to that of a human observer's perspective.

With the observation room cameras, on the other hand, what is produced is a bird's-eye view, in which teacher and students alike are reduced, diminished. It also seemed that the cameras were set up, or had been directed, in such a way as to focus primarily on the teacher's performance: relatively little attention, in the footage I have observed, is paid to the students' part in the lesson, other than when they are responding directly to the teacher.

I therefore continued to use my own camera, even when filming in the observation room. It seems to me that this decision was not primarily a technical one: what it reflects, in part at least, is the commitment, outlined above, to conceptualising those involved in the research as participants, not as objects of investigation. And it was important to me that my research did not seem to the participants to be associated with institutional regimes of observation and monitoring (Yandell 2000, 2010).

When filming in Neville's classroom, there was also an issue about the placing of the camera. In the first couple of lessons that I filmed, the camera was placed at the side of the room, near the front. I had put it there because it was the point from which I could include the greatest number of students. It was Darren, a student in the class, who suggested to me that it would be better to place the camera at the back of the room, from where it would be possible to film more of the teacher. I explained that I was most interested in filming what he and the other students were doing – but I adopted Darren's suggestion. I made this decision because I was interested in filming Neville's performance, but also because I wanted to show some respect for Darren's contribution as a participant in the research. So the decision was, in some sense, and like so much else in real-world research, something of a compromise (Robson 2002).

Data analysis and interpretation

As I indicated at the start of this chapter, what I am presenting is not an ethnography, but it does draw on ethnographic perspectives. Geertz (1973: 20) identified three characteristics of ethnographic description:

> It is interpretive; what it is interpretive of is the flow of social discourse; and the interpreting involved consists in trying to rescue the 'said' of such discourse from its perishing occasions and fix it in perusable terms.

In what follows, I say something about the interpretive method and tradition in which I would want to locate my work, before moving on to consider how I have identified, selected and represented the 'said', in Geertz's terms, which I wish to rescue and render perusable.

Vygotsky and elaborated description

In his analysis of Piaget's theory of egocentric speech, Vygotsky makes the point that 'he who considers facts, inevitably considers them in the light of one theory or another' (Vygotsky 1987: 55). His critique of Piaget is, in effect, that Piaget viewed his empirical data through the lens of a bourgeois idealist consciousness, a consciousness that took as axiomatic the primacy of the (asocial) self. For Piaget, then, the central and defining trajectory of development was from the individual to the social: speech begins as egocentric, only later, under the pressures of the environment becoming socially orientated. For Vygotsky, on the other hand, the primary movement is from the social to the individual (though the relationship between these poles remains a more complex, dialectical one). But Vygotsky does not content himself with a challenge to Piaget's philosophical/ideological premises; he seeks to ground his challenge to Piaget in his own experimental data. What is interesting is the way in which Vygotsky reports on such data:

> Consider, for example, the following episode. In one of our experiments, a child of five-and-a-half was drawing a picture of a tram. While drawing a line that would represent a wheel, the child put too much pressure on the pencil

and the lead broke. The child attempted, nonetheless, to complete the circle by pressing the pencil to the paper. But nothing appeared on the paper other than the imprint of the broken pencil. As if to himself, the child quietly said, 'Broken.' Laying the pencil aside, he took a paintbrush and began to draw a broken tram car that was in the process of being repaired after an accident, continuing to talk to himself from time to time about the new subject of his drawing. This egocentric utterance is clearly related to the whole course of the child's activity. It constitutes a turning point in his drawing and clearly indicates his conscious reflection on the situation and its attendant difficulties. It is so clearly fused with the normal process of thinking that it is impossible to view it as a simple accompaniment of that thinking.

(Vygotsky 1987: 70)

A number of aspects of this account are noteworthy. There is the accidental nature of the event: it occurred during an experiment, but was not a planned part of the experiment. The account relies on close observation, but this is no straightforwardly objective catalogue of the subject's actions. There is an attentiveness to the interests (Kress 2010, and see Chapter 2) and agency of the child, and the child's acts are interpreted by the observer, who infers motives and who adduces a causal relationship between the child's words and his subsequent behaviour.

When I first read *Thought and Language*, more than 25 years ago, I blithely attributed the subjective, anecdotal character of Vygotsky's accounts of his experiments to the fact that he was writing a long time ago (a notion of historical distance that I have since encountered in school students, for whom 'the old days' can mean anything from the 1960s to the Pleistocene era).[3] But this really won't do. Vygotsky's approach to and presentation of his data are products not simply of his academic background as a literary scholar nor of the stylistic models available to him, but of conscious choices on his part. This becomes clear from the most cursory glance at Piaget's *The Language and Thought of the Child* (Gruber and Voneche 1977), the work to which Chapter 2 of Vygotsky's *Thought and Language* is a direct response. Piaget presents, clearly and forthrightly, the qualitative and quantitative data on which his conclusions are based – the 'facts' that are so conspicuously lacking from, or at the most sketchily presented in, Vygotsky's account.

What is foregrounded by Vygotsky's account is the work of interpretation on the part of the observer/experimentalist: the data of the child's actions cannot easily or straightforwardly be coded, classified (as Piaget had done), without in the process oversimplifying what is actually going on. Vygotsky remains committed to a scientific approach; what he rejects is an approach that is reductive of the complexity of the empirical field.[4] The Vygotskian approach is attentive to the concrete realities of the classroom; more than this, though, it stakes out a ground that is distinct from an empiricist tradition of research with which, I suppose, I have a longstanding quarrel (see Yandell 1999). As Tolman (1999) has argued, this approach is one that accepts that the data that are to be presented are, as it were, fully subjective data – that the research evidence is compelling not because of any notion of replicability but because of the plausibility of the cultural-historical account that is offered. And in this notion of an account is embedded both the act of narrative and – inextricable from this narrative – an interpretation. My role as researcher has thus been as a reader (and re-reader) of these data.

The interpretation of digital video data

The following chapters present analysis of the data I gathered at Wharfside School. Through this analysis, I attempt to get closer to an adequate account of the ways in which literary texts were read by the two classes I observed, and of the uses to which these textual encounters were put. The data are specific, local, situated in particular histories. My analysis of them attempts to attend to these specificities because, as Burgess and Hardcastle (1991: 46)[5] have argued,

> as long as we continue in our thinking to abstract language from its context in culture and history and to think of it just as language, or as skills, or predominantly a matter of forms, we shall restrict our view of pupils' learning. We shall not attend adequately to the difference which lies in classrooms, whether of class or ethnicity or culture or gender. It is necessary to be specific.

Doecke *et al.*, in the 'position paper [outlining] a framework for research on English teaching' (2007: 4) to which I have referred earlier in this chapter, take a fairly disparaging view of the affordances of digital video as a research tool:

> We conceptualise classroom observation as an interpretive process, which acknowledges the perspectives of those who may see a classroom differently. We also assume the value of enabling practitioners to view their classrooms outside their habitual frames of reference, sensitizing them to the complexities of 'framing' and 'interpretation', and thereby enabling them to see their classrooms differently . . . Paradoxically, this is to abandon any notion that classrooms can be 'captured' by employing an array of ever more sophisticated technology, as though an observer can somehow get closer to the 'reality' of classrooms by resorting to audio and video recording. This appears to be the claim made by Kress *et al.* for their 'multimodal (semiotic) approach' to classrooms, which they distinguish from 'the linguistic approach that has dominated so much research on English classrooms since the 1970s' (Kress *et al.*, 2005: 3).
> For all the variety of semiotic sources on which they draw, the standpoint from which they construct their accounts of classrooms remains that of the research team. The voices, bodies and practices of teachers are interpreted from the perspective of the researchers, providing at best a somewhat

troubling surplus of meaning that threatens to deconstruct their master narrative of 'English in urban classrooms'.

(Doecke *et al.* 2007: 14–15)

From the earlier part of this chapter, in which I discuss my role as researcher and my relationship with the teachers involved in the research that I conducted, it should be clear that there is a part of this critique of Kress *et al.* (2005) that I would tend to support. The distance between that research team and the teachers on whose work they report is, I think, much greater than the distance between either Monica or Neville and me: my interpretive perspective is significantly different from the one that informs *English in Urban Classrooms*.

Where I would disagree with Doecke *et al.*, on the other hand, is in relation to the use – and usefulness – of digital video technology. The issue here is not whether the technology can 'capture' the 'reality' of a lesson, whether the video footage forecloses, or renders superfluous, the act of interpretation: it can't and it doesn't. But what it made possible for me as a researcher was significant. It enabled me to revisit a lesson that I had observed, to review and to notice things that I had not noticed in the real time of the lesson. So, to take one example among many, it was only in reviewing the footage of Monica's lesson on 1 December 2005 that I paid attention to Foyzur's intervention in the discussion of *Richard III*. My interpretation of this moment, which is the focus of analysis in Chapter 9, prompted me to review the footage of the lessons that had preceded this one. I wanted to look for moments in the earlier lessons that might plausibly be construed as contributing towards the understanding of Richard's role that Foyzur produced on 1 December.

What makes digital video footage so valuable as a resource in exploring and interpreting classrooms is precisely the complexity of classrooms, the complexity of the 'social discourse' (Geertz 1973) that flows through them. This complexity is the complexity of multimodal social semiotics: meanings are made multimodally, and, as I seek to demonstrate in the analysis that follows, particularly in Chapters 8, 9 and 10, an adequate interpretation of this meaning-making might reasonably be said to rely on the repeated review of the data that digital video facilitates. This is an argument about research method, but it is also an argument about the theoretical field: there is a congruence between my use of digital video data and the theory of the sign sketched out in the preceding chapter. The meaning of the data gathered in the empirical field did not – could not – reside in those data themselves; the different and developing meanings that have been made (and contested) are products of repeated, recursive and collaborative readings of these data.

Digital video technology has also, *contra* Doecke *et al.*, made it possible for me to enable 'practitioners to view their classrooms outside their habitual frames of reference . . . thereby enabling them to see their classrooms differently' (Doecke *et al.* 2007: 14). Both Monica and Neville have viewed and commented on some parts of the footage that are analysed in the following chapters. Over the past eight years, I have also shared some of these data with a wide range of teacher colleagues: with teachers in Wharfside School; with PGCE students as part of a lecture on classroom observation; with experienced English teachers in Cambridge and London; at seminars, conferences and research symposia in London and in Melbourne. Always, the issue of interpretation has been to the fore: it has been what we have argued about. And my interpretation – the interpretation presented in the remaining chapters of this book – has been shaped, modified and refined in these discussions.

The selection of significant moments

I am particularly interested in forms of pedagogy that enable students to make their own meanings, to contest meanings, to move beyond script and counter-script (Gutierrez *et al.* 1995, and see Chapter 5). The lessons, and the parts of the lessons on which I have focused attention, have been chosen because they are moments in which students' meaning-making can be observed, moments that reveal something of the pedagogy that encourages and is attentive to such processes.

So these are, in some sense, the moments that I was interested in before I started this research. There are continuities, then, with my earlier work as a teacher and as a researcher: with my earlier accounts of my own practice (Yandell 1994, 1995, 1997b, 2001) and of others' practice (Yandell 2005). But there's a problem with conceptualising the process in this way, in that it doesn't quite allow for the extent to which it is a *process*. My sense of the salience of particular moments was a product of my history, and especially my history as a teacher, but was also constantly being developed by the data, by what I was observing and the sense that I – and others – were making of it. That is, I was both 'rely[ing] on prior professional practice knowledge' and continuing to 'search for saliences' – that is, to 'search for knowledge in and through practice to correct and amend practice in the light of changing circumstances and new perspectives' (Kemmis 2005: 421).

This search involved understanding Monica's and Neville's practice differently, and understanding my own interpretation of their practice differently, because of becoming aware of others' interpretations, and because of the need to render more explicit the sense that I was making of their practice (and of the video data as evidence of this practice).

There are two other aspects to this question of the selection of significant moments that are worth a mention here. The first is I have discovered that, for me as a researcher, being there matters. Monica and Neville have both, very kindly, supplied me with digital video footage of lessons that I was unable to observe. I have viewed the footage with interest, and it has, of course, supple-mented my knowledge of the students' work, their encounters with literature and with each other. But I would not feel at all comfortable using such footage as my data, attempting to subject it to the same forms of analysis that I have used on video gathered in lessons when I was present. I could, I suppose, justify such reservations fairly easily, on the grounds that I would have only the perspective of the camera and therefore would miss out on the triangulation provided by my own observations in real time, by my awareness of things that happened out of shot. So, for example, in Monica's lesson on 1 December 2005, I was able observe the transmission round the class of Perry's counterscript (see Chapter 9). But I think there is more to it than that. Is it a not completely rational reservation about the inauthenticity of my position in relation to such data – in other words, some vestigial attachment to the truth-claims of the eye-witness? Or is it – and I think this is plausible – that the video data was always used by me to confirm, extend, enrich, complicate my own sense of the lesson that I had observed? So it perhaps is not accurate for me to describe my approach as one that centred on the analysis of video data, since these data were never my starting-point.

I also need to qualify what I have said about the selection of significant moments. I would want to argue that there are interesting things to say about almost any moment of any of these lessons, the lessons that I observed at Wharfside. In other words, I am making a claim that I could have focused attention on other moments, on other students. Entailed in this is the claim that the moments on which I have focused are in important ways representative of other moments, other lessons. (I return to this point in my concluding chapter.)

Notes

1 Wharfside (not its real name) is a coeducational 11–19 comprehensive secondary school in East London. At the time the research data were collected, it had about 1,200 students, from a wide variety of ethnic backgrounds, with slightly more boys than girls. Well over 50 per cent of students were entitled to free school meals (the most widely-used proxy indicator of poverty in the UK). Within the English Department, mixed-ability grouping was used for all years up to and including GCSE.

2 For some instances when I intervened in lessons, see Chapters 7 and 9.

3 The version that I read during my PGCE course was, of course, Vygotsky (1962).

4 My argument about Vygotsky and method was made 20 years ago by David Bakhurst, in an elegant and persuasive footnote (see Bakhurst 1991: 83–84).

5 Burgess and Hardcastle's emphases here find an echo in Bakhurst's explication of the two central features of Ilyenkov's dialectical method:

> First, the method is *particularist*. That is, it cannot be formulated as a set of general principles neutral with respect to subject. How it must be applied is entirely determined by the specific nature of the subject under study . . . Second, his position is *historicist*, that is, he presents human knowledge as a historical phenomenon, evolving through a relentless process of immanent critique, with each new stage responding to contradictions in the last.
>
> (Bakhurst 1991: 163, original emphasis)

Investigating literacy practices within the secondary English classroom, or where is the text in this class?

To begin to examine how literary texts are read in urban English classrooms, I investigate what happens in a single lesson, one that I observed in June 2005, very near the start of my data collection. I make the claim that what happens in the lesson is recognisable as a version of English and of English pedagogy, a version that is underrepresented – indeed, scarcely acknowledged – within the dominant, policy-oriented discourses of literacy and literacy instruction. The description of the lesson, and the literacy practices inscribed in it, is thus linked with an exploration of issues of pedagogy.[1]

As I noted in Chapter 3, a great deal of attention has been paid in recent years to literacy practices outside the classroom, while, as Kress *et al.* (2005: 117) observe, 'little attention has yet been given to the study of literacy practices as experienced by pupils . . . in secondary-school English classrooms'. Kress *et al.* argue the need to observe what does go on in English classrooms, since, despite the extent of regulation by policy, curriculum and pedagogic frameworks, 'English teachers actively construct their subject day by day, *differently* in the settings of the different classrooms'.

To describe the lesson, I will make use of the multimodal approach adopted by Kress *et al.* (2005, see also Kress and van Leeuwen 2001; Kress *et al.* 2001); to explain what I think was going on in the lesson, I refer to the much cited and much contested Vygotskian concept of the ZPD, discussed in Chapter 2.

The class, a mixed-ability group of 30 12- and 13-year-olds at Wharfside School, is in the middle of work based around Shakespeare's *Julius Caesar*. In previous lessons, students have read extracts from the first half of the play, up to the assassination of Caesar, using the script of the BBC *Animated Tales* version; they have watched the assassination scene and Brutus' funeral oration from the 1953 Marlon Brando film.

The lesson begins, in accordance with a routine that is departmental policy in the school, with time for individual reading. Without prompting, most students produce a book from their bag, settle at their appointed seat, and start reading. Those who arrive without a book are given one by the support teacher, Morlette. Though scarcely providing sufficient time for any sustained reading, the activity is effective in calming the class, enabling an orderly start to the lesson proper, and possibly reinforcing messages about the value attached to 'private' reading within the English curriculum. This opening provides an interesting contrast with what is to come. Here, for a few minutes, is something that approximates to the dominant model of reading within our society: each individual communing in isolation with a book that has, to a greater or lesser extent, been chosen by the reader.

After five or six minutes, the teacher (Monica) takes the register, then asks the students to put their books away. She is sitting on a table at one end of the room. The students are sitting in well-defined groups of three or four; all can make eye-contact with the teacher. In addressing the whole class, Monica's voice is only slightly raised: there is an expectation that she will be listened to, and she is. She says that in the lesson we will be thinking about Brutus and doing some role-play; first, though, she says that she wants the class to think about things that are really important. Religion, suggests one student; Morlette raises her hand and says 'Human rights'; 'The right to be gay,' adds Nazrul. This prompts Kemi to talk about the new Pope: she doesn't approve of him because of his prejudiced attitude to homosexuality. Monica listens to each of these contributions (as do the other students) but does not make any explicit response. She says that she wants the students, in their groups, to talk about violence: 'Is it ever right to use it?' She suggests, quite casually – in a way that might indicate that these issues are already common currency within the class – that they may want to think about situations where a country has been invaded, or about the apartheid regime in South Africa: 'Ms Lindsay might want to say something about that,' she adds, alluding to the fact that Morlette is South African.

And the students do talk. At Billy, Jo and Paul's table, where I am sitting, the conversation stutters into life. They talk about bullying, and how they would respond if a younger brother or sister were being attacked in the playground. Elsewhere, Nazrul's group discusses the situation in the Occupied Territories and the violence of the *Intifada*.

After about seven minutes, Monica stops the group talk and asks for reports from each group. Kirsty talks about the right to use violence to defend one's family. She refers to the recent news story about Abigail Witchalls, a young mother who had been stabbed in Surrey while out walking with her young son (Pallister and Jones 2005). In Kirsty's view, the Abigail Witchalls story is one that illustrates the need to resort to violence. Chris responds that everything can be talked over, and so violence cannot be justified; Kemi disagrees with this position, arguing that there are times when the only way of dealing with a bully is to confront the bully physically. Morlette refers to the case of Tony Martin, the Norfolk farmer who shot and killed a burglar (Gillan 2000): she says that she thinks he was wrong to do what he did, but she recognises that people have different moments of last resort. Lisa introduces a personal anecdote about the police failing to respond adequately to a violent situation; this encourages Billy to tell the class about his grandmother, who was robbed while she was in hospital, and again the police had not acted as Billy's family expected them to.

It is worth drawing attention to two aspects of this moment: firstly, the space that existed for Billy to tell this story, to be listened to, for this intensely personal family experience – weighed down with the family's sense of their grandmother's vulnerability, her dignity, her particular right to claim assistance from the police – to become part of the lesson, not extraneous to it; secondly, the extent to which Billy's story was taken up by others – it found echoes in other students' experiences of the police not being there when they were needed.

What is striking about this part of the lesson is not just the quality of individual interventions in the discussion or the maturity with which students can signal disagreement with each other– though these features of the students' talk are impressive – but the level of engagement shown by all the students in the room. This is evident in the quiet seriousness with which each contribution is received. If this is a product and manifestation of the social relationships within the class, it is also something that the class may well have learned from Monica. When a student is speaking, her gaze and posture indicate that she is giving them her full attention; when Perry, a relatively new arrival to the class who seems to find it difficult to stay still and listen quietly to other students, interrupts or distracts other students on his table, Monica's quiet admonitions to him emphasise that he needs to be quiet so that *she* can hear what is being said, and concentrate properly on it. Something of the processes of socialisation that have created this environment are discernible in the lesson itself. In reporting back on her group's discussion, Lisa, who is in the same group as Perry, says, in an entirely matter-of-fact way, that she had started off holding the view that violence was always wrong, but she had listened to Perry and he had convinced her. Similarly, Morlette's contributions to the discussion model what is expected of the students in this lesson, this classroom.

In this part of the lesson, Monica says very little. She ensures that each group gets a turn, and shows that she is listening to what they have to say. When Foyzur offers a rather confused (and confusing) explanation of an Islamic justification for the *Intifada*, reporting that he found this information on a website, Monica merely suggests that he might need to do some more research by checking out some other websites. When someone from each group has spoken, Monica announces that we will come back to this discussion at another time, but now we must turn our attention to Brutus. There is, thus, no forced closure of the debate, no attempt to resolve or summarise all the contributions; neither is the relationship of this part of the lesson to what follows rendered explicit in any way.

Why did Brutus decide to kill his friend?

Almost 30 minutes of the hour-long lesson have passed before Monica simply poses the question: 'Why did Brutus decide to kill his friend?' She explains that each group will be allocated a part of the play, a key moment in the period before the assassination, and that their task will be to prepare a role-play of that scene.

Copies of the scripts are distributed, and each group is assigned their scene (Brutus talking with Portia, Cassius persuading Brutus to join the conspiracy, and so on). At first, the groups rely heavily on the script. Students sit, heads bent over the text, with little obvious interaction within the groups. They locate their section of the script, sometimes unaided, sometimes with help from Morlette or Monica. Some students read a few lines aloud to the other members of their group. And then, at different moments over the next 10 minutes, each group leaves their seats, moves into the spaces between the furniture and begins to improvise their scene. The move is spontaneous, in the sense that it emerges from the group, not in response to a suggestion from the teacher, and it is accompanied by a marked shift in the relationship of the students to the roles that they are playing. Leaving the scripts behind, they are able to use the resources of movement, pose, gesture and gaze as they begin to inhabit the characters. Kirsty and Jenny become versions of Portia and Brutus, versions informed and inflected by the girls' knowledge of other married relationships, whether their parents' or the representations of adult male-female relationships in soap operas or films or cartoons. Kirsty's Portia maintains a physical distance from Jenny's Brutus that enacts her displeasure, her anger and disappointment in Brutus for his failure to share his thoughts with her; Jenny, in turn, guilty because of this silent breach of trust, cannot meet Kirsty's eye. Billy and Jo work together on the scene in which Cassius first raises the possibility of the conspiracy with Brutus – and Billy finds a linguistic register but also a way of holding his own body that seem more Brutus-like than I could possibly have anticipated.

In these role-plays, there is a doubleness to what is going on. On the one hand, students are drawing on experiences and emotions that are part of their own subjectivities – bringing themselves into the lesson, as it were. How this happens is also worth dwelling on: each group starts with the script and then moves away from it as the group members begin to inhabit the roles; each group starts sitting down, the scripts prominent in the interactions within the group, scripts guiding and structuring these interactions. Then, at different moments in each of the groups, the students get up and start to draw on other semiotic systems (gesture, movement, pose, expression) as they construct the interactions between Cassius and Brutus, Brutus and Portia, and so on. Does this movement into theatrical spaces – if that is what they are – enable students to draw on other resources, other possible ways of being the character, other roles and possibilities? This is where the other part of what is going on seems to rise to prominence, as students relish the opportunity of *being someone else*. The moment is one which allows for continuities with experiences beyond the classroom while also providing students with the liberating potential of an alternative persona or identity. In this lesson, there is Nazrul's Caesar, whose elaborate costuming effects have been created with two tops zippered together to create an impromptu toga; there is Kemi as Cassius, playing Brutus for the self-important fool that he becomes under the spell of her sly persuasion; there is Billy as Brutus, assuming a more public – almost pompous – manner of speech, quite distinct from the register he uses for normal classroom interactions; and there is Kirsty as Portia – both wifely and resolutely refusing to be patronised or excluded by Brutus. In all these cases – and many more – there is the pleasure of playing another person that I have described elsewhere in writing about a different class's experience of reading *The Demon Headmaster* (Yandell 2005; see also Barrs 1987; Gee 2003 and Chapter 12 of this volume on the liberating potential of adopting roles).

In the final 10 minutes of the lesson, the groups get to perform their role-plays, with the rest of the class as audience. Before each group begins its performance, the students arrange themselves in a freeze-frame that is intended to capture the essence of their scene, and Monica photographs them.

Heteroglossia, classroom scripts and ways of reading

Gutierrez *et al.* (1995) have explored the ways in which power is constructed between the teacher and students. Using Bakhtin's ([1975] 1981) concepts of dialogic meaning and social heteroglossia, they present a view of the classroom as 'inherently multi-voiced' and suggest that 'social heteroglossia, or the inherently intertextual and interdiscursive nature of social interaction, is not only a feature of novelistic writing, but a feature of the world' (Gutierrez *et al.* 1995: 446). Their observation of classroom interaction leads them to argue, however, that in most classrooms what is produced is a 'rigidly monologic teacher script', through which the teacher's power is maintained and in which the 'dominant cultural values' are reflected:

> While some students contribute to and participate in the teacher script, those who do not comply with the teacher's rules for participation form their own *counterscript*. In this context, members of the classroom community hold varied expertise in the form of local knowledge, but the inscribed knowledge of the teacher and classroom regularly displaces the local and culturally varied knowledge of the students.
>
> (Gutierrez *et al.* 1995: 446–447)

It is easy to see a parallel between the monologic practices described by Gutierrez *et al.* and the 'scaffolding' version of the ZPD inscribed in policy. The assumption, for example in the *Literacy Progress Units* (DfEE 2001d) from which I quoted in Chapter 2, is that students' acquisition of (approved) literacy depends on the elimination of error and compliance with rules. In such contexts, it is, perhaps, not surprising that 'counterscripts' have proliferated – counterscripts that are experienced by teachers as disruptive and anti-educational.

In place of the unproductive, discordant coexistence of monologic teacher script and disaffected student counterscript, Gutierrez *et al.* propose a 'third space' – a place which seems to bear more than a passing resemblance to the fully social, dialectical version of the ZPD outlined by Daniels (see Chapter 2).

The only space where a true interaction or communication between teacher and student can occur in this classroom is in the middle ground, or 'third space,' in which a Bakhtinian social heteroglossia is possible. Conceiving the classroom as a place for social heteroglossia reveals the potential for the classroom to become a site where no cultural discourses are secondary. Acknowledging the inherent cognitive and sociocultural benefits that come from the multiple discourses is of particular importance, especially in classrooms populated largely by African American, Latino, and mixed-race students.

(Gutierrez *et al.* 1995: 447)

As an example of the teacher's monologic script, Gutierrez *et al.* provide a 'current events' quiz in a ninth-grade classroom. There is, it seems to me, a direct and illuminating contrast between the cultural practices of the quiz, where the teacher asks questions about stories selected from that day's *Los Angeles Times*, in which the teacher defines knowledge in such a way as to construct the students as ignorant, and the ways in which 'current events' are introduced into Monica's lesson. In the lesson that I observed, no single source or script is privileged to the exclusion of others – though Monica does question the reliability of Foyzur's internet-based sources. The world is allowed into the classroom, not as a prepackaged entity but as material to be constructed, interrogated and contested within the dialogic discursive practices of the classroom. Thus Kemi's fierce criticism of the Pope builds on Nazrul's assertion of gay rights, and Monica introduces Morlette's autobiography – her experiences in South Africa – as potential subject matter for the class's exploration of violence. When I listened to Nazrul and his group talking about the situation in the Occupied Territories, it was clear that Nazrul saw Palestine as different from the cases cited by other students, where violence was construed as legitimate if it were a direct response to, a reciprocation of, equivalent violence (defending one's friend in a playground fight, standing up to bullies, and so on). What Nazrul was arguing was that the *Intifada* was justified because of the *general and historical* denial of Palestinian rights by the state of Israel. I would want to argue that this represents a more developed, more political, view of violence within a nexus of historically situated power relationships – not fully articulated, perhaps, but there nonetheless.

Curriculum, as social heteroglossia, is a constructed text, a mosaic of the multiple texts of the participants; it is the social practice of the classroom. Redefining curriculum as social practice forces the abandonment of monologic instruction and provides the social and cognitive rationale for including and constructing multiple forms of knowing.

(Gutierrez *et al.* 1995: 468–469)

The lesson that I observed has to be understood in the context of the history of the teacher's relationship with the class (the argument that was made in

Chapter 2). Monica had been teaching the class since the beginning of Year 7 – so for nearly two years. What one sees in one lesson is the product of, or stands in a relationship with, the students' collective experience of other lessons in which they have participated in similar activities. In discussion after the lesson, Monica suggested that lessons such as this one can only be achieved with a class that the teacher has 'trained up' since Year 7; qualifying this, though, was her recognition that classes have their own identities, that this is a good class – which is a way of gesturing at the social dynamics of the group, the class's sense of its own identity. Monica talked of a girl who had been in the class until her family moved out of London, a girl with Tourette's syndrome. She told of the girl's behaviour, of how upsetting other students found it but how they had accepted it over time. The story is about the class's – the students' – inclusive attitudes and behaviours, but it also reveals Monica's sense of the history of the class and its (social) development.

For me as an observer, the characteristics – and the quality – of this lesson were thrown into sharp relief by the fact that this was the eighteenth lesson I had observed in a three-week period, and all the others had been taught by students on the initial teacher education course on which I taught. The fundamental contrast here is not one of competence but rather of the widely differing timescales involved – and hence of the difference in the classroom relationships established. Continuity is an enabling condition – it permits the possibility of the development of a relationship, of shared experiences and expectations becoming part of the discursive fabric of individual lessons (Freedman 1995).

I indicated at the start that what I observed in this single lesson seems to me to be a recognisable version of English. I am reminded of Tony Burgess' description of a series of lessons in another East London comprehensive school, lessons in which 'the activities of literature are constructed from within deepening and elaborating classroom discourses' (Burgess 1984: 59). In urban classrooms in the United States, likewise, the practices recorded by Suzanne Miller (2003) and by Carol Lee (2001) share important points of correspondence, in the sense of development over time, in the respect with which students' contributions were treated, in the collaborative construction of richly intercultural meanings and understandings, with the practice that I observed in Monica's classroom.

All of this might appear to have very little to do with the reading of *Julius Caesar* – and yet, it seems to me, it is fundamentally important in determining the character of that reading. What is constituted in these interactions is the social arena of the classroom, the social relationships of the classroom, not as preconditions for reading/English/work but as inextricably bound up with the experience of subject English. More specifically, the first part of the lesson creates the parameters, the fields of reference and of relevance, for the reading of the text. It announces that students' views, experiences, knowledge of the world outside and of the social relations within and beyond the classroom, are implicated in their reading. And that links with something else identified by Monica after the lesson – the fact that the class is enjoying *Julius Caesar*. Is there a connection between the seriousness with which the students are treated in their English lessons – the fact that they are expected to discuss things that matter and discuss them in an 'adult' way – and their enjoyment of 'adult' – both difficult and high status/elite culture – texts?

Whatever else this lesson is, it cannot be construed as an exercise – it is not presented as a preparation for something else, as a way of honing students' skills of debate or role-play, but rather as the thing itself (Edelsky 1996; Moll and Whitmore 1993). And this also suggests a link with Vygotsky's tendency to look at development through the lens of problem-solving: the complex relationship of language and learning is tested (and visible) in contexts where participants are presented with problems. So here what Monica does is to suggest that the lesson is part of an investigation of Brutus: Brutus is a problem to be explored. Why did he decide to kill his friend? It is significant, too, that the question is posed by Monica in these terms – not why did he kill his friend, even, but why did he *decide* to: the emphasis is placed on an intellectual process, on how the decision was made. This approach is common to both parts of the lesson: each is introduced by Monica posing a question. Also significant, perhaps, is that this is the only explicit or marked commonality: there is no – inevitably reductive – attempt to articulate the relationship between the two halves of the lesson, save only in the structural parallel: a question is posed, and then students are invited to explore answers to it.

Of course, it would be possible to construe these activities and the lesson in which they were situated not as literacy practices but as something else – as 'speaking and listening' (in the jargon of the National Curriculum, a separate attainment target, not to be confused with reading – DfEE 1999a). For only a few minutes in the hour-long lesson were students in Monica's class focusing their attention directly on the printed words of the script of *Julius Caesar*. And yet every part of the lesson functioned to create the opportunity for students to explore the play and to collaborate in the construction of a reading of it, a reading that paid attention to its dynamic and difficult interplay of perspectives, its movement between personal and political, a reading that amounted to full engagement with the text. It is important, I think, to stress that what the lesson demonstrated was that there simply is no necessary connection between accessibility and dumbing down. This was not a twenty-first century equivalent of *Lambs' Tales,* not Shakespeare domesticated or trivialised (Bottoms 2000), but a way of reading that enabled students to draw on a vast array of social semiotic resources to make the text meaningful.

The question posed by the second title to this chapter alludes to Stanley Fish's *Is There a Text in This Class?* (1980). I have already indicated, in Chapter 3, something of what seems to me to be problematic about Fish's concept of an interpretive community, though I would want to argue that the Year 8 class that I observed was indeed acting as – had become – an interpretive community. The text that they were reading, though, was not one that was instantiated merely on the pages of their partial scripts of *Julius Caesar*, in the course of the lesson, the text was read as it became, as it were, productively multimodal – its multimodality, instantiated in talk, in movement, in gesture, in the images of the tableaux, inextricably linked to the meanings that the class produced.

Wertsch *et al.* (1993) draw a contrast between the passive responses that are required of students in most classrooms and situations where more active participation is demanded. In the latter, as in Monica's classroom, learners:

> are required to take on an increasingly active responsibility for the strategic processes involved in reading comprehension precisely because they are required to participate in intermental functioning by ventriloquating through a social language that presupposes their taking on cognitive authority.
>
> (Wertsch *et al.* 1993: 349)

Learning is happening in the semiotic work of Monica's students – in their interactions, not (merely) in their heads. And in this process, the text of *Julius Caesar* is being remade: it is a sign that 'maintains its vitality and dynamism and the capacity for further development' (Vološinov [1929] 1986: 23, quoted in Chapter 2) precisely because of this remaking in the intersection of different accents, different interests.

Note

1 An earlier version of this chapter appeared in Yandell (2007).

Chapter 6

Literature and representation

The text, the classroom
and the world outside

In this chapter I want to do three things.[1] First, developing an aspect of the discussion of literature and reading position that figured briefly in Chapter 3, I will discuss the issue of representation in literature. Second, developing one of the themes from the previous chapter, I want to look further at the relationship between texts, teachers and school students. And third, again touching on an aspect of the previous chapter, I want to suggest ways in which the literature read and written in the classroom can contribute towards students' understanding of and engagement with the wider world. In exploring these questions, I will be exploring the categorisation of literature enacted in policy, and how policy envisages that different categories of literature will be read differently, for different purposes. I will be comparing what policy has to say on these matters with the ways in which texts that might be construed as multicultural are read in particular classrooms, by particular groups of students.

Representing otherness

In 1985, when I started work as a teacher in a boys' comprehensive in Tower Hamlets, one of the first texts that I chose to read with my Year 8 group was *Young Warriors* (1967). The novel, by Jamaican author V. S. Reid, tells a coming-of-age story of five Maroon warriors who help their people to outwit and ambush the occupying Redcoat army. At this distance, I do not know why I chose it – whether it was to do with the boys' adventure story format of the novel, with its anti-imperialist narrative and positioning, whether it seemed to be accessible enough, to my highly inexpert eyes, for my students to be able to cope with it (whatever coping with it might mean). I asked my students to look at the front cover, to describe what they could see and then to predict as much as they could about the novel they were about to read (see Figure 6.1). It's an interesting exercise, both as a way of activating students' prior knowledge and as an opportunity to render explicit some aspects of the conditions of literary production. The content of the image – the foregrounding of the Maroon boys, the adoption of their perspective on the advancing Redcoats, the extent to which the image represents a particular moment in the novel – all provide useful ways

Figure 6.1 The front cover of *Young Warriors* (Reid 1967)

into the written text, productive foci for the students' conversation. But there are also issues about the style of the illustration – the use of primary colours, the lack of individuation in the four Maroon figures in the foreground (and maybe even the problematic, racialised stereotype of the Maroons in the treetops). When students returned to the front cover after reading the novel, many felt that the illustration marked a dumbing down of the content, a means to market the text as 'safe', unthreatening, childish.

What immediately attracted the attention and interest of my first Year 8 group, however, was not the front cover but the back, and more particularly the photo of V. S. Reid in the centre of it (Figure 6.2). 'Who is this?' they asked. I explained that this was the author. What was completely clear from my students' responses was that, for them as for me, encountering black authors was something of a novelty. The class was almost entirely composed of students of Bangladeshi origin. There was an identification on their part with the author; but what was the basis of this identification? It was not a product of language or geography or religion or ethnicity, in any straightforward sense. It was not, in other words, an issue of any narrowly-defined identity politics. But the students' obvious surprise – and pleasure – was related to their sense of themselves, like V. S. Reid,

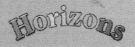

Five Maroon boys pass tests of skill and endurance to become warriors in their village. When they go out hunting to celebrate, they suddenly discover that the forest is full of their enemies, the English Redcoats. In the campaign that follows, the defeat of the Maroons seems certain, but the young warriors help to bring about a great victory.

V. S. Reid is a leading Jamaican writer, and another of his novels, *Sixty-Five*, is also published by Longman Caribbean.

Longman Caribbean

ISBN 0 582 76569 2

Figure 6.2 The back cover of *Young Warriors* (Reid 1967)

being defined as 'other' by the dominant culture in which they lived. They understood, I would argue, that in a clear, political sense they were black.

Is there, then, a very simple definition of multicultural literature? Is it just a way of referring to literature written by black authors? What, though, of the subject-matter of such literature? Is it also an element in the multicultural identity of *Young Warriors* that it tells a story of Maroon people? And what of the presence of the white Redcoat soldiers in the narrative? Does the fact that the novel enacts a conflict between organised groups of runaway Maroons and the colonial power make it more multicultural? To put it another way, would it have been a less multicultural text if Tommy and the other warriors had restricted themselves to hunting coneys?

Versions of multiculturalism had been given prominence in the Bullock Report (DES 1975), with its a recognition of the relevance of students' out-of-school identities and experiences to what happens in the classroom (see Chapter 1). But such pluralist notions were always contested. Barely a year after the publication of the Bullock Report, the speech that James Callaghan, the then Prime Minister, made at Ruskin College, signalled an agenda for education that has continued to dominate the discourse of policy throughout the intervening decades: the focus on basic skills, on standards and reductive versions of accountability has left little space for more nuanced considerations of curriculum and pedagogy. Shortly after I started work in Tower Hamlets, the Bullock Report's commitment to more locally accountable, student- and community-centred approaches was effaced in official discourse by an entirely different model of the relationship between students' lives and identities outside school, on the one hand, and, on the other, the school curriculum. When the consultation paper on the National Curriculum was published (DES 1987), it used the language of progressive identity politics in a statement of entitlement that denied any curricular space for the exploration of difference, of subjectivity. This was, quite explicitly, to be a one-size-fits-all curriculum, one that ensured 'that all pupils, regardless of sex, ethnic origin and geographical location, have access to broadly the same good and relevant curriculum and programmes of study' (DES 1987: 4).

In this paradigm, the school curriculum, detailed in the programmes of study, derives its validity not from its responsiveness to local interests but from its universality. And, if the curriculum is to be 'broadly the same', little space is left for any serious attention to be paid to what Bullock termed 'the language and culture of the home'. The key word here is 'regardless': local differences – of gender, history, culture – are to be disregarded. One might be permitted to wonder about the meaning of 'relevant' in this context. Relevant to what, or to whom? What does such relevance look like? This formulation has, nonetheless, been massively influential. If one enters 'curriculum' and 'regardless' as link terms in an internet search engine such as Google, one finds hundreds of UK school websites, all of them proclaiming their commitment to providing a curriculum that is beneficial precisely because it is delivered 'regardless' of the identities and specific characteristics of its students.

Perhaps part of the reason for this universalist curriculum promise/premise is that it distances schooling from the dangerously controversial territory of identity politics while simultaneously colonising the language of equality of opportunity. What could be more egalitarian than a commitment to a common curriculum? And what, at the same time, could be more comforting to those who fear social fragmentation and who regard the curriculum as a means of both asserting and re-establishing a single, national identity?

And yet, of course, even for those most vehemently committed to a notion of a curriculum that is 'good' because it pays no regard to the histories of the students to whom it is to be delivered, the plain fact of actually existing social diversity cannot be avoided completely. So, from the earliest incarnation of the National Curriculum there has been a small plot labelled 'multiculturalism'. It appeared in the first version of the National Curriculum for English in the 'Programmes of Study for Reading', in the instruction that at Key Stage 2:

> The reading materials provided should include a range of fiction, non-fiction and poetry, as well as periodicals suitable for children of this age. These should include works written in English from other cultures.
>
> (DES/Welsh Office 1990: 30)

In the National Curriculum Council's *Non-statutory Guidance* that accompanied the publication of the first version of the National Curriculum, the section on literature contains this advice: 'Texts should reflect the multicultural nature of society, including home-language and dual-language texts' (NCC 1990: D2). In the version of the National Curriculum that was current at the time of my data collection, there is the following statement of entitlement:

Texts from different cultures and traditions
Pupils should be taught:

a   to understand the values and assumptions in the texts
b   the significance of the subject matter and the language
c   the distinctive qualities of literature from different traditions
d   how familiar themes are explored in different cultural contexts [e.g. how childhood is portrayed, references to oral or folk traditions]
e   to make connections and comparisons between texts from different cultures

(DfEE 1999a: 49)

It is worth comparing this with the preceding section:

English literary heritage
Pupils should be taught:

a   how and why texts have been influential and significant [e.g. the influence of Greek myths, the Authorised Version of the Bible, the Arthurian legends]

b   the characteristics of texts that are considered to be of high quality
c   the appeal and importance of these texts over time

(DfEE 1999a: 49)

When exploring texts 'from different cultures and traditions', the student is placed in the role of cultural anthropologist; when encountering the 'English literary heritage', it would seem that awe and wonder are more appropriate responses. The assumption is that the student will encounter difference in reading texts from different cultures, but will be inducted into her or his own 'heritage' in worshipping at more canonical shrines.

This schematic distinction is tendentious, to say the least. The same version of the National Curriculum lists as 'major writers from different cultures and traditions' Arthur Miller and Tennessee Williams alongside Athol Fugard and Wole Soyinka, Hemingway and Steinbeck together with Achebe and Ngugi wa Thiong'o. Meanwhile, the 'major playwrights' named as part of the 'English literary heritage' include Congreve, Goldsmith, O'Casey, Shaw, Sheridan and Oscar Wilde.

Among post-1914 writers of fiction, there is James Joyce; among the poets, Sylvia Plath. What I am not doing here is requesting a re-classification exercise, a literary equivalent of the bureaucratic madness of the apartheid regime in South Africa. What I am suggesting is that such lists are inevitably arbitrary. A line is drawn between what is part of an 'English' tradition and what belongs elsewhere.

When school students began their GCSE courses, they found in their English *Anthology* a section headed 'Different Cultures' (AQA 2002: 5–18).[2] In the earlier versions of the *Anthology*, this had been entitled 'Poems from Other Cultures and Traditions' (NEAB 1996: 17–28; NEAB/AQA 1998: 17–26). The change might be regarded as progressive – a recognition, at any rate, that the ascription of otherness to certain cultures made an assumption about the cultural positioning of the reader. The move was, nonetheless, a slight one. The *Anthology* continued to operationalise the National Curriculum's distinction between the canonical and the multicultural: all that united the poems selected for inclusion in the 'Different Cultures' section was difference. The *Anthology* encouraged particular ways of reading the poems contained therein. They were stripped of history, of specificity. Did it matter that Tatamkhulu Afrika's 'Nothing's Changed' (AQA 2002: 6) was written in the immediate aftermath of the end of apartheid in South Africa? Or that Achebe's 'Vultures' (AQA 2002: 10) moves from the lived experience of the Nigerian Civil War to pose a more universal question about the ethical status of 'kindred love'? Apparently not. 'Vultures', bizarrely, was accompanied by an illustration of vultures, as if, somehow, it should be read as a nature poem.

The problem of all anthologies is that they are someone else's selection, and that, in consequence, the meaning of the anthologised text becomes determined by the anthologist's criteria for inclusion. This tendency becomes much more acute when the reader's response to the anthologised texts is to be assessed through an examination question. When the anthologist chooses thematically, or historically, or geographically (war poetry, Mersey poets, or whatever), there is some room for manoeuvre on the part of the reader, some space in which the complexity and the uncertainty of the relationship between the text and the world beyond the text might be negotiated. In this section of the AQA *Anthology*, though, cultural difference is the sole criterion, and in its wake are dragged some fairly disreputable assumptions about culture and identity. If these are poems from different cultures, then, presumably, there is a one-for-one correspondence between the poem and the culture which it represents – the culture that it is, so to speak, 'from'. Culture thus becomes like a replica football kit, an instantly recognisable index of affiliation: the badge signals membership that is, simultaneously, inclusive and exclusive: one poem, one poet, one culture. Such a view of culture – stable, single and essentialist – would be questionable in any context. What makes it seem positively perverse is that many of the poems contained in the *Anthology* problematise precisely these assumptions, as they enact within themselves processes of cultural negotiation and contestation, exploring shifts in identity and cultural positioning and relating these shifts both to global historical processes and to individual subjectivities.

'Half Caste': contested readings, contested identities

What happened when these poems were read in the classroom was shaped by the immediate context of the *Anthology* and the overarching context of the GCSE examination. Sometimes, nevertheless, school students' (and even teachers') purposes were less narrowly instrumental than these contexts might suggest. I want to turn now to describe what happened when one of the *Anthology* poems, John Agard's 'Half Caste' (AQA 2002: 13) was read in Wharfside School, in April 2006. In analysing what was happening in the lesson, I want to indicate the importance of approaches to teaching and learning that are attentive to the cultures, histories and subjectivities of the learners. I also want to draw attention to the complexity of the processes involved in the reading that went on, the complexity of the meanings that were made and contested.

It is a mixed-ability Year 10 English class (14- and 15-year-olds), halfway through their GCSE course. They have just started work on the 'Different Cultures' section of the *Anthology*, and Agard's is the first poem that they will study. Before looking at the poem, however, their teacher, Neville, asks them to devise an improvisation:

[08:15]
TEACHER: . . . it can be about anything you like, *anything*, but it must end with the two words, someone saying the two words, 'Excuse me' and preferably a freeze frame, because I know how good some of you are at drama, you know

how to use body language and gestures . . . if you can end with 'Excuse me' and a freeze frame, that's exactly what I want.

(Transcript from videotaped lesson, 21 April 2006)[3]

After 10 minutes of rehearsal, groups of students present their role-plays to the class. Jamal's group creates a newsreader's desk, signifying a studio, at the front of the room, from where the anchorman introduces Patrick as the roving reporter, interviewing a football manager. Patrick's questions about the team's recent poor results is met by an angry, defensive and dismissive 'Excuse me'. Amina's group goes next. She and three other girls of Bangladeshi heritage organise themselves into two pairs who encounter each other in the undefined public space – a corridor, a street – that the classroom has become. Neither pair can give way, and the slight physical contact of their meeting is accompanied by this dialogue:

[23:30]
SARAH: What?
AMINA: Why're you barging us for?
SARAH: You're the ones who's barging us.
AMINA: Excuse me, *bitch*.

Amina's last word, delivered with particular emphasis, is lent even more power by the fact that it breaches the rules of the game that Neville has established – the instruction that the role-play should end with 'Excuse me'.

Mutib's group has devised a scenario in which Salman has a met a girl (Susan) whom he fancies. His attempts to chat her up are interrupted by the arrival of Mutib, who informs Salman that the girl is his sister. 'Excuse me!' says Salman, with an exaggerated politeness that is belied by body language that indicates that no ground will be conceded.

After the presentations, Neville encourages his students to think about the different ways of saying 'Excuse me' that they have explored. Mutib comments:

[32:20]
MUTIB: It's like manners . . . you say excuse me instead of swearing . . . it's a way of showing that you're angry without swearing at him or shouting or saying anything that might upset him.

Tariq reminds the class of Mutib's much earlier suggestion, that 'Excuse me' could be 'flirty', and Neville asks Mutib to explain what he meant by this:

[34:50]
MUTIB: Say I was a girl, and a man come to me and put his hand like on my leg and that if, if he was ugly you'd say 'excuse me', *[raises pitch of voice, rising intonation, signalling rejection]* like, but if he was good-looking you'd say

'excuse me' *[again raises pitch of voice, this time attempting to sound seductive, interested]*.
SALMAN: No you wouldn't, *I* wouldn't.

Was Salman contesting Mutib's view of women, his assumption that a woman's response to physical harassment would vary according to her judgement of the man's appearance? Or was he contesting the generalisation, Mutib's confidence in speaking for all women? Or was he uncomfortable with Mutib's gender-switching performance? I don't know. What does emerge from these moments is a sense of how much the students already know about the layered nuances of language, how it is used to enforce and contest power relationships and how these exchanges are situated in a dense web of culturally-specific, multimodal meaning-making. As Vološinov argues:

> *Verbal communication can never be understood and explained outside of this connection with a concrete situation.* Verbal intercourse is inextricably inter-woven with communication of other types, all stemming from the common ground of production communication. It goes without saying that word cannot be divorced from this eternally generative, unified process of com-munication. In its concrete connection with a situation, verbal communica-tion is always accompanied by social acts of a nonverbal character . . . and is often only an accessory to these acts . . . Language acquires life and histori-cally evolves precisely here, in concrete verbal communication, and not in the abstract linguistic system of language forms, nor in the individual psyche of speakers.
>
> (Vološinov [1929] 1986: 95, original emphasis)

Vološinov's argument with Saussurean linguistics, discussed in Chapter 2, helps to illuminate the tensions between the abstractions of policy (instantiated in the National Curriculum and in the GCSE syllabus) and the concreteness of classroom interactions: the latter exemplify Vološinov's concept of an 'eternally generative, unified process of communication'.

The students' improvisations, and the discussion arising out of them, seemed ideal preparation for reading Agard's poem. The students, given time and space to investigate and imagine other scenarios in which 'Excuse me' might carry a heavy semantic load – and the opportunity to draw on their knowledge of sites beyond the classroom – arrive at the poem already sensitised to the multiaccented, socially determined character of the sign.

When Neville puts a new slide on the interactive whiteboard (IWB), there is an immediate, explosive response to what is displayed – the title of the poem:

[38:13]
MALCOLM: That is so racist, that is so racist.
TEACHER: Malcolm, do you want to say a bit more?

MALCOLM: No I don't want to say a bit more, that is so disgusting, despicable.
MUTIB: You might as well call someone a Paki or something, it's the same thing.
MALCOLM: I don't care – I don't know what it means, anyway.

It matters, in this exchange, that Malcolm is a mixed-race student and Mutib is of South Asian heritage: it matters, but what they say is not explained by such facts. There is, in their reaction, genuine outrage; equally, there is a *performance* of outrage. The outrage and the performance are both equally inseparable from the context of the classroom, from the fact that the offensive words have appeared on the IWB and hence are part of the formal script of the lesson: outrage enables the students to contest the power relations of the classroom, to stand in judgement on the text that they are supposed to be reading, rather than be judged by the accuracy, sensitivity or plausibility of their reading of it.

When the uproar subsides, Neville perseveres with an exploration of what the title might mean. It becomes apparent that there is not a consensual view on this:

[40:17]
TEACHER: Malcolm, I would like you to say if you agree with what Tariq says this means.
MALCOLM: What did he say?
TEACHER: Tariq—
TARIQ: When somebody, when you call someone a half caste it may be a different religion, or they might be, they might have two religions, two backgrounds.
GAVIN: You can't have two religions.
TARIQ: {You can.
SALMAN: {Course you can, your mum might be a Muslim and your dad might be a Christian.
GAVIN: Well *you* can't have two religions.
SALMAN: Yeah, I know, that's what I'm saying.

In the current climate of licensed Islamophobia, it is not surprising that Tariq, a relatively recent arrival from Afghanistan, should foreground religious identity, or difference in religion, as the primary line of divide. He is quite clear, too, about the force of the term 'half caste': 'when you call someone a half caste' directs attention to the context for the utterance, a context where the label is attached by another as a term of abuse. In the ensuing debate, countering Gavin's insistence on an individual's brand loyalty to a single religion, both Salman and Tariq show an awareness of religious affiliation as sociocultural, historically produced and situated.

The matter, though, is far from settled, and it is Malcolm who re-opens the debate:

[46:37]
MALCOLM: What's the difference between mixed race and half caste? Is mixed race just the colour of your skin?

TEACHER: Does anyone want to answer that?

TARIQ: Mixed race is when you are from, when you have two backgrounds, when your father, your dad is from one country and your mum is from another, like me from London and—

SALMAN: No, it's not, though, mixed race is two different, like your mother being a different colour from your dad.

TARIQ: That's what I just said.

SALMAN: No, you didn't, you said backgrounds, as in countries.

TARIQ: Yeah, that's what I mean, backgrounds and—

SALMAN: {No.

For Tariq, 'race' only makes sense in terms of history, origins, background; for Salman, on the other hand, it is all a question of skin colour. Neville lets the discussion run for a while. Gavin and Salman explore whether someone with one white and one Chinese parent should be categorised as mixed race. Gavin, who is white, thinks not, presumably because he associates the term only with the children of liaisons between white and black (African or African-Caribbean) people. Salman convinces him that the term is more elastic, but maintains a distinction between 'race' and nationality ('you could be white Chinese though'). Neville encourages the class to explore this further:

[48:29]

TEACHER: Is a race anything other than a colour? Could you have two people of the same colour who were different races?

[murmurs – confusion – then]

MUTIB: Yeah – Indian and Pakistani.

TEACHER: OK, Mutib, tell me about that.

MUTIB: Well, I don't know, that could be like half caste, or it could be like normal, because brown is brown.

TEACHER: OK, Ben and Sarah, we'll come to you in a moment, I want you to take Mutib's idea, if someone has an Indian mum and a Pakistani dad, are they mixed race?

[a mixture of yeahs and nos]

Mutib suggests that the answer to the question might be arrived at by consulting a dictionary, or by searching on the internet. (In effect, he is making an appeal to the higher linguistic authority that Vološinov argues does not exist: Mutib pins his hopes for a resolution of this difficulty, momentarily, on language as a stable, already-defined, system of signs. But the sign is being re-made in the course of this dialogue.) Salman, meanwhile, makes explicit the connection between his sense of himself – the identity which he wishes to present – and his definition of mixed race:

[49:16]

SALMAN: I'm British but I'm black, I'm born in England, I've lived in England the rest of my life, and from my passport, I'm British – that's just like you could say a British man and a British woman, but er I'm still thingy, I'm still black and if I was to go fuck some white bird and have some mixed race kids, they're gonna be mixed race, innit.

Mutib's response is both diplomatic and thought-provoking, as he insists on the contingency of all such labels:

[49:40]
MUTIB: Yeah. For a black person and a white person, that's mixed race, innit. But if there's an Indian man and a Pakistani woman, then for them that's mixed race.
GAVIN: No, if they're the same colour, it's not mixed race.
[there is a pause – a long one – silence: there's a lot of thinking going on]
MUTIB: That's a hard one, man, innit.

The conversation continues. Malcolm attempts to explore a hypothetical question that is, simultaneously, a way of teasing Salman about his insistence on his British identity:

[50:05]
MALCOLM: Say if Salman, I dunno where he's from, Nigeria, wherever.
SALMAN: No, no.
MALCOLM: Kenya.
SALMAN: NO.
MALCOLM: Congo.
SALMAN: NO!!
MALCOLM: Angola.
SALMAN: NO not Angola!
TEACHER: Malcolm, why don't you ask him?
SALMAN: —Britain, man, England!
MALCOLM: All right, England, then. Say if someone was born Nigeria, right, and like the bird was born Kenya, and they had sex, does the child, it wouldn't come out mixed race?

Rebecca talks about having an English mother and an Irish father, and Malcolm responds by making a distinction between culture and race: in his view, Rebecca's heritage is culturally mixed, but not racially. Martin, however, voices uncertainty about whether this is, in practice, an absolute distinction. Gavin shifts the terrain – while also returning the discussion to what is going on in Agard's poem – with an appeal to the common-sense view of other people's perceptions:

[51:35]
GAVIN: See when people look at you, they don't turn round and say you're mixed race, do they – they say you're white . . . because people wouldn't walk down

the street and say Martin was mixed race even though he might have, I don't know, a German dad or a Polish mum or something like that.

Gavin, who is white, is a powerful and often somewhat truculent presence at the back of the room. What he says here is, in some sense, nothing more or less than the truth, the truth of the categories that operate beyond the school gates, on the streets of East London. But these categories are neither neutral nor unproblematic, in the world outside as in the classroom. The 'people' to whom Gavin refers are, presumably, people like him: he shares their confidence in deploying the categories of race to determine others' identity. It is not coincidental that Gavin found it difficult to accept Salman's examples of different versions of 'mixed race' such as Chinese/white: for Gavin, the superordinate categories are white and black. He has some distance to travel, I suspect, before he can acknowledge the justice of Agard's ridicule of such external, reductive ascription of identity. But at least, in this lesson, the students' dialogic enquiry into the category of 'race' opens it up for further perusal.

In the course of the discussion, neither Gavin nor anyone else in the room has been expected to 'cast off the language and culture of the home', in the words of the Bullock Report (DES 1975). It matters, too, that Neville, their teacher, is black, and that he is prepared to talk to the students about his parents' background in Goa and his sense of his own cultural identity. He is a participant in the dialogue:

[52:36]
TEACHER: So here's a question. I've told you about my background yesterday, didn't I. My family, parents would describe themselves as Goan . . . but all I know is London, and England.
SALMAN: So you class yourself as British.
TEACHER: So what if I were to go to Goa, and have a child with someone who had only known Goa, would the child be mixed race?
[several nos]
TEACHER: . . . but my culture would be entirely different because all I really know is London.

The debate has continued to acknowledge, indeed to be structured around, the students' sense of their historically situated identities. There is nothing cosy about this. Mutib's insistence on the relevance of the divide between India and Pakistan to the subject under discussion involves him (and his peers) in strenuous intellectual work at the same time as demanding considerable resources of diplomacy: he manages to disagree with Gavin, to suggest that Gavin's notion of what mixed race means is too narrow to be universally applicable, without causing offence. Equally, the students are prepared to tease out the inconsistencies and silences in their peers' presentation of self – as when Malcolm prods Salman to acknowledge his African heritage.

From one perspective, Salman's insistence on defining himself as British – and not as African – can be seen as analogous to Tariq's earlier presentation of himself as 'from London' or to Amina's feisty, assertive role-play persona ('Excuse me, *bitch*'). It is not possible simply to read off students' classroom identities from data on their histories, their heritage, their home identities. The selves that they perform in the classroom are inflections of those other, out-of-school identities, and, as such, they can legitimately be construed as indications of the students' agency and of the classroom's potential as a site within which different versions of the self can be fashioned and experimented with. Individual students' room for manoeuvre should not be exaggerated, though. There is powerful pressure on them to produce approved versions of their identities. Within the classroom, as in the outside world, the new arrival has a lowly status. There is a strong urge to belong. How could it be otherwise in a society where government and mainstream media habitually present both refugees and migrant workers as a problem, as drains on the nation's resources? And these, too, form the concrete situation within which the students' utterances must be construed: no wonder, then, that Salman insists on his Britishness and Tariq presents himself as a Londoner.[4]

And, in this situation, the social and affective dimensions of classroom interaction and hence of learning seem really rather important. There is much more to be done if all the students in the class are to understand what Martin is already reaching towards, in his suggestion, made after listening to Agard's performance, that Agard's 'Excuse me' has an element of 'retaliation – like he's taking the confusing points and using them against him'. There is, equally, more work to be done if the students' everyday concepts of race, culture and ethnicity are to be brought into a dialectical relationship with more scientific understandings of these terms. (Whether all of this work would best be accomplished in the English classroom is not clear: both history and science departments might have contributions to make.) The claim that I am making, though, is for the importance of the work that was being done in Neville's classroom in this lesson, work that enabled the students to begin to grasp Agard's poem while also grappling with questions of identity and difference that continue to exert a shaping influence on our society. This is, it seems to me, the work of cultural production (and contestation), to which I alluded in Chapter 2.

The world beyond the classroom

When I started teaching in London, a novel that was widely used as a class reader in London schools was Beverley Naidoo's *Journey to Jo'burg* (1985). Telling the story of Naledi and Tiro, a sister and brother who travel from their village to Johannesburg to find their mother, a maid for a white family, so that she can return to the village and save the life of her youngest child, the novel lays bare the grotesque, savage inequalities of the apartheid regime. And that, of course, was the point. English teachers chose to read it with their classes for reasons that lie beyond the approaches to 'texts from different cultures and traditions' proposed by the National Curriculum. Educating London school students about apartheid South Africa was both a contribution to antiracist education and a natural extension of the ethical commitments that have historically shaped English teachers' conception of their subject and, in particular, of the role of literature.

These same ethical commitments have underpinned teachers' selection of class readers from Hans Peter Richter's *Friedrich* ([1961] 1971) to, more recently, John Boyne's *The Boy in the Striped Pyjamas* (2006).[5] Whatever other – aesthetic – criteria may have been in play, part of the justification for such choices was, without doubt, teachers' sense of the importance of teaching about the Holocaust. Now, some English departments have started to explore Elizabeth Laird and Sonia Nimr's *A Little Piece of Ground* (2003). Set in the Occupied Territories, it tells the story of Karim, a Palestinian boy from a middle-class family in Ramallah, and his friendship with Hopper, a boy from the nearby refugee camp. Their shared passion for football takes them to the 'little piece of ground' of the title, the stretch of wasteland where they play together until their games are interrupted by the arrival of an Israeli tank. The makeshift pitch thus functions as a synecdoche, standing for the state of Palestine itself, as the novel attempts to represent the impact of the occupation on the lives of ordinary Palestinians. Such multicultural texts demand a place within the English curriculum, not for the anthropological interests recommended by the National Curriculum but for reasons of solidarity. It is the rationale provided by Atticus Finch in that classic – if deeply problematic – piece of multicultural literature, *To Kill a Mockingbird*:

> Atticus stood up and walked to the end of the porch. When he had completed his examination of the wisteria vine he strolled back to me.
> 'First of all,' he said, 'if you can learn a simple trick, Scout, you'll get along a lot better with all kinds of folks. You never really understand a person until you consider things from his point of view—'
> 'Sir?'
> '—until you climb into his skin and walk around in it.'
>
> (Lee 1960: 36)

Solidarity, quite distinct from sympathy, is the recognition of common interest: 'your struggle is our struggle'. It is the movement from the binary opposition of 'I'/'not I' to the collective point of view. And Atticus's prescription of empathy is, perhaps, the literary route whereby this broader perspective might be attained.

As Atticus Finch's words indicate, such claims for the power of literature are nothing new. An adequate account of how (and why) literary texts are read in urban classrooms must not neglect this dimension of the reading experience. What this chapter, particularly in the section that focuses on the discussion of 'Half Caste' among Neville's students, has sought to emphasise is the need to attend equally carefully to the points of view, the positions, of the readers. This emphasis is explored further in the following chapter.

Notes

1 An earlier version of this chapter appeared as Yandell (2008b).
2 I focus on the AQA examination board's GCSE English syllabus (specification A), which was followed by 60 per cent of UK candidates at the time of my data collection. See www.jcq. org.uk/attachments/published/397/JCQ%20GCSE%20Results.pdf, and www.aqa.org.uk/ over/stat_nat.php, both accessed 24 September 2007.
3 Subsequent quotations in this chapter are from the transcript of the same lesson, unless otherwise indicated. In this and in subsequent chapters, excerpts from transcripts of video data are prefaced by an indication of the time that had elapsed since the start of the lesson. The symbol | is used to indicate an overlap in speech between two people.
4 I was working on this chapter on the day after Gordon Brown's first speech as Prime Minister to the Labour Party Conference, a speech in which there were 80 references to Britain and Britishness – and a speech which contains the line, 'I stand for a Britain where it is a mark of citizenship that you should learn our language and traditions' (<http://www.labour.org.uk/ conference/brown_speech>, accessed 25 September 2007). The shift from first to second person and back again is as interesting as the assumptions about language and traditions.
5 See also Vicky Obied's (2007) account of the use of Brecht's magnificent sonnet, 'Emigrant's Lament' as part of an English department's contribution to Refugee Week in an East London school.

Chapter 7

Class readers

Exploring a different *View from the Bridge*

... the written word travels gratifyingly farther than anything else and can be invested with surprising new meanings, some that illuminate the writer to himself.

(Miller [1987] 1990: 350)

Very often a child writes badly because he has nothing he wants to write about.

(Vygotsky 2004: 46)

Different readers, different readings

The survey of literary theory and of ethnographic approaches to literacy in Chapter 3 indicated the widespread acceptance of the proposition that different readers read the same text in different ways. Texts, likewise, are not considered as stable repositories of authorial meaning; they have become slippery shape-shifters, holding up a mirror not so much to nature as to the reader. Reading is semiotic activity, the construction of meaning motivated by the interests of the reader; reading is a process in which the whole subjectivity of the reader is implicated (Kress 2010; see also Chapter 2 of this volume). Each reading is thus necessarily gendered, racialised, historicised: the product of a specific historical subject, reading in a specific historical context.[1]

What happens, though, when different readers, different readings meet? At worst, there may be sound and fury and little else, as rival theoretical positions and idiosyncratic interpretations bounce off each other like marbles in a jar. Richard Levin (1979) long ago poured scorn on the academic competition to produce new readings of old texts. At best, however, a new reading can illuminate for all of us aspects of a familiar text that had previously escaped our notice. Edward Said's (1983) reading of *Mansfield Park*, say, enables other readers to attend more carefully to Sir Thomas Bertram's trips to Antigua – and to grasp the significance of geography as an organising principle in Jane Austen's novel. Said's reading stands, moreover, in an explicitly dialogic relationship to Raymond Williams' reading of Austen in *The Country and the City* (1973). Said argues that

Williams seriously underestimated the extent and importance of global imperialist concerns in English literature from the sixteenth century onwards (and also that Austen's morality is not, as Williams maintained, separable from its socioeconomic basis). That there might be a relationship between Said's own history and his desire to broaden the horizons of Williams' analysis is not reductive of either's contribution: it is to recognise the particularity of each reader's interest, to understand each reading as necessarily and inevitably motivated.

Are some readings, then, better than others? Are some, indeed, permissible and others illicit? And if so, what are the criteria by which they are to be judged? Plausibility? Internal coherence? Impact? Other, more tacit criteria? Just as important, whose criteria are to be used, and how do these criteria operate?

Does different mean worse?

In this chapter, I want to address these questions in relation to an English lesson in Wharfside School and to return to Neville's Year 10 class whose discussions of 'Half Caste' were the focus of the preceding chapter. Before I do so, however, I want to indicate some possible parameters of this discussion by reference to an incident that occurred over 20 years ago, at the boys' secondary school in East London where I had just started working as a teacher. In an end-of-year examination, students were asked to read 'Yellow', a poem by Robert Service (1979: 21–22) which uses an incident in which a man shoots a dog to explore the nature of cowardice.

The students' reading of the poem was assessed through a series of comprehension questions. Even at this distance, it is possible to reconstruct the reasons why my colleagues had chosen this text: it has a strong narrative line, dealing with guns, dogs and death; there is nothing complicated about its poetic form; its language is, for the most part, accessible. At the same time, there is an introspective quality and an emphasis on moral responsibility, both of which could be construed as instantiating central values in the experience of reading within the school English curriculum. So, perhaps, the choice of text both implies a set of values and assumes a particular subjectivity in the reader(s): the choice constructs the (adolescent) masculinity to which the text is supposed to appeal.

When I came to mark my students' exam papers, I encountered a problem. Most of the students in my class were of Bangladeshi heritage. Some had been born in the UK; most had not, and a significant proportion were relatively recent arrivals in this country. In the context of the bizarre literacy practice of the examination, where students are expected to commune in complete isolation with a previously-unseen text, they had encountered a false friend, the word 'yellow'. For my students, yellow denoted a colour: connotations of cowardice were a thing unknown. The more confident, adventurous readers moved from initial attempts to link the title with the location (the yellow, sandy beach) to theories of the salience of racial identity: perhaps, they speculated, the poetic persona was Chinese. For all of them, though, their ignorance of the intended meaning of 'yellow' rendered futile their attempts to arrive at a meaningful reading of the poem. There is a long and rather dishonourable tradition, in staffrooms and in the pages of the education press, of mockery of the howlers perpetrated by examination candidates. What had happened in this case, though, is an example of a much more serious blunder on the examiner's part – an unwarranted assumption of shared meanings that vitiates the whole process of assessment. Another way of presenting this incident is to say that my students struggled because they lacked the appropriate linguistic/cultural capital (Bourdieu and Passeron 1977). What is problematic about this is the fact that lack of familiarity with a single lexical item made the whole text inaccessible – and so the chosen poem was not, in the current parlance, fit for purpose. Because my students did not know that 'yellow' could mean cowardly, they read the poem differently. Although it would be true to say that they made different sense of it, such a statement strikes me as perverse. Their readings were not just different – they were flawed and inadequate. (After the exam, when I explained that yellow was associated with cowardice, my students instantly discarded their earlier readings: better informed, they read the poem differently.)

The story of 'Yellow' indicates a tension that is present across educational sectors in the ways in which the reading of literary texts in particular is framed. It picks up the threads of the discussion in Chapter 3 about the Wordsworthian values that inform the dominant paradigm of reading and response to literature. On the one hand, teachers value students' engagement and originality. We want students to make texts their own, to enter into the act of reading on their own terms, to read the text through the prism of their own lifeworld. On the other hand, we know that there is stuff that they need to know if their readings are to be adequate, informed, meaningful. Sometimes that knowledge is lexical; sometimes it relates to the formal and generic properties of the text (how sonnets or science fiction work); sometimes it is about the conditions of a text's production (Jacobean theatre or Victorian novels, say); and sometimes it is knowledge of wider cultural, social, political, economic and intellectual history: Swift's *A Modest Proposal* is more, as well as differently, meaningful if the reader knows something of the history of British imperialism in Ireland.

Sometimes, too, we seem to act as if the story of 'Yellow' were paradigmatic of all differences in reading – as if all such differences were merely the product of differential access to the right sort of knowledge – as if different readings were simply better(-informed) or worse(-informed) readings. My observations of Neville's Year 10 class at Wharfside School challenge such assumptions.

Class positions in reading *A View from the Bridge*

I want to focus on a single lesson, but before turning to the reading that happened in the lesson it is necessary to sketch out some of the contexts in which that reading happened. Indeed, to describe the circumstances of the reading as contexts is itself problematic to the point of being misleading. It suggests that the reading is in some way separable from the contexts in which it occurs, when part of my argument is that the act of reading is shaped and informed by networks of interlocking, inextricably linked con/texts (see the discussion of social theories of the sign, from Vološinov to Harris, in the first part of Chapter 2).

It has become fashionable to make reference to the importance of student voice. What happens, though, when the student voice expresses resistance to the exigencies of assessment criteria and exam boards? How is the teacher to reconcile the imperative to produce coursework, to get through the syllabus, with his principled commitment to education that is open, accountable and dialogic?

At the start of the lesson there is a moment that is both wildly atypical and deeply revealing. It is early March: Neville, in his first year of teaching, has worked hard in the previous six months to establish a relationship with this very diverse, very challenging group of 14- and 15-year-olds. He is trying to convince the students that they should complete – or at least attempt – the homework tasks that he sets:

[05:11]

TEACHER: OK, I'm going to say a couple of words about this homework, I've asked Mr B— to come in and say a couple of words about this homework as well.

REBECCA: Who?

TEACHER: Mr B—, he's the Head of English, because the last time I set a homework, three people did it, and I didn't get any homework from anyone else after despite asking, this is absolutely serious, the homework isn't optional, I don't know what you think I do with homework but I do not set it just to keep you busy, my interest isn't in keeping you off the street, it's crucial, crucial to what we're doing that you do this bit of homework, hopefully, before the end of the lesson Mr B— will come in and say a few words about what will happen if you don't, but it seems to me that for some reason I have done something with you that makes you think you don't need to do the work.

(10 March 2006)

This is Neville at his sternest. More than this, though, it's uncharacteristic of his approach that there is an attempt to use the hierarchical structures of the school to persuade his students to produce their assignments. But it doesn't work:

[05:58]

DARREN: Sir, why did you say '*hopefully*' he'll come?

TEACHER: Because he's teaching at the moment and it depends whether or not he gets a moment.

DARREN: So why're you *hoping* that he'll come?

TEACHER: *[2 seconds]* Because I think that something that's happened is that you seem to think when I set you work it doesn't matter. I want you to realise that it does, so I've asked someone else to come in and tell you that it does.

DARREN: What, because you can't control us, you have to bring in someone else?

TEACHER: Is it control, is it a question of control? Or a question of you taking the work seriously?

DARREN: Question of status.

TEACHER: *[1 second]* Definitely there is status involved, I'm asking the head of department to come and talk to you. *[3 seconds]* OK, what we're going to do today is we're going to finish reading.

(10 March 2006)

Darren, like many of his classmates, is intrigued by Neville and his way of being, a way of being that is deeply respectful of students' views and identities, a way of being that leaves a space for – indeed, invites – students to scrutinise the usually taken-for-granted purposes and inequalities of classroom interactions. There are, then, continuities with past conversations in Darren's attentive discourse analysis – but there's also an edge to it, an impatience with the perceived evasion of Neville's first response to the interrogation of 'hopefully', a forensic skill in peeling aside the surface niceties of timetabling issues to the heart of the matter: the work of the English classroom, Darren insists, cannot be divorced from questions of power, of status. 'What is to be done?' is here displaced by 'Who decides what is to be done?'

In an earlier version of this chapter, I suggested that it was perfectly possible to see Darren's intervention as nothing more than a disruptive tactic. The suggestion is one that Neville has challenged:

I am so certain that you are right not to read Darren's intervention as a disruptive tactic that I wonder if you should (even parenthetically) suggest that it might be. I think I've never mentioned this because I've attributed my certainty to my insider's understanding of the exchange; I've accepted that you may need to acknowledge the potential misreading of readers who weren't there in the lesson, who don't know Darren. But what struck me this time was the 3-second pause at the end of the transcript: it feels like I deliberately leave a space – an invitation – for Darren to respond to what I've said. If his agenda here was to disrupt, he would have filled that space. But his agenda was exactly the one you describe: he wants to inquire into who decides what is to be done, and he challenges me to be more honest with him than he had thought I was being. I think he doesn't reply because my response was more honest, and I did enter into his inquiry. I suppose what I'm saying is: I don't think it *is* perfectly possible to see his intervention as nothing more than a disruptive tactic; to do so isn't just a different reading, it's a flawed and inadequate one.

(NG to JY, 18 March 2013)

Before the class can start to read the remaining couple of pages of *A View from the Bridge*, they need to resolve the issue of who is to read Catherine's part:

[09:45]
TEACHER: . . . so we'll start from Catherine's reaction to Eddie saying this, um *[pause]* would anyone like to be Catherine – Mutib's absent?
[4 seconds]
SALMAN: Mutib will always be here in our hearts.
TEACHER: Amina, can I ask you?
AMINA: No.
TEACHER: You were a great First Officer yesterday.
AMINA: I wasn't.

(10 March 2006)

And what follows is a discussion, lasting over a minute, as to who is to read Catherine's lines, before, eventually, it is decided that Sarah will. This is a classroom where roles, within and without the play, are negotiated. It is a time-consuming and a messy business. At one point, Susan says, 'Sir, you're the teacher, you decide.' But that is not how things are done here. Mutib is absent from the lesson in a fairly specialised sense: he is in the exclusion room, a place where he spends, it would seem, a fair amount of time. Salman's elegiac comment is delivered for comic effect, but the layers of irony cannot quite conceal a truth about the identification of student and role. The part has become Mutib's, and so the reluctance to replace him might be attributable to a sense that to do so would constitute a theft. Students are, of course, able to distinguish between the roles and their extratextual selves. But in their reading of the play there is an enjoyment of the opportunity to inhabit a character and a possessiveness about the role that they have chosen, or that has been allocated to them.

Further evidence of this is offered a few minutes later when Salman, who is reading Marco's part, remarks, with complete matter-of-factness, to the student who is reading Eddie, 'No, it's all right, I'm going to shank [colloquial for stab] you anyway.' There is a playfulness about Salman's identification with the role, a relishing of the power that this will give him – and of the impunity with which, in role, he can utter such threats to another student. I wonder, too, how much Salman's cool assumption of another identity in the classroom might be attributable to his familiarity with the multiple identities of the video games he plays – and discusses with his peers (Gee 2003).

When the hurly-burly's done and the reading of the play is finished, Neville wants to focus on Alfieri's role. He prompts Martin to repeat the point he had made in the previous lesson, to the effect that Alfieri reports on Eddie's story because Eddie is no longer in a position to be able to tell it himself. What Neville is working towards is an exploration of Alfieri's choric role. He re-reads, to the class, Alfieri's final speech. As he finishes reading, Darren intervenes:

[26:25]
DARREN: Why is it called *A View from the Bridge*?
TEACHER: Great question, what else could it be called? *[5 seconds]* Based on that last bit that I've just read, what else might you call the play? *[3 seconds]* Whose story is it?
[2 seconds]
DARREN: Alfieri's.
TEACHER: Alfieri's story about?
[3 seconds]
SALMAN: *[shouts]* Eddie.
TEACHER: Why Eddie in particular?
SALMAN: Snitching.
TEACHER: It's a story about snitching.
SALMAN: Loyalty.
MARTIN: Not snitching.
TEACHER: How do you mean, Martin?
MARTIN: Like the story about Billy whatever.

(10 March 2006)

Salman's take on the play as a tale about snitching has a history (and a morality) attached to it. When I started observing the class, they had finished reading (and watching the Baz Luhrmann film of) *Romeo and Juliet*. Discussing with other students on his table the question of who was responsible for the lovers' deaths, Salman was vehement that Benvolio was to blame. 'Why?' I inquired. 'Because he grassed Romeo up to the Prince.' As far as Salman was concerned, what Benvolio had done in providing an accurate account of the fights in which Mercutio and Tybalt had died was, quite simply, wrong – a fundamental breach of ethical values. To divulge to a representative of judicial authority – of the state – information about violent acts that one has witnessed is not, for Salman, the duty of every citizen but rather the behaviour of a reprobate: it is an offence against the code of loyalty. I could not tell how much Salman's reading of the play was influenced by Luhrmann's representation of the Prince of Verona as an American chief of police. But his reading cannot be dismissed as aberrant or wilful, particularly when it is a reading that took place in a city where so many citizens lack confidence in the forces of law and order.[2] What this earlier moment also suggests is that the class has a collective history of exploring issues through their shared reading of texts, and, perhaps, particularly through texts in which ethical conflicts are realised in and through drama.

(After the lesson, Neville explained to me that the interpretation of Benvolio as the villain of the piece had not originated with Salman but with Claudia, a girl who had since left the school. In class, she had reacted with outrage to the scene in which Benvolio talks to the Prince, expressing the same views which I had later heard from Salman. Rather oddly, none of this judgement survives in her writing about the play: in her exercise book, responsibility for the tragic deaths is attributed, more conventionally, to Friar Laurence and to Lord Capulet. One might speculate whether Claudia was aware of 'mainstream' interpretations, and of the desirability of conforming to them in written assignments. Or was it that it was harder for her to explain, in writing, a reading that drew its strength from a moral code that she might assume was not shared by her reader, the teacher? Or had she just changed her mind?)

Qualifying Salman's 'snitching' with his suggestion that Miller's play is a story about '*not* snitching', Martin is emphasising that this is, in his view, a play with a moral. This is the significance of his reference to the story of Vinny Bolzano ('Billy'), told to Catherine by Eddie and Beatrice as a warning of the dire consequences of speaking to the Immigration Bureau: Martin proposes that *A View from the Bridge* carries the same message.

The space provided by this conversation allows students to explore, assemble and develop their readings of the play.

[27:03]
SALMAN: It's a story about how it was in those times . . .
TEACHER: Can you relate that to Darren's question?
SALMAN: What was Darren's question?
TEACHER: What was your question, Darren?
DARREN: What does *A View from the Bridge* mean?
TEACHER: What does it mean to give somebody a view?
SARAH: Like, their point, your opinion.
TEACHER: Your point, your opinion.
SALMAN: No, a view, something for them to see.
TEACHER: OK, so keep thinking about how this works, your point, your opinion, something for them to see, Darren, what do you think, do you think this is beginning to answer your question? *[4 seconds]* A view from the bridge, this is how things are from *[3 seconds]* this is how things are from the Brooklyn Bridge, it's *a* view from *the* bridge, there's only one bridge.
MARTIN: They're talking about what the view is, like it's an everyday thing.
TEACHER: Sorry, Martin.
MARTIN: It's like it's an everyday thing . . . it's like this is what it's like, it's an everyday thing. *[shrugs shoulders]*
TEACHER: Thanks, Martin, do you know what this is reminding me of? Our very first lesson on this play, where we were talking about Eddie coming home, taking off his cap and jacket, and Gavin was saying, that's just a normal thing, it's the normal thing he does, and I wrote on the board, 'normal, everyday thing'. *[miming the act of writing]*

(10 March 2006)

There are important things going on here. It is worth emphasising Neville's skill in orchestrating the discussion, his tolerance of the long pauses that are signs not of boredom but of the necessary spaces for thinking, his ability to reflect back to the students the length of their engagement with the play. He seizes the opportunity presented by Darren's question about the title of the play and uses it as another way of thinking about how the story is told, about Miller's dramatic technique and the mediating role of Alfieri. And, equally, we should pay attention to the students' contributions, to what they know and to the serious intellectual work that they are doing. As Nystrand *et al.* (2003: 140) argue:

> In an ideal dialogic learning environment, especially in open discussion as opposed to tightly cast recitation, teachers treat students as potential sources of knowledge and opinion, and in so doing complicate expert-novice hierarchies.

And yet, Darren still is not satisfied. As Neville continues to explore the significance of the title, Darren interjects: 'I think Alfieri makes no sense, man, he don't make sense to me.' Darren's meaning needs to be unpicked carefully. One strand of his response concerns the issue of narrative and dramatic technique. At first, his position might appear to be one of naïve realism – an attack on an implausibly omniscient choric narrator. 'How,' he asks, 'does Alfieri know all this detail?' How can Alfieri be privy to events that occur behind closed doors – the closed doors of the tenement where Eddie and Beatrice live? But Darren's dissatisfaction with the title re-emerges here in a form that reveals more clearly its origins in his quarrel with Alfieri:

[29:52]
TEACHER: . . . so Alfieri talks about it all as if it is in the present tense, he appears, narrates something that's happened, he was involved because he bailed out Marco and Rodolpho, he was involved because he was there at the end, he was involved because Eddie came to see him.
DARREN: Way you was talking like he was there in the house.
TEACHER: He was, wasn't he, {so what does that mean?
DARREN: {He weren't, weren't in the house, so this this title don't make sense then if your view, you're viewing from the bridge, you ain't seeing no detail are you?
TEACHER: Sorry Darren.
DARREN: Said, like, if they're saying it as a view from the bridge, if you're viewing from a bridge, it's not much detail is it?

(10 March 2006)

What my transcript fails to capture is the way Darren speaks in this part of the lesson. There is an angry urgency about it that explains the interruptions of Neville here:

he's not, in these exchanges, trying to be rude, or to challenge Neville's teacherly authority: he is struggling to communicate his idea – and what he is challenging is not Neville's authority but Alfieri's. It is, in part, the intensity of Darren's interest here that makes me reluctant to construe this as merely a discussion about dramaturgy. What Darren is contesting, I think, is not only the question of verisimilitude (how could Alfieri be privy to these events?) but also – centrally – Alfieri's privileged perspective. Who's telling whose story is, for Darren, a class question. When he complains that Alfieri 'makes no sense, man' the words he uses draw attention to Alfieri's speech – speech that marks him out as different from, detached from, the other characters.

Darren's problem with Alfieri is explored further as the discussion about the title continues:

[31:24]
TEACHER: Darren, what if it were called a day in the life? A day in the life of
    Eddie Carbone? What might that mean?
MARTIN: Everyday things that Eddie does.
DARREN: It would make more sense, innit.
TEACHER: How, how would that make more sense?
[4 seconds]
DARREN: Cause, I dunno, it would just make more sense than this.

(10 March 2006)

'Make more sense': Darren's words here echo his first attack on Alfieri. Despite Neville's promptings, though, he does not expand on or explain what he means by this. I will return to this point later, but first I want to track the continuing discussion:

[31:50]
TEACHER: These are {really
AMINA: {Why the bridge, anyway?
TEACHER: Anyone got any ideas?
SALMAN: Yes! A view from the other side of the side of the world from the
    Brooklyn Bridge, I mean, like bridge, a lead way into this is my city, a view
    from the bridge, you don't, not, it may look good, but that's not the half
    of it.
JY: So, Salman, what's on the other side of the bridge? If where Eddie and the
    rest of them live is what the play is looking at, what's on the other side of the
    bridge?
DARREN: Sicily.
TEACHER: If you call out you're denying Salman a chance to think.
DARREN: I'm not denying . . .
SALMAN: Immigrants looking at . . . in the beginning, the other half of it.
TEACHER: Tariq.

TARIQ: On the other side are people who are rich, yeah, so I think when the immigrants come from Sicily to New York they pass under it, so that's why there's a view from the bridge . . .

(10 March 2006)

Amina's question is unusual. Her interest in the official business of the lesson is often, it would appear, fairly minimal; again, what the transcript does not capture is her tone of voice, which might best be described as insistent, almost angry. In the various suggestions that are made as answers to Amina's question, there is an awareness of the gulf, economic as well as geographical, that separates Sicily and New York within the world of the play. But there is also, less fully articulated, an exploration of New York as a city divided along class lines. It is this sense of the bridge that Neville brings to the fore by asking students to consider the two different cover illustrations on the edition of the play that they are using (Miller [1955] 1995):[3]

[33:06]
TEACHER: Thank you, Tariq, we've got two totally different book jackets here. *[holding them up for the class to see]* I think that these book jackets give us two

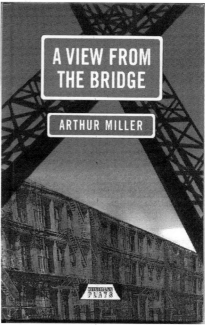

Figure 7.1 *A View from the Bridge* (Miller [1955] 1995, redesigned cover)

Figure 7.2 *A View from the Bridge* (Miller [1955] 1995, older cover)

different sides of the bridge, have a look at them, you may have one in front of you . . . what can you see on one side of the bridge?

(10 March 2006)

The cover of the newer edition is a photographic image. In the foreground is the water, beyond it a waterfront with high-rise buildings; the point of view is only slightly above the water line, and directly underneath the bridge, which looms above. The whole image is monochrome, variations in ochre – almost as if the landscape were bathed in a soft, golden light. The older edition represents a 'classic' tenement, with its lattice of fire escapes; above there is a blue sky, while in the foreground intersect two huge black steel girders. It is reminiscent of Miller's description of the set for Peter Brook's 1956 production of the play:

> The play began on a Red Hook street against the exterior brick wall of a tenement, which soon split open to show a basement apartment and above it a maze of fire escapes winding back and forth across the face of the building in the background.
>
> (Miller [1987] 1990: 431)

The newer cover might, then, be construed as representing the city as aspiration: seen from afar, its towering buildings signify wealth, development and opportunity. The older cover is, in contrast, Alfieri's view of Eddie and Beatrice's tenement: it may have prompted Darren to start thinking about Alfieri's perspective and positioning, the outsider who is somehow allowed a privileged view inside the tenement – and even inside the psyches of its inhabitants.

Prompted by Neville's question, the students report what they can see:

[33:26]
SEAN: Crap buildings and good buildings.
TEACHER: OK, crap buildings and good buildings, all right, what did we call this kind of housing?
AMINA: That's the view and {that's the bridge
DARREN: {Poor side and the rich side.
TEACHER: Good, and which side are we on? which side are the characters living on?
AMINA: On the other, the blue side. *[referring to the dominant colour of the older cover]*
TEACHER: That's right, do you remember the tenement housing, all the housing that's crammed in, people living in no space, illegal immigrants, very little space . . .

(10 March 2006)

And Sarah, picking up the thread of a conversation from an earlier lesson, reading the scene in the first act where Marco explains to Beatrice about sardine-fishing, reminds us of the possibility of reading the sardines as emblematic of the constrictions of life in the slum:

[33:54]

SARAH: Like sardines.

TEACHER: Like sardines, thank you, to go back to that bit of the play, sardines, you never think sardines swim in the sea *[3 seconds]* it's, I feel that my job at the moment is a bit difficult.

MARTIN: I think I know what he means by that.

TEACHER: Tell me, go on.

MARTIN: I think he means, you wouldn't think that many people could live in these small houses.

TEACHER: Good, that's exactly it, they're squished in there. *[gesture to demonstrate the packing of sardines in a tin]*

AMINA: Like sardines.

(10 March 2006)

As evidence of learning, evidence of Neville's success in creating a classroom environment in which talk is productive, in which students can engage fully with the play, in which meanings can emerge over long spans of time, this is impressive. Neville's practice recalls that described by Suzanne Miller (2003: 296):

> Teachers who mediated the discussion successfully listened well, providing support carefully when it was needed – after waiting to see whether other students might provide a next step or move. These teachers showed continual respect for students' emerging new abilities, allowing room for students to take responsibility for posing and pursuing questions.

Within the lesson, it encourages Neville to elaborate an account of the play, and of Alfieri's role within it, that provides the students with a context of theatrical history:

[35:20]

TEACHER: I've not figured out how to do this, but a lot of the reasons for the things we are talking about is to do with Greek tragedy, erm, which Tariq picked up and mentioned in the introduction, I'm not sure how to open this up, Becky, can you stop that, but the ancient Greeks, a bit more than two thousand years ago, they kind of invented drama, instead of just reading out poetry they had people acting it out and they had certain rules for where it was and the person, like the prologue in *Romeo and Juliet*, who explained what happened, also took part in the action, just like Alfieri does, he narrates it, and he takes part in it, in Greek tragedy all the action happened in real time I think . . . so you'd see this play, Salman, where there were no breaks, no leaps from one time to another at all, it all happened *[gesture]* and it would be about immovable objects and unstoppable forces, people coming to terms with something they couldn't come to terms with, and *A View from the Bridge* is written like that, as a Greek tragedy.

(10 March 2006)

What is happening in this moment is, from one perspective, the transfer of cultural capital. What Neville knows about the history of western drama enables him to place Alfieri's role – and Miller's intentions – in a specific context. There would be a way of presenting the students' responses to the play as partial, naïve, uninformed: thus what Alfieri says 'makes no sense' to Darren because he does not understand the mediating (and simultaneously distancing) role of the chorus, because he is not reading *A View from the Bridge* from a position of knowledge about a set of (very largely uncinematic) dramatic conventions. Neville is, in this account, filling in some of the gaps, thereby enabling his students to acquire a useful sense of context in which their reading of the play can be filled out, deepened, informed.

The influence of the examination board

But there are also other, more pressing imperatives motivating Neville's intervention. The GCSE examination board provides clear and detailed guidance not only on the texts to be read but also on the coursework tasks to be completed:

Texts chosen must be of sufficient substance and quality to merit serious consideration, and tasks must conform to the specific requirements set out below . . . The range of coursework tasks should enable candidates to show their understanding of literary tradition, and to show their appreciation of social and historical influences and cultural contexts.

(AQA 2005a: 26)

It is worth quoting in full the specific guidance offered on the 'Post-1914 Drama' coursework – the category within which *A View from the Bridge* fits:

This task should enable the candidate to demonstrate their response to the study of at least one play published after 1914. Candidates should respond to plays as drama as well as published texts. Appropriate assignments might include the following:

- An analysis of how character, language, setting or structure contribute to the dramatic effect of a text and how these aspects relate to literary conventions or traditions, such as the device of the Common Man in *A Man For All Seasons*.
- A study of the significance of a particular scene to the play as a whole in a play such as *The Crucible* which will explore how it relates to its social and historical context.

- A study of the importance of stage directions and effects in a play such as *Equus* which will show the candidate's awareness of dramatic conventions and the cultural context.
- An exploration of the dramatic effectiveness of one or more scenes in *The Madness of George III* which will show the candidate's awareness of the historical context and the ability to relate these scenes to the whole text.
- A study of a key scene from *An Inspector Calls* which will explore Priestley's dramatic methods and explain how an understanding of the historical and social context of the play might help shape audience response to the key scene and to the play as a whole.

(AQA 2005a: 28–29)

The examination board requires particular kinds of knowledge – knowledge of contexts both sociohistorical and literary – and particular kinds of response – response that is attentive to matters of form and structure and that is able to evaluate questions of dramatic effectiveness. It is these requirements that Neville attempts to satisfy, and he does this in a very deft and engaging way. I worry, though, about these specifications, firstly because the readers they envisage and assume are so different from the students in Neville's class – and from the vast majority of 14- and 15-year-olds. Most GCSE students are not in a position to place the text they are studying within a literary or dramatic tradition, nor necessarily to have anything other than the very sketchiest notion of the social, historical and cultural contexts of the text's production. They are, therefore, reliant on their teacher to do what Neville does here: to provide potted histories. In itself, this seems to me to be a perfectly legitimate aspect of the teacher's intervention. But what is problematic is that this potted history then becomes central to the student's 'response': the good student is the one who digests the gobbets and can regurgitate them appropriately – and we are left with something that looks uncomfortably like an English Literature curriculum for bright parrots.

We might wish to consider, then, what kind of literature curriculum, what kind of engagement with texts, would be appropriate for 14- and 15-year-olds, not just in urban schools such as the one where Neville teaches. Vygotsky argued strongly that educationalists needed to pay attention to the vital role of imagination in the intellectual development of adolescents. Those who neglected it, or who associated it merely with development in early childhood, were, he insisted, mistaken:

This false interpretation of fantasy is due to it being viewed one-sidedly, as a function which is linked to emotional life, the life of inclinations and sentiments, but its other side, which is linked to intellectual life, remains obscure. But, as Pushkin has aptly remarked, 'imagination is as necessary in geometry as it is in poetry'.

(Vygotsky 1994: 270)

One might, then, wonder if imaginative and creative engagement might find a place in the spectrum of responses to drama approved by the GCSE syllabus. The exam board's examples of 'good' assignments, however, carry the clear implication that what is being sought is a literary critical essay, dealing with aspects of context and focusing on an analysis of the playwright's technique. Candidates are invited to show that they know *how* a play is structured, *how* its effects are created, *how* it communicates to its audience. It is less clear whether there is any room in such essays for any exploration of *what* the play might mean – that is, of the meanings that are made by groups of students in their engagement with the play. This leads me on to the second, and even more worrying, implication of the specifications: what becomes marginalised or, frequently, left out altogether. Evidence for this is supplied by a GCSE examiners' report:

> Whilst it has to be said that many moderators are seeing responses to the same small range of texts across hundreds of centres and thousands of candidates, there is a feeling that task setting – at the heart of good approaches to coursework – is continuing to improve. The worst kinds of assignment – dubious creative responses masquerading as analysis; multiple pieces of Original Writing; descriptions of why Tom Cruise would be a better Hamlet than Brad Pitt and why he should wear black – have largely disappeared, ending up, thankfully, in the same bin as Eva Smith's Diary. Many moderators reported this year that task setting was improving as centres devise tasks which enable candidates to address key assessment objectives.
>
> (AQA 2005b: 30)

There is a cheery circularity about the process: teachers use the assessment objectives to set tasks that enable candidates to meet the assessment criteria. Outside this virtuous circle lie the unauthorised responses at which the examiners sneer. The examiners are here rejecting not merely less successful examples of a type, but 'kinds of assignment': they have determined that responses framed within particular genres – creative responses, pieces that might encourage students to draw on wider cultural resources, more imaginative or creative explorations – are inappropriate because they do not enable candidates to meet the assessment objectives. Some years ago, in investigating school students' reading of Shakespeare, I expressed concern at the turn against empathetic writing (Yandell 1997b). 'Eva Smith's Diary' has now officially been consigned to the dustbin of English studies, but I remain bothered by the binary opposition of creative and critical, the assumption of the automatic superiority of the essay form – and less than convinced by a simple hierarchy of values in which putatively objective analysis is privileged over forms of response that allow more scope for students to enter into a relationship with the text on their own terms.

The issue of the assessment of students' reading of literature is one to which I return in Chapter 11. For now, though, I want to return to Darren and his problem with Alfieri. Neville, using the contrasting front covers to explicate the title (and hence the mediating role of Alfieri), asks, 'Which side are we on? Which side are the characters living on?' Both cover designs might suggest that we are on a different side from the characters, that we, in effect, share Alfieri's detached perspective. And this is, I think, the assumption that Darren challenges. He knows whose side he is on, in the sense both of where his allegiances lie and also of whose lifeworld more closely resembles his own. For Miller, presenting working-class characters to a middle-class, theatre-going audience, Alfieri's choric role serves the purpose of mediating an unfamiliar social world and representing the story within the frame of a classical western dramatic tradition (hence, for example, Miller's original title for the play, *An Italian Tragedy*). For Darren, Alfieri is the intrusive other: no wonder that what he says 'makes no sense'. This does not mean that questions of dramatic structure and technique are irrelevant to Darren's reading of the play – any more than they were irrelevant to students who once grappled with writing 'Eva Smith's Diary'.

Miller's observations on the casting for the first English production of the play are worth remembering in this context:

> The *View* auditions were held in a theatre whose back faced the vegetable stalls of Covent Garden. I would sit beside Peter Brook listening in some pain as one actor after another who seemed to have arrived fresh from Oxford recited the words of Brooklyn waterfront Italo-Americans. One day in desperation I asked Peter if we couldn't interview some of the Cockney hawkers in the hive of working-class types behind the theatre, exactly the kind of men the play needed. 'Doesn't a grocer's son ever think of becoming an actor?' I asked.
>
> 'Those are all grocer's sons,' Peter replied, indicating the group of young gentlemen awaiting their turns at one side of the orchestra, 'but they have trained themselves into this class language. Almost all the plays are written in that language and are about those kinds of people.'
>
> (Miller [1987] 1990: 430)

Darren does not need to turn himself into a Brooklyn waterfront Italo-American to recognise his (class) affinity with Eddie and Marco, say – an affinity that is, of course, also gendered. Perhaps he needs the chance to explore, play with – and enjoy – this affinity before he can even begin to engage with questions of technique, of structure, of theatrical tradition. And when he does begin to engage with the play in this way, it still might be on his terms, from his reading position.

Notes

1 An earlier version of this chapter appeared as Yandell (2006).
2 See, for example, two reports in the *Guardian* newspaper, both published a few months after the observed lesson: one (Jeevan Vasagar 19 June 2006) is headlined 'Thousands march with family raided by police', the other (Will Woodward, 27 June 2006), 'Police have no right to rush into action on dubious intelligence, say most Muslims in poll.'
3 The different covers are from different issues of the Heinemann Plays edition of *A View from the Bridge*: no information is provided as to the date of the issue with the redesigned cover.

Chapter 8

Embodied readings

The multimodal social semiotic work of the English classroom

In this chapter, I continue to describe, and account for, the work that is involved in the reading of literature in urban English classrooms.[1] In paying close attention to these events, I suggest that the richness of the cultural work that takes place in the classroom demands a theoretical synthesis of, as it were, old and new semiotics: to make sense of these English classrooms, to describe and theorise the reading that is accomplished in them, we need to use both the multimodal lens of recent social semiotics and Bakhtinian perspectives on language and culture.

The multimodal turn in social semiotic theory has, to a large extent, been promoted as a necessary response to new times, new technologies. The prominence of the screen rather than the page as a site of semiotic activity, the salience of the image, still and moving, across a broad spectrum of media, and the concomitant marginalisation of written (printed) text are taken as facts of cultural life in the twenty-first century. Hence, it is argued, there is a need for a multimodal lens through which the new signifying practices, new combinations and ensembles of semiotic material, can be investigated and analysed (Hodge and Kress 1988; Kress and van Leeuwen 1996 and 2001; Kress 2003).

But at the same time as multimodality is presented as a necessary response to a changed semiotic landscape, it has also been argued that multimodal activity is nothing new (Coupland and Gwyn 2003; Franks, 2003; Jewitt and Kress 2003; Kress 2001; Kress *et al.* 2001). From this perspective, multimodal theory reveals truths at least as old as Cicero, to whom it was perfectly clear that rhetoric was not just a matter of what was said but of how it was said, and of the mutually complementary systems of word and gesture (Kendon 2000). In this version of multimodality, to treat language, either spoken or written, as a monomodal system was always to deal in abstractions: monomodal assumptions thus amounted to a failure to recognise the materiality of the book or the *billet-doux*, to ignore the simple fact that words are spoken (and heard) by physical bodies situated in specific (and semiotically significant) spaces. It is this second, older version of multimodality which will inform much of what follows.

There is, of course, no fundamental contradiction between these two sides of multimodality; indeed, it is reasonable to suggest that it is precisely the affordances of the new media that have alerted us to aspects of social semiosis that previously it had been easier to ignore. This last point has a general application in relation to the sociocultural world; it also has a particular relevance to questions of research method within the social sciences. The new technologies that have made multimodality an unmissable feature of contemporary life have also made it possible for the researcher to pay proper attention to the multimodal meanings that have always been in front of our noses. Where once we had to rely on audio tape recordings of significant interactions (and hence transcripts that perforce privileged the spoken word), now the availability of digital video enables us to record and analyse a much wider ensemble of semiotic resources as they are deployed – and remade (Franks and Jewitt 2001; Goodwin 2001; LeBaron and Streeck 2000).

In what follows, I want to suggest that an adequate account of reading, of pedagogy and of learning within secondary English classrooms needs to pay attention to the multimodal work that goes on in them. This chapter is also, therefore, a return to the methodological argument I developed in Chapter 4 in response to Doecke *et al.* (2007) (see pp. 62–64). I want to focus attention on two lessons, one taught by Neville and the other by Monica. In the following presentation and analysis of data from two of these lessons, I make use of some of the still images, taken from the video footage and supplemented by description, to capture something of the complexity of the video data.

Year 10 explore Arthur Miller

In the first of these lessons, from January 2006, Neville's Year 10 class is exploring Arthur Miller's *A View from the Bridge* (the lesson took place nearly two months before the one that was the focus in the previous chapter). I have indicated that the main emphasis of my investigation will be on what I have characterised as the older multimodality of embodied social semiotic activity. At the start of the lesson, however, there is a sequence that is only rendered possible because of the multimodal affordances of the new information and communications technologies. As the students enter the classroom, they notice – and pay attention to – the image displayed on the IWB. It is an aerial view of the school and the surrounding area, downloaded from the Google website. Its presence on the IWB, and the students' reading of it, produced an opening to the lesson that differed noticeably from what I had observed on other occasions in this class's English lessons.

In the normal course of events, the students do not enter the classroom *en masse*; they trickle in, individually or in small groups. Partly this is because they come from different lessons, and hence from different parts of the school building; partly it is because, at the times when one lesson ends and another begins, the corridors and stairways function as a social space, where students meet and interact. For this Year 10 class, the social spaces and interactions of the corridor tend to permeate the classroom. Conversations begun outside the classroom continue within it, and there is a fairly leisurely attitude taken towards whatever it is that the teacher has decided should be the business of the English lesson. It takes time for seating arrangements to be sorted out, time for coats and the other 'non-uniform' items, which the school rules decree should not be worn in class, to be removed. And, of course, the teacher's relationship with the class is implicated in all of this. His arrangement of the furniture – café style, as it is sometimes termed – with clusters of tables around which students sit, together with his markedly respectful, quiet and polite way of addressing the students, lies at a particular point on the spectrum of possible approaches towards classroom management and organisation. The students, meanwhile, can be seen as contesting the official script, the power relations of the institution, in a myriad of tiny actions – the length of time taken to remove a jacket, to end a conversation, to sit in an assigned seat – each of which seems to signal a desire to hang on to other identities, other ways of being, and a reluctance to accept the particular *habitus* of school student that the institution seeks to impose on them.

In today's lesson, as usual, students' arrivals in the classroom are dispersed across a two-minute period. What is unusual is that their attention is more or less immediately caught by the image on the screen. This difference is manifested in speech, in that the first conversations in the room are about something that is present – the image on the screen:

[00:24]
REBECCA: That's the football pitch.
JAMAL: *[sitting down by window]* What's that from?

(24 January 2006)

Much more obvious, though, is the difference in the orientation of students' posture and gaze. Ten seconds into the lesson, Rebecca is standing in front of the IWB, looking at it; Sean enters; Imran is sitting, also looking at the IWB. Sean walks across the room towards his seat; he turns towards the board as he does so – following Rebecca's gaze; Halima enters and also looks at the IWB. Rebecca approaches the board; Halima and Sean are all standing directly in front of the board, as Rebecca points at a spot on it (it is at this moment, 25 seconds into the lesson, that she makes the utterance transcribed above). Tariq approaches the board, stands to Rebecca's left.

Forty seconds later, more students have entered the room. Almost all are congregated around the board; those who are further away are also looking at it.

Contrast this moment with an equivalent moment, two minutes into the lesson, from the class's English lesson two weeks later: more or less the same students are in the room, but there is simply no single focus of activity or attention. What is salient, I think, in this juxtaposition is the question of gaze. In the first moment, there is a single focus for the students' gaze – and it is clear from this where the students' interest lies; in the second moment, two weeks later, the dispersed gazes of the students reveal the extent to which there is not, at this moment, a common, unified interest in what is going on in the lesson.

The second moment, I want to suggest, is much more representative of the early parts of the class's English lessons.

The IWB was also switched on in the later lesson, but it clearly did not function as a pole of attraction in the way that it had in the lesson under consideration. Why was this? The answer, so obvious that it might appear banal, is that the aerial view of the school meant something to the students. The IWB acted as a node, as it were, a meeting point of local, everyday knowledge and school knowledge (Vygotsky 1987; see also Chapter 2 of this volume). Questions of representation and provenance, inevitably and inextricably the business of English lessons, were here located in the students' sense of their immediate environment – and hence both Rebecca's identification of *the* football pitch and Jamal's question about where the image came from, how it arrived on the screen in the classroom.

The image was not part of the planned lesson. As Neville, the teacher, says:

[02:08]
TEACHER: OK, I had absolutely no intention of having this map up at the beginning of the lesson, I had it up at the end of the last lesson, but it's made me think . . .

(24 January 2006)

And, as he speaks, he zooms out from the view of the school to an image of most of the northern hemisphere:

[03:02]
TEACHER: OK, when we did the lesson on Alfieri's speech and I was showing you those maps, I didn't know about this bit of Google, which I just might use instead . . . we talked about how Alfieri said he lived in New York, how he came from Sicily, he was born in Italy, he said, and he lived in New York, and this wasn't Sicily he said, this was Brooklyn, this was Red Hook . . . OK we've just about in this picture we got Sicily there. *[he points at the board]*

(24 January 2006)

What Neville is doing is exploiting the interest that the students have shown in the image to enable them to make connections, connections between this lesson and earlier lessons as well as connections between local/unschooled knowledge and more disciplinary knowledges, between geography and the literary text that the class is studying:

[04:58]
TEACHER: And that there is Manhattan, the posh expensive bit, the island where the Empire State Building and the World Trade Centre were . . . and Brooklyn . . . Manhattan's up there, and this is Brooklyn, have a look at it, what can you see?
MARTIN: Buildings.

TEACHER: Buildings, anything else?

AMINA: Water, river?

TEACHER: OK where's the water?

REBECCA: Forest.

TEACHER: There's lots of trees . . . but look at the buildings, how they are laid out . . . in rows, and rows and rows, so this, I'd say, I'm pretty sure, that's the Brooklyn Bridge – that's the bridge in *A View from the Bridge* . . . and this would be the waterfront, those would be the docks that Eddie works in, the shorefront except of course that this was, this is probably a couple of years ago, as opposed to 1955, OK, something to bear in mind.

(24 January 2006)

The whole episode takes only seven minutes. It is, I think, an adroit pedagogical move, using the affordances of the technology (the IWB linked to the resources of the internet) to provide students with a bridge between their own sense of place and the places of the play – from the contemporary dockland of East London to a historical New York waterfront. Simultaneously, the technology is used as a bridge between the possibility of representing their local area through aerial images and the representation of 1950s Brooklyn in Miller's play.

I want to explore this last point in a little more detail. There is, it is true, little in the spoken interaction in this section of the lesson that directs explicit attention towards questions of representation or perspective. What I would like to suggest, though, is that the activity itself foregrounds these questions. Much of what is achieved here could have been presented by other means. Neville could have arrived at the lesson equipped with a globe, an atlas and a collection of photographic images of mid-twentieth-century New York (though such resources could not have been easily assembled in the impromptu manner that defines Neville's response to students' interest here). Had he done so, it would have been highly unlikely that anyone would have asked the question that Jamal poses right at the start: 'What's that from?' By interrogating the provenance of resources, the question opens up questions of agency: who has assembled these resources, for what purposes? Moments later, as Neville, responding to students' interest in the IWB image by improvising a geography lesson, begins to change the image from the close-up aerial view of the school, one of the students asks 'What's the point of zooming out?' The question does much more than reveal a shared technical language and a shared expertise in manipulating images and perspectives: it focuses attention on the activity, and hence on the agency of the viewer. And these questions – from whose point of view are these objects being seen, and for what purposes? – are, as has been indicated in Chapter 7, pertinent questions to ask in relation to *A View from the Bridge*. The fact that these questions are asked is itself evidence of what this episode makes possible. What I am also suggesting here is that students can ask these questions because of the way that the teacher uses the affordances of the technology to render visible the viewer's agency in selecting and framing particular views and particular subjects. There is a relationship, therefore, a complex and productive interaction between the different social semiotic modes in play in the classroom, between the teacher's and students' language-as-speech, their use of gaze and posture to signal engagement, the images on the IWB and the printed text of the play.

The interactivity here, then, is what Moss *et al.* have termed 'Conceptual interactivity – where the focus is on interacting with, exploring and constructing curriculum concepts and ideas' (2007: 40). In reporting on one of their case study examples, taken from a Maths lesson, these authors argue that:

> What is important for learning is how the design of the text reshapes curriculum knowledge. What is to be learnt and how it can be learnt become clearer. The images . . . and the opportunity to manipulate these images dynamically offer the students a different representation that is central to the learning task. This representation offers the possibility of making connections between the specialised knowledge of Maths and the everyday knowledge of space and design. It also enables them to draw on other knowledge and experiences and to connect them with mathematics, which in turn repositions them in relation to the production of knowledge.
>
> (Moss *et al.* 2007: 42)

In the next part of the lesson, attention shifts away from the IWB and onto the printed text. Yet, even here – especially here – we need a multimodal lens if we are to investigate how Neville and his students explore *A View from the Bridge* in the following 20-minute segment of the lesson. Neville explains that the activity is a continuation of work started in the previous lesson:

[07:46]

TEACHER: I'm going to take the register, and instead of replying here or yes or nothing, I want you to um tell me the name of either Eddie, Beatrice or Catherine, one thing they did with their hands, and either what it says about them or one reason that you think Arthur Miller has included this, OK, so either Eddie, Beatrice or Catherine, one thing they do with their hands, in those first ten pages we've read, and one reason why the playwright might have told the actor to do this.

(24 January 2006)

In issuing these instructions, the dominant mode employed by the teacher is language-as-speech: he tells the students what they are to do, how they are to respond to their names. The message – a message about the task but also about power relations in the classroom – is, however, echoed in other modes. Neville has taken a position at the front centre of the room, in front of the IWB. He sits on the teacher's desk, facing the class. While he talks, he uses his fingers to enumerate the three parts of the task. All of these other modes – positioning, posture, gaze and gesture – have clear regulatory functions: they are part of the ensemble of

Table 8.1 Salman's exit, 24 January 2006

Time	Teacher movement/gesture	Student movement/gesture	Speech
04:17	Gestures towards the door; stands by Salman, gesturing towards the door with his thumb Places both hands over his eyes Teacher closes the door after Salman, returns towards the board	Another student arrives in the doorway, says something Salman, still sitting, turns towards teacher Salman gets up and leaves the room, apologises as he does so	Salman: Shut up you fat cunt Teacher: Salman, get out Salman: What, no, I'm sorry, I'm sorry Salman: Sorry

multimodal resources whereby the teacher organises and manages the work of the class. I want to focus attention on one of these modes, gesture, because what Neville accomplishes through gesture is much more than the maintenance of power relationships in the classroom. In this instance, too, gesture has a special place because it is directly implicated in the content of the lesson: gesture functions, then, as a managerial and an heuristic tool as well as being an object of study.

Something of the power of gesture can be glimpsed at an earlier moment in the lesson (see Table 8.1).

While ascribing causality to any one 'turn' within such an interaction is fraught with difficulty, it seems that the moment when Neville convinces Salman that he does indeed have to leave the room is not when he issues the injunction to leave, nor even when he gestures towards the door with his thumb, but when he makes the much more theatrical gesture of covering his face with his hands. This movement breaks the eye contact between student and teacher; it signals disengagement but also, possibly, despair. It achieves meanings that words could not: words would prolong the conversation, keeping the possibility of dialogue – and hence, as it were, of plea-bargaining – alive. Neville's gesture tells Salman that the time has come to beat a tactical retreat, and he does so. (There is something slightly exaggerated, pantomimic about the whole interaction – as, indeed, there is about Salman's return to the class, a couple of minutes later, when he tiptoes in while Neville's back is turned.)

When Neville invites students to give examples of what the three main characters do with their hands, the first few contributions are made and received largely through the mode of language-as-speech. Other modes are at play, but operate entirely in a regulatory function as a means whereby the teacher organises the discourse. He directs his gaze towards the student whom he has invited to speak; he stands at the front of the room, register cradled in his left elbow, pen in his right hand, and appears to tick off students as each offers their example of a gesture. What is being emphasised here is not simply a power relationship but a concern to establish an inclusive practice: Neville uses the register as a sign that this is an activity in which all can participate, and in which all are expected to participate.

Something else happens when Rumina refers to the moment in the play when Catherine leads Eddie to the armchair. Neville raises his right arm, extends it horizontally to his side, and looks along it, to a point beyond his hand: he performs, in other words, the gesture that Rumina has chosen as her example. Here, then, gesture has moved from a regulatory to an heuristic function: this is, Neville indicates, what the stage direction means, this is what the moment in the play might look like.

A little later in the lesson, Neville draws the students' attention to Eddie's words to Catherine: 'Turn around, lemme see in the back.' The teacher's interest here is primarily linguistic – he wants students to be able to identify, and talk about, the grammatical and lexical means whereby Eddie's character is established. But Neville notices, and capitalises on, the fact that Amina explicates Eddie's speech gesturally:

[19:43]
TEACHER: OK, good, Amina, do what you did – I just saw you move your arm, didn't you?

(24 January 2006)

And Neville repeats Amina's gesture, lifting his right arm and making a circling motion with his hand.

Such sequences are significant. They suggest the beginnings of a move towards a reconceptualisation of the written text as a performance text – just as the focus throughout this part of the lesson on the stage directions and hand movements of the characters emphasises the extent to which the play's meanings are made multimodally. And yet Amina's single gesture, her interpretation of the hand movement that might accompany Eddie's words to Catherine, is, I think, the only moment in the lesson when a student makes such a move: it is the only time when a student makes, as it were, an embodied contribution to the learning.

Why this might be the case is suggested at another moment in this part of the lesson, when Neville steps back from the activity itself, from the identification and explication of gesture within the playscript, to provide students with a rationale for the activity:

[15:52]
TEACHER: Lots of people yesterday, about three different people . . . were asking what's the point of this? I don't get it, what's the point of this? Um, the examining board give us a few objectives, and this is actually, this is what I'm supposed to be teaching you, not necessarily in *A View from the Bridge*, but as part of the course, it's one of the GCSE objectives, I've made it a bit shorter. *[reading from a slide he has put up on the IWB]*

Understand how writers use devices to achieve their effects and comment on ways language changes – it's my job to teach you how to do that, according to the exam board.

(24 January 2006)

The activity, then, is located in the learning objectives prescribed by the GCSE examination board (and, though Neville does not say this, derived by the board from the National Curriculum). The way in which the teacher frames the activity helps to explain why, in exploring the meaning of gesture in the play, linguistic modes (language-as-speech, language-as-writing) have tended to remain dominant. The focus of the students' attention is on the play as a written text, the work of Arthur Miller, and not, primarily, the play as a performance text, the collaborative work of an acting company. Again, this is something that Neville is quite explicit about:

[22:52]
TEACHER: . . . we're not watching it, so we don't see the actors doing this, we're reading it and thinking about it as something that Arthur Miller has written, *[Neville returns to the IWB, making a circling motion with his hand around the words that refer to the writer's use of devices]* in which these stage directions are the devices, OK, the devices he uses to have an effect, because we're reading it, because we're not watching it . . .

(24 January 2006)

In itself, this is a remarkable instance of accountability, of a teacher offering to the class an account of the processes in which he and the students are involved. It is an account that points in two directions, both towards the requirements of the examination syllabus and towards the material conditions in which the reading of the text is being produced. What this move accomplishes is the creation of a space in which the complexity, the Bakhtinian multi-voicedness of this reading (Bakhtin [1975] 1981; se also Chapter 2 of this volume) can be explored and reflected upon.

Having spent time focusing on Eddie's 'Turn around, lemme look in the back' as a way of eliciting the linguistic particularity of the character, the voice that the actor playing Eddie must inhabit, Neville directs the students' attention to the stage directions:

[23:13]
TEACHER: . . . so as we read it, as Rebecca has been reading out all the stage directions, Rebecca – you're not reading it in Eddie's voice are you?
REBECCA: *[??]*
TEACHER: Are you reading it in B's?
REBECCA: *[??]*
TEACHER: So whose voice are you reading the stage directions in?

REBECCA: My voice.

TEACHER: Yours, excellent, OK so one voice could be the reader's. Who's talking to us as Rebecca is reading this, who's putting these words into her mouth?

TARIQ: The er, the writer.

TEACHER: Good, so another voice could be the writer's, all words, I think, are in someone's voice . . . or in several voices, and as we've said, this is in Rebecca's voice, it's in Arthur Miller's voice, we're hearing them all at the same time – this one [*pointing to Eddie's words on the IWB*] is in Tariq's voice, it's in Eddie's voice, and also it's the writer's voice

AMINA: Tariq?

TEACHER: Because he's been reading the part of Eddie, just like Rebecca has been the stage directions [*pause*] and as well as all that, it's in the voice that we imagine Tariq may be trying to achieve, sometimes when he reads it you may feel oh I don't think Eddie would say it like that, so we've got, um, the reader, the character, the writer, the actor, the audience and probably loads of others, OK?

(24 January 2006)

The development here is from Rebecca's straightforward, common-sense response (she reads the stage directions, so obviously they are in her voice), through the idea of the ventriloquism that is inherent in scripted drama (actors speaking someone else's words, the words put in their mouths, authorised by the writer), to a much more subtle model of polyphony, of the simultaneous presence and apprehension of multiple voices inhabiting the text.

This model situates the students differently from the position allocated to them in Neville's earlier version of the author-text-reader relationship, where 'we're reading it and thinking about it as something that Arthur Miller has written, in which these stage directions are the devices . . . he uses to have an effect'. In the earlier version, authority rests with the writer. In this model, on the other hand, the interpretive space offered to both reader and audience is not merely the opportunity to construe the intentions of the playwright, but rather to compare actual readings with a range of other possible readings, readings that are products of the readers' own interpretive decisions. Within this heteroglossia, Neville's earlier distinction between reading and performance also becomes less clear-cut. The students to whom parts have been assigned are represented as actors, the rest of the class as audience.

And yet, of course, the modes of performance are constrained: for all the attention paid to stage directions and to gesture, the students only get to do (and hear) the voices. There are many reasons why this is so – to do with examination syllabuses and assessment criteria, the social dynamic of the class and the fact that Neville, in his first year as a teacher, is still establishing a relationship with the class and developing a sense of what might be possible within the parameters of secondary English as it is instantiated in his classroom.

Year 9 explore *Richard III*

I want now to turn to a different lesson, one in which students draw on a different range of multimodal social semiotic resources in making sense of a complex text. I will focus on 14 minutes of a Year 9 English lesson from November 2005. The class had recently started work on *Richard III*. They had read the first part of Act 1, and had watched the openings of two film versions, starring Laurence Olivier and Ian McKellen respectively in the title role. In the first part of this lesson, students were analysing still images taken from the two films, discussing the ways in which Richard was represented in each. This is how Monica, the teacher, sets up the final activity of the lesson, an activity that is intended to prepare students for reading the next part of the play, the scene in which Richard woos Anne:

[36:19]

TEACHER: OK, we can do this quite quickly, all right, and you can be in a three and you can be in a three, what I want you to do, just very quickly, I want you to do a very quick role-play

BILLY: Yes!

TEACHER: I want one person, listen, one person has to persuade the other person to do something that they really, really, really, really don't want to do, OK, so I want you think about, you can be anything, anything at all, not want to do whatever it is you decide and I don't want it to end up with punching somebody and forcing them to do something. *[Nazrul throws punch and makes appropriate sound effect]* You have to do it with words, OK?

STUDENT: Can I be anything?

TEACHER: You can be girls, boys . . .

KIRSTY: *[holding up image that they have been analysing]* Have you got to base it on the picture?

TEACHER: No, it's not based on the picture, it's not based on anything, you can pick any situation with any characters you like but one person has to be persuading another person or other people to do something that they do not want to do.

KIRSTY: Has it got to be Richard and them lot?

TEACHER: No, it can be anybody, anybody you like.

(22 November 2005)

Billy's positive response to the news that the class is to work on role-play is representative of the class's attitude: students are both used to, and enthusiastic about, such activities. It is interesting, too, that there is an assumption on the part of at least some of the students that the improvisations that they devise should be obviously related to the work they have been doing on *Richard III*: Monica has to repeat, four times, that the students are free to choose any role at all – that they do not have to base their work on the characters or the events of the play. The activity is thus different from the role-play I described from an observation of the class's exploration of *Julius Caesar* some six months earlier (Chapter 5). In that earlier lesson, students took on the roles of characters from the play, at specific moments in the play. Their improvisations there were thus more constrained, explorations of the interactions of given characters at defined moments leading up to the assassination of Caesar.

In another respect, it might seem that the teacher is being highly prescriptive. Her injunction that the students have to achieve the persuasion 'with words' might appear to indicate that the only mode available is language-as-speech. While there is an emphasis here on the persuasive power of language, the main force of this warning is clear from the context – 'I don't want it to end up with punching somebody and forcing them to do something'. In any case, what happens next is anything but monomodal.

In the preceding 35 minutes of the lesson, the organisation of the classroom had conformed to a paradigm that is instantly recognisable from the vast majority of secondary school lessons, not only within English but across a broad swathe of the curriculum. With very few exceptions, students remained seated throughout. Their attention was focused, to a greater or lesser extent, on the teacher at the front of the room, introducing the lesson and explaining the activities, on the materials on the tables in front of them, and on their partners (while working on the analysis of the images taken from the productions of *Richard III*). Their contribution to the lesson had been almost entirely through the modes of language-as-writing, in annotating the images, and language-as-speech, in discussing the images with their partners and with the rest of the class. Legitimate activity – work – might reasonably have been construed as participation in these modes. Other semiotic resources are deployed by the students, but only in ways that are strictly ancillary: hands are raised to indicate that the student has something to say; aspects of the images are identified by pointing gestures; participation in pair work or in whole-class talk is signalled by the direction of gaze and by changes in the orientation of the body. A sense of this can be gleaned from what is going on in the classroom immediately after the teacher has set up the role-play activity. Where the groups have already been constituted, the students have tended to turn towards each other, thereby both signalling the identity of the group and enabling planning talk to happen within the group. In other parts of the room, students have not yet established their group: negotiations are being conducted across the tables, as is evident from the intersecting directions of gaze.

These, though, are merely slight variations. Within two minutes, the classroom as a site of social semiotic activity has been utterly transformed. All the students are now on their feet. This has not happened all at once. Some students had moved around the room as they formed their groups. Then, at different moments during the two minutes, groups of students moved from their seats to spaces in between the tables as they began to develop their role-plays. No one has told them to stand, to move – but they know that this is both allowed and also, in some sense, expected of them. (The activity has a history: it is part of a pattern of such activities, part of the class's experience of English with Monica as their teacher: see Chapter 5.) The expectation can be inferred from the decision that the teacher makes about where to intervene: the groups where she lingers, where she chooses to interact with the students, are those who have remained seated when others have begun to move around. It would seem that standing up indicates a specific stage in the activity, reached when the group has decided on the scenario and on the allocation of roles.

For five minutes more, the rehearsals continue. The classroom is noisy, bustling, seemingly chaotic. Then, with the minimum of fuss, Monica brings the class back together again so that the performances can begin:

[46:16]
TEACHER: If we're quick on the swapping over, we can get them all in, come on, and we'll talk about them tomorrow in the lesson, right, ready, go . . .

And the first role-play starts. A performance space has been created along one side of the classroom. In the first scenario, three female friends meet. Lucy and Helen know that Jo's boyfriend (whose name is Richard) has been unfaithful to her, and they want to persuade her to end the relationship:

[46:34]
LUCY: Tell her about Richard.
HELEN: He was cheating on you.
JO: You just want me to break up with him.
LUCY: He was in the cinema, with some other girl.
JO: I don't care, I've heard it all so many times, I don't care . . . he's rich.
LUCY: Just because he's rich, it doesn't mean you have to be his bitch, man, you're such a gold-digger.

(22 November 2005)

The scenario and the roles that the girls adopt are familiar from the stock situations and characters of soap opera. Their dialogue achieves all of this with great economy, establishing Helen and Lucy as the loyal friends, Jo as the conflicted lover. To acknowledge this, though, is merely to recognise that the students are able to draw on a stock of shared cultural knowledge. The activity provides an opportunity for the girls to explore relationships and the difficult ethical questions that arise from them. What are the obligations of friendship? How can competing claims – of loyalty, of economic well-being, of romantic ideals – be reconciled?

But the social semiotic work that the group does is not reducible to the dialogue that they have improvised. As Anton Franks has argued: 'In improvised drama, the body acts as a form of representation and allows the possibility of transforming everyday spaces (everyday classrooms, for instance) into theatrical spaces' (Franks 1996: 107).

They use the physical resources of their bodies and of the performance space to make meanings. The solidarity and intimacy of the three friends is represented by their physical closeness, Lucy's power by her central position within the group as well as by her insistent eye-contact with Jo, whose reluctance to accept her friends' counsel is communicated as much by gaze and body language, her tendency to avoid eye-contact and to turn slightly away from the other two, as it is by the words she speaks. When Lucy says, 'Just because he's rich, it doesn't mean you have to be his bitch' the epigrammatic force of her words is emphasised by a dismissive flick of her left hand. The implication of the gesture is that the choice that confronts Jo is not simply over whether to continue the relationship with Richard, since what she decides about Richard will affect how she is seen by her friends, and therefore how they will relate to her in the future: Lucy's gesture, therefore, can be construed as a warning, or even a threat. It has been enough to persuade Jo, who moves away from the group, meets Richard and informs him that it is all over between them.

In the following improvisation, the performance space becomes a shopping centre, where Ali is walking with his father. They pass a window where a new video game is displayed, and Ali attempts to convince his father that he should buy the game for him. If in some ways this scenario seems to draw more on the out-of-school lives and interests of the students, the style in which the scene is acted suggests something rather less mundane. Alongside the words with which he promises, in effect, to become the perfect son, Ali produces the most supplicatory of facial expressions, his eyes beseechingly wide; and, when these do not achieve the desired outcome, he prostrates himself, kneeling before his father. There is an arch knowingness about Ali's heightened use of facial expression and body language that might, perhaps, owe more to Bollywood than to first-hand experience.

In the third group's improvisation, three chairs are rearranged to form the interior of a car. Kemi, driving, informs Kirsty, her front-seat passenger, that there is a job for her:

[49:41]
KEMI: Kirsty, the boss has called you in for some special business, there's a man you have to cap . . . to join the crew . . . you need the money for your mother's breast cancer, so I don't wanna hear . . . your cousin could just disappear, you know, Kirsty, that would be so unfortunate, don't you think . . . now, Kirsty, here's the gun, and they're coming now, I better not hear you flop, the boss won't be happy.

(22 November 2005)

There is much to admire about the performance. Kemi's speech shows that she knows a thing or two about the language of persuasion: there is the lexis of the criminal underworld, as represented in a wealth of texts from *The Big Sleep* to *The Bill* ('the boss . . . special business . . . to cap'); there is an appeal to an economic motive that operates simultaneously as an assumption that family loyalties trump any adherence to wider social or ethical concerns ('you need the money for your mother's breast cancer'); and there is the deliciously minatory use of polite understatement ('that would be so unfortunate, don't you think'). Equally impressive, though, is the way that the group has marshalled its resources to produce an improvisation within which Kemi can create so menacing a character. The hand movements that represent her manipulation of the steering wheel function as a reminder of the claustrophobic car interior that is the setting, while simultaneously emphasising her character's dominance and control. Clothes, meanwhile, become signifiers of gang membership: Jenny, silent and impassive on the back seat, wears a hood, Kemi is muffed in scarf and woolly hat – while only Kirsty, the novice, is bareheaded. In rehearsal earlier, Kirsty had also worn a scarf as a makeshift hood: the decision to discard this for the performance itself is one that emphasises her character's precarious status on the periphery of the gang. In the exuberant profusion of reasons offered in Kemi's speech, Kirsty's lack of headgear reinforces the importance of one motive in particular: 'to join the crew'. (Among other effects, then, what the role-play activity does is to create the possibility that students' non-uniform items, which generally, as I indicated above, intrude on the lesson only as part of the students' counterscript, their contestation of the identity imposed on them by the disciplinary regime of the school as institution, become resources for cultural making – and hence for learning within the official script of the lesson.)

The body as dialogic classroom resource

Neville, in the lesson on *A View from the Bridge* which I discussed in Chapter 7, makes explicit to the class the connection between, on the one hand, the focus on gesture and the stage directions through which Miller specifies gesture, and, on the other, the overarching framework of the GCSE syllabus and its assessment objectives. There are, as I have suggested, other things going on in the lesson, other ways of thinking about the script and its realisation in the particular conditions of performance that pertain to the classroom. Nonetheless, the teacher is at pains to ensure that students understand that the stage directions that they read in their copies of the play are 'devices' whereby the writer achieves identifiable 'effects'. He is thus teaching in the manner promoted by current government policy (the *Framework for English*'s encouragement of 'teaching to objectives that are shared with pupils' – DfEE 2001b: 18).

In Monica's lesson, in contrast, the students' work on role-play is not informed by any explicit learning objective. What, then, is the relationship between these performances and what might be construed as the teacher's objective? In relation to the learning that the teacher plans, the connection has to be inferred from two sources. Firstly, there is Monica's instruction when she sets up the activity: 'One person has to persuade the other person to do something that they really, really, really, really don't want to do.' Secondly, there is the place that the lesson occupies in the reading of *Richard III*: the class is about to read Act 1, Scene 2, in which Richard woos Anne. He does this over the corpse of Henry VI, who is, in Shakespeare's version of history, her father-in-law.[2] It would have been perfectly possible for Monica to have said to the class something along the lines of: 'We are about to read a scene in the play in which Richard manages to persuade somebody who hates him, someone whose husband and father-in-law he has killed, to marry him. I want you to explore how he might manage to do this, so I would like you to try improvising such a scene.' She does not do so; more than this, as I noted above, she emphasises to the students that there is no necessary connection in character or situation between the improvisations and the play.

What happens in the lesson is that the students produce a wide variety of situations and characters. Apart from the three I have already described, there is a scene in a nightclub, where a reluctant dancer succumbs to peer pressure and takes to the floor; a conversation where someone is cajoled into taking drugs for the first time; and another where a young man agrees to participate in a violent attack on an elderly neighbour. I want to say something, later, about the creativity of these performances. Even within the narrower context of the class's developing understanding of *Richard III*, however, this 14-minute section at the end of a lesson seems to me to have been remarkably effective as a means of preparing students to grasp the astonishing seduction scene in the play. It would be tempting to conclude that the students' performances show how much they already knew about persuasion, about the multimodal semiotic terrain wherein relationships are instantiated and whereby power is established and contested. But it might be more accurate to suggest that the performances enabled students to learn (more) about these things: in the performances, concepts are being developed.

Eight months later, when I was feeding back some of the preliminary results of my research to the class, I explained that I had already shown some of the footage of their role-plays to different groups of teachers. I said that there had been some discussion among the teachers as to whether the activity could be construed as a legitimate part of English lessons. The students assured me that it could. Kirsty commented:

> Role-play lets you like express yourself more in words that you can't say, like, you can act, you can act something out that you don't know how to say, it helps you more to explain.
>
> (7 July 2006)

Foyzur added:

> It's like you're saying something through your actions and you can hear them and . . . see what's going on instead of just reading so you understand in a different way.
>
> (7 July 2006)

Terry Eagleton has made an argument for the importance of embodied experience that intersects interestingly with the students' justification for role-play:

> The body is the most palpable sign that we have of the givenness of human existence. It is not something we get to choose. My body is not something I decided to walk around in, like a toupee. It is not something I am 'in' at all. Having a body is not like being inside a tank. Who would be this disembodied 'I' inside it? It is more like having a language. Having a language, as we have seen, is not like being trapped inside a tank or a prison house; it is a way of being in the midst of a world. To be on the 'inside' of a language is to have a world opened up to you, and thus be on the 'outside' of it at the same time. The same is true of the human body. Having a body is a way of going to work on the world, not a way of being walled off from it. It would be odd to complain that I could come at things better if only I could shuck off my flesh. It would be like complaining that I could talk to you better if only this crude, ineffectual stuff called speech did not get in the way.
>
> (Eagleton 2003: 166)

For Eagleton, 'Having a body is a way of going to work on the world'. The emphasis on the materiality of existence, and hence of semiotic production, is helpful. I wonder, though, if Eagleton has gone quite far enough. Though he sees it as 'like having a language', for him the givenness of the corporeal seems to be its dominant, defining property. What Kirsty's conception of role-play suggests, on the other hand, is a view of the body as a semiotic and heuristic resource. This is precisely what Monica's students exemplify and enact: with extraordinary economy, they use a wide range of resources – language, gesture, movement, clothing – to inhabit and explore the roles and relationships that they create. These resources are both irreducibly physical and, at the same time, inescapably cultural. The students' meanings are made and mediated intertextually, in and through culture. That is true of the words spoken but also of the gestures made – of Kemi spinning an imaginary steering wheel or of Ali going down on his knees to beg a video game from his father.

From one perspective, then, this is just another strategy, a remarkably circuitous way of preparing students to read a section of a Shakespeare play. But it is a strategy that, by implication, offers different answers to the question of what English is for, and to the question of what literary texts are for. There is an unfashionable inexplicitness in relation to learning objectives, in contrast with Neville's practice noted above: Monica asks the students to rehearse and perform their improvisations, but does not even hint at the rationale for this activity. Because of this, the students remain free to draw on a wide repertoire of cultural resources, to make meaning with all the means at their disposal. And thus, when the class gets to read Richard's scene with Anne, his words are filled with a much denser semiotic load, a much richer and more complicated network of cultural understandings of persuasion and power relations. Around Richard's voice echo the voices of the students' role-play characters and of the diverse texts and genres on which these improvisations drew. When the students see Richard fall on his knees before Anne, their sense of the complex and contradictory meanings of this gesture, the irony of Richard's apparent submission working as a sign of his control, is informed and inflected by their memory of Ali kneeling before his father in the classroom-become-a-street. I want to suggest, therefore, that the Bakhtinian concept of heteroglossia (Bakhtin [1975] 1981, and Chapter 2 of this volume) applies here not just to language but also to the other modes employed by the students in their role-plays. Furthermore, this multimodal multivoicedness is rendered possible by the teacher's generous – loosely-defined, unprescriptive – conception of the activity.

I want to suggest, too, that what happens in these role-plays is precisely the dialectical movement between the everyday (or 'spontaneous') and scientific concepts that Vygotsky identified as the salient property of instruction (see Chapter 2). Students make new meanings from the material at their disposal: that is what is happening when they draw on the cultural resources available to them to create the situations, characters and interactions of their role-plays. If these role-plays then enable them to make sense of Richard's wooing of Anne, to understand more, and differently, what such a scene might mean, their reading of Shakespeare then enables them to understand more, and differently, the performances that they have created.

Barthes' distinction between readerly and writerly texts is of relevance here:

> Our literature is characterized by a pitiless divorce which the literary institution maintains between the producer of the text and its user, between its owner and its customer, between its author and its reader. This reader is thereby plunged into a kind of idleness – he is intransitive; he is, in short, *serious*: instead of functioning himself, instead of gaining access to the magic of the signifier, to the pleasure of writing, he is left with no more than the poor freedom either to accept or to reject the text: reading is nothing more than a *referendum*. Opposite the writerly text, then, is its countervalue, its negative, reactive value: what can be read, but not written: the *readerly*. We call any readerly text a classic text.
>
> (Barthes [1973] 1990: 4)

The distinction, though, is not between categories of text but between ways of reading. In the lesson that I analysed in Chapter 7, *A View from the Bridge* remains, to a large extent, readerly: the divorce between producer and user is one that the assessment criteria, attended to by the teacher, enforce: the students' task is, from a distance, to identify and appreciate (as a customer, a user) the devices whereby the writer achieves his effects. And yet, even here, the divide threatens to break down, to collapse under the weight of the multivoicedness of the production of the text in the classroom. What Monica's pedagogy does is to transform *Richard III* into a writerly text: in her classroom as they produce the multimodal texts of their role-plays, students gain access to 'the magic of signifier, the pleasure of writing'.

What emerges from both lessons is a version of English that cannot be encapsulated within the official discourse of current policy. These are ways of engaging with literary texts, these are forms of pedagogy, these are moments of learning that are worth attending to, worth describing and attempting to theorise. There are, to be sure, significant differences between the two lessons: differences in emphasis, differences in the extent to which assessment regimes exert a prominent, shaping influence, differences, too, that are the product of the particular histories and institutional positioning of the participants. But there are also important points of commonality: in the insistence on the importance of specific acts of cultural making (rather than on tasks designed merely to inculcate generalisable skills) and in the attention that is paid to the agency of the learners, an agency that is historically situated and made manifest in multimodal social semiotic activity.

Notes

1 An earlier version of this chapter appeared as Yandell (2008c).
2 She was betrothed to Edward, Henry VI's son, at the time of his death at the battle of Tewkesbury (1471). And not, as the Standards website informs us, 'his dead brother's widow' (Lesson 2 PowerPoint, slide 9, downloaded from 'Teaching Shakespeare to able pupils: Lessons to provide challenge for pupils working towards Level 7 in reading Shakespeare': / www.standards.dfes.gov.uk/secondary/keystage3/subjects/english/shakespeare/teaching_ learning/able_pupils/>, accessed 12 April 2007.)

Chapter 9

Reading together over time

In earlier chapters, I have tended to focus attention on events within a single lesson. In this chapter, I make an argument for the importance of attending to longer timescales in making sense of the reading, and the learning, that is accomplished within a single lesson.

The 'everyday' in *A View from the Bridge*

In Chapter 7, I looked at the way the students in Neville's class were developing a reading of Miller's play, a reading which was significantly inflected by their sense of their own social class positioning. When Darren asks about the meaning of the play's title, his question opens up a discussion of representation, of the society that Miller represents and the perspective from which it is represented. Martin's contribution to this discussion, as Neville acknowledges, carries an echo of an earlier lesson. Martin suggests that the view from the bridge is of 'an everyday thing' (see p. 98). In the context of the single lesson, the force of this suggestion is not apparent: what gives it a greater (and different) semiotic load is the associations that derive from its place in an earlier argument.

Two months earlier, in the class's first encounter with the text of *A View from the Bridge*, Neville had used a brief extract from the opening few pages of the script to induct his students into the practices of close reading and textual annotation. In that lesson, speculating on Eddie Carbone's state of mind as he returns home after a day's work on the docks, Malcolm had drawn attention to the stage direction, '*EDDIE . . . hangs up his cap and jacket*' (Miller [1955] 1995: 5):

[22:57]
MALCOLM: I think he looks forward to going to work, sounds like he's got a
    boring life.
GAVIN: Oh yeah, that's what I was going to ask.
MALCOLM: Like some normal things, he goes into his house, hangs up his jacket,
    and that's the end, like.
TEACHER: Excellent.

MALCOLM: Boring.

TEACHER: Just a sec, Gavin I'll be with you in a second . . . OK . . . I want to look carefully at what Malcolm has just said. He has picked out a line in the stage direction and Malcolm has used the word normal. Malcolm, would you mind if I used the word 'everyday'? Yeah, normal, everyday things. Just, Mutib, just in this line, he hangs up his hat and jacket, Malcolm has seen a kind of routine, OK, another day left on that ship, he hangs up his hat and jacket, I haven't got a copy with me, *A View from the Bridge* is a very, very thin play, every single word matters, Arthur Miller has put every word there for a reason.

(6 January 2006)

But Neville's use of 'everyday' as a synonym for 'normal' is contested by Gavin:

[24:39]

GAVIN: You shouldn't put everyday, though, everyday things, you should just put normal things, because when we watched that film last time *[On the Waterfront]* everyone wears jacket and hat.

TEACHER: Good, excellent, Gavin, it's not just him, but by everyday I mean they do it day in, day out, it's like coming to school is an everyday thing, you just do it day after day, does that make sense?

SALMAN: We're not allowed to wear non-uniform, getting told to take off your jacket . . .

JY: So, Salman, follow that through more, when Eddie comes in, hangs up his hat and jacket, what's that signalling?

SALMAN: That *[3 seconds]* he's a normal person.

JY: But, what's the act of hanging up his hat and jacket, what is he moving from to?

MARTIN: Work to home.

TEACHER: OK so it's a symbol, in a way, isn't it? This is saying, the jacket and cap he wears at work, he hangs it up, that is the end of my working day, I am at home now.

(6 January 2006)

I confess that I am still not sure of Gavin's grounds for contesting the use of the word 'everyday'. What is clear, though, is that the word does not have the same sense for him that it has for Neville.[1] Gavin's interest, at this moment, is in a normativity that is historically situated. Neville had shown *On the Waterfront* to the class as a way into the world of *A View from the Bridge*: one of the things that Gavin has taken from the film is a sense of what longshoremen were likely to have worn in the 1950s. Is it, then, that 'everyday' fails to communicate the historical specificity of Eddie's clothing? I don't know. I am also uncertain about the motives for Salman's intervention: to what extent is he exploiting the discussion to indulge in one of his favourite counter-scripts (the unfairness of school life) and how much is he drawing on his knowledge of the codes and conventions of schooling to make sense of Eddie's actions? But the effect of Salman's contribution is to enrich the semiotic significance, for the class, of the stage direction: to emphasise the sense of the normal and to encourage an identification with Eddie and with the class whom he represents. And thus the attention that was given to the word in that earlier lesson means that when, two months later, Martin suggests that what the play represents is the everyday, Neville is right to take this as, in effect, a referencing of the earlier discussion: the *everyday* here has a meaning that is specific to the class's shared history of engagement with Miller's play.

This is a small, slight example of the importance of attending to the accumulation of meanings across time in capturing a class's experience of a shared text. I turn now to a more substantial instance of this phenomenon in Monica's Year 9 class, in the early weeks of their reading of *Richard III*.

What does Richard want?

By 1 December 2005, Monica's class had watched the first act of *Richard III* in two versions (Olivier 1955 and Loncraine 1995). They had read the script as far as the end of Act 1, and had analysed still images, some from a wide range of productions and some that were frames taken from the two film versions.

In the lesson on 1 December, the students were in groups of four. Monica started the lesson by giving each group a large piece of sugar paper and a pen. 'What does Richard want?' she asked. The students talked about the question in their groups, then wrote answers on the sugar paper. After about four minutes, the pieces of sugar paper were passed around the class, so that each group had a different piece in front of them. This gave them the opportunity to read another group's answers to the first question as they began to address Monica's second question, which was about the obstacles that lay in Richard's way. After four minutes, the process was repeated, the pieces of sugar paper were passed on again, and Monica asked her third question: 'What has Richard achieved so far?' The groups were given four more minutes and then the class was brought together to share their answers to these three questions.

[12:38]
TEACHER: OK, right, let's see where we are . . . Nazrul, can you give me, um, what did Richard want?
NAZRUL: Power. *[indistinct – others are talking – volunteering answers]*
TEACHER: All right, one at a time. Right, you think he wanted power. Ali?
ALI: Um, to marry Anne.
TEACHER: He wanted to marry Anne. Billy?
BILLY: He wanted a family.
TEACHER: He wanted a family. Um, Anhar?
ANHAR: To become king.

TEACHER: He wanted to become king. Kemi?
KEMI: He wanted to be noticed.
TEACHER: To be noticed, good.
HELEN: He wanted fame.
TEACHER: Fame.
HELEN: And luxury.
TEACHER: OK, good, the things that go with being a king.

(1 December 2005)

These answers, deftly orchestrated by Monica, come thick and fast. Students are keen to contribute, confident that they have things to say. The answers show something of the students' knowledge of the play, of Richard's character and motives. The responses are framed, then, by ways of reading a literary/dramatic text such as *Richard III* that are well-established, familiar, part of the routine business of English classrooms. In a tradition stretching back to A.C. Bradley (and beyond him to Coleridge), Shakespearean roles are discussed as if they were stable, psychologically consistent characters, whose motives can be known, analysed and deployed to understand and explain their actions.[2]

What is noticeable about the answers provided by the students is the extent to which they seem to build on previous contributions. Billy's 'He wanted a family' could be construed more as a response to Ali's point, that Richard wanted to marry Anne, than to any information directly present in the text or the films. And, it should be said, it is not easy to interpret the force of each contribution, the evidence of learning that it provides. Is the connection that Billy makes between marriage and family/procreation merely the reiteration of a cliché, or does it have particular reference to the significance of the family within the feudal system? Is Billy, in other words, harking back to Nazrul's original claim that what Richard wants is power? And is Anhar's contribution, that Richard wanted to become king, in any sense related to the previous focus on marriage and family? His later intervention (see below) would suggest that he was, at the very least, working towards an interpretation of Richard's motives in which these different strands were integrated.

What, then of Kemi's 'He wanted to be noticed'? Where does this phrase come from, and why did she choose it? Kemi, a dominant personality in the class, usually seems intensely aware of others' interest in her. Is she seeing Richard through the lens of her own classroom persona? Is she demonstrating an awareness of the rules of the literary critical genre – the psychological interpretation of character – and even of the specific sub-genre in which moral iniquity becomes reinterpreted, reframed, as psychological deficit – the depraved recoded as the deprived? Is she dipping into her plentiful cultural reserves to find the most appropriate cliché? Helen's suggestions both corroborate Kemi's – the goal of fame accentuates a social (and even theatrical) perspective on kingship, while 'luxury' complements this with a nod in the direction of the material benefits to be gained.

What Monica does next is to push harder:

[13:34]

TEACHER: OK, good, the things that go with being a king ... Chris, do you think you can separate out the, this is a hard question, I'm going to give you a little minute to think about it, all right, and if Chris doesn't know the answer and you think you might be able to, see if you can come up with the answer. Do you think you can separate out the wanting to be married and the wanting to have a family from the wanting to become king? *[2 seconds]* Have a think about that question because it's quite a hard question. *[3 seconds]* Do you think you might have an answer, Chris?

(1 December 2005)

Responding to the catalogue of desires produced by the students, Monica wants to explore with the class the relationship between the items on the list. Signalled very clearly as a 'hard question', and explicitly directed towards one of the high-achieving students, Monica's intervention transforms the activity into something much more intellectually demanding than a mere report-back. She is making clear that there are ways of participating in this discussion that go beyond reading the words written on the piece of sugar paper. Chris is being invited to synthesise the findings, and in so doing to develop a better understanding of the relationship between family and power within a feudal context, within the world of the play. For the moment, at any rate, Chris does not rise to the challenge; instead, he might almost be taking his cue from Kemi's use of the discursive practices of problem-page psychology:

[14:10]

CHRIS: Maybe he was lonely.

TEACHER: So, you think, you think you can separate, that maybe he was lonely and he wanted a wife and ...

[Kemi raises her hand]

TEACHER: { ... he wanted a family.

CHRIS: {King was about wanting power.

TEACHER: Yeah, OK, good.

(1 December 2005)

In this interchange, both Monica and Chris are quoting the words and phrases of earlier contributors. This is a development, then, but it is one that alludes to its connection with what has gone before. Chris's answer is not what Monica was looking for, but it is not dismissed. Other students are invited to participate:

[14:24]

TEACHER: Anybody got any other ideas about that? *[points at Kemi, whose hand is still in the air, Kemi starts to speak]*

No, hang on, we'll take, all right, cos you answer lots of questions, sorry, I'll come to you second, I'll ask Anhar first.

ANHAR: I think no because, because he just married her because he wants to become king. If he didn't marry her, he can't be king.

(1 December 2005)

Monica's conduct of the discussion is mindful of timescales and developments beyond the single lesson (see Chapter 5); her explanation of the decision not to take Kemi immediately places this exchange within a longer-term perspective: this is one of many such occasions, and part of the teacher's role, it is implied, is to encourage a more equal access to speaking rights. Anhar's contribution here renders explicit the link between marriage and the throne that was, as I indicated above, possibly implicit in his earlier intervention.

[14:37]

TEACHER: OK, he just married her because {he wanted to become king.

BILLY: {Miss, what was the question?

[Subhan raises his hand]

TEACHER: The question, it was a hard question I think, I don't know if I phrased it right, but I was asking if you could separate out the wanting to be married and have a family which Chris sort of said you could by saying{that he was lonely . . .

? ALI: {?? *[indistinct]*

TEACHER: . . . from wanting to be king, so Anhar is disagreeing and saying he doesn't think you can separate {it out because . . .

BILLY: {that's what I think . . .

TEACHER: All right . . . {the wanting to be married to Anne is part of . . .

PERRY: {Do you know what he done, man?

TEACHER: Ssh! Wanting to become king,

[Caroline raises her hand]

TEACHER: Just a minute, Perry, we don't need to have that kind of comment and don't make it again, please, it's disruptive to other people's work . . .

(1 December 2005)

It is worth dwelling on what Monica is doing in this sequence. She echoes Anhar's point, then, in response to Billy's question, acknowledges that what is being discussed is difficult. She draws attention to the fact that Anhar's view is opposed to that of Chris. What Monica doesn't do at this stage is equally significant: she doesn't rebuke or criticise Billy for not paying attention; she doesn't move on as soon as she has received the answer she is looking for; she doesn't present herself as the fount of all knowledge. There is a deep modesty, and an open acknowledgement of the shared struggle with and through language, in her 'I don't know if I phrased it right'.

There are aspects of the exchange with Perry that are simply not captured by the transcript as I have presented it. I am not even sure if the sexualised meaning of Perry's words is clear – I am not sure how much of this meaning was conveyed through tone – but what he is alluding to is that Richard had sex with Anne. The tone of Monica's response is very calm and measured; the emphasis is firmly on the inappropriateness of his contribution to the conversation, rather than, say, on any transgression of the bounds of decency. More than this, though, Monica's response affirms that what is going on in the classroom should be construed as 'work': meanings are being made, struggled over, contested.

[15:19]
TEACHER: *[acknowledging Subhan's raised hand]* Yeah.
SUBHAN: I agree with what Anhar said, yeah, because in the film, yeah, he says 'I will have her but I will not have her for long' and if he marries her and becomes the king, yeah, and if he doesn't like stay with her he can still be king, so like they couldn't get him out from the king.

(1 December 2005)

Subhan's hand had been raised for 37 seconds. He waited patiently for his turn, and when it came his first move was to signal agreement with Anhar. To see this as (merely) good manners, or obedience, or a display of, in the current jargon, appropriate learning behaviour, does not seem to me to be adequate. There is, I think, a seriousness about it which is to do with taking the discussion seriously and, simultaneously, to do with taking other students seriously. The point I have made elsewhere (Chapter 5), in observing the class six months earlier, about the development of a relationship with Monica over time, and about the development of ways of working, is instantiated here in Subhan's intervention. And what he does, unprompted, is to provide textual evidence to support his point. It may not be word perfect, but he has remembered Richard's 'I'll have her but I will not keep her long' (Act 1, Scene 3, 233).

[15:36]
TEACHER: OK, good, good answer . . . um, Caroline, what do you think?
CAROLINE: Um, yeah, I think you can't either because, um, part of becoming the king is to get with Anne so that is why he wants to get with Anne so that he can become king and to get further into that particular plan, so . . .
TEACHER: OK, good, what about you, Lucy?
LUCY: I was going to say that if he marries Anne he can have his own kids and he will be remembered because he had sons.
TEACHER: And they'll become kings after him so that's sort of connected to that as well, excellent, can you think, how was he in the film after he had been chatting Anne up in the play?

(1 December 2005)

There's a marked inclusiveness about these interventions. Both Caroline and Lucy are less concerned to introduce new material than to support others who have already spoken and to synthesise the earlier contributions with the interpretation offered by Anhar and Subhan.

What is revealed by an analysis of the language in this three-minute segment of a lesson is very impressive. In what the students say, in the ways in which they interact with each other and with Monica, there is a great deal of evidence of well-established practices. This is a class which is used to talk, used to listening carefully to one another: even Perry's transgressive intervention tends to emphasise that the rules by which this talk is conducted are well understood. This is a group of students who are able to use talk as the medium through which important intellectual work can be accomplished collaboratively; these are students who are confident in their ability to make sense of a complex text, confident that they will have things to say about it.

But the digital video recording of the lesson enables other perspectives. Sitting at the front of the classroom, underneath the IWB, were Jo, Mutib and Foyzur, none of whom contributed to the whole-class talk in this segment of the lesson. For most of the time, Foyzur was leaning forward, his head resting on the table in front of him. At one point, just before Perry makes his comment, Jo, sitting opposite Foyzur, also leans forward, her head on the table, her posture mirroring Foyzur's. She maintains this position for a few seconds, then sits up again and opens her copy of the play. She browses through the pages, looking at the pictures (it is a recent Cambridge School Shakespeare edition, illustrated with images taken from performances). Twenty-five seconds later (just as Caroline is beginning to speak), Foyzur lifts his head from the table, opens his copy of the play, yawns and begins to flip through the pages. Mutib, sitting to Foyzur's left, follows suit. Glances are exchanged between Mutib and Jo.

As Monica moves on to take responses to her second question ('What's stopping him from getting it?'), Jo has put her head back down on the desk. Then Perry, who is out of camera, towards the back of the room, passes a message to Mutib, who is looking at Perry: he suggests that they should look at the image on page 147 of their copies of *Richard III*. Subhan also exchanges glances with Perry and with Mutib. As the students find the image, there is a burst of fairly loud laughter – and a further exchange of (conspiratorial, knowing) glances. At this point, Foyzur turns his head around towards Subhan and Caroline, who are sitting together, directly behind him. The book is open in his hands, and he grins at Subhan and Caroline before turning back, making eye contact with Jo. These movements are echoed, almost immediately, by Mutib, who turns his whole torso around so that he is facing Subhan and Caroline.

The laughter has alerted Monica to the fact that something else is going on. She notices Mutib, and stops to reprimand him:

[17:16]

TEACHER: . . . Mutib, Mutib, if you were speaking you would really want people to be listening to you.

MUTIB: What? I didn't know no one was speaking.
TEACHER: No, well I was speaking, OK, and then I'm going to ask Ian a question.

(1 December 2005)

Monica carries on with the lesson. While she does so, Foyzur balances his book on his head and Mutib turns round to smile at Subhan. The book stays on Foyzur's head for a few seconds, then falls to the ground. He picks it up, places it over his face, then pushes it to the back of his head while he leans forward. Briefly, he rests his head on the table, then sits up again and exchanges glances with Jo.

About 50 seconds have elapsed since Monica last spoke to Mutib. In this time, the discussion has continued, focusing on the obstacles confronting Richard. Now she seeks to bring Mutib into that discussion:

[18:15]
TEACHER: Mutib, what did you have for what was stopping him apart from the king, the brother being a king?
MUTIB: Um *[3 seconds]* what stopped him? *[reading from the paper in front of him]* He was short and ugly.
TEACHER: *[2 seconds]* OK.
MUTIB: I didn't write that it was someone.
TEACHER: You didn't write that, you can't think back to your own writing on that?
MUTIB: No, but what stopped him was . . . *[4 seconds] [to Foyzur, sitting next to him]* What did you write for what stopped him?
TEACHER: You can't remember, OK, um, Ali, um sorry, yeah, Ali.

(1 December 2005)

Put in the spotlight by Monica, Mutib has tried to respond appropriately. But he hasn't been following the conversation, so he has to resort to the sugar paper that is on the table in front of him. He picks up the paper and reads ('He was short and ugly'). Realising that these words are not adequate, he distances himself from them: 'I didn't write that . . .'. Monica tries to elicit a different response from him, and he turns to Foyzur for help. Foyzur shrugs his shoulders, shakes his head slightly, and Monica moves on to another student, and to the third of her questions: what has Richard achieved so far?

A further 70 seconds go by, in which Ali and Helen suggest answers (Richard has won Anne over, and he has got respect). Foyzur, Jo and Subhan continue to exchange glances, to smile at each other, and there is a short, mouthed conversation between Caroline and Mutib (again turning round to face her). There is no indication that any of them is paying attention to the formal business of the lesson – the teacher's script, in Gutierrez *et al.*'s (1995) terms. And then Foyzur raises his hand.

[19:53]
[Foyzur puts his hand up]
TEACHER: Anhar.

ANHAR: He's the king.

TEACHER: He hasn't yet become the king, not in the bit that we've watched so far.

FOYZUR: I think that he's like the main character, he's taken over, like the audience are more interested in him than the other characters.

(1 December 2005)

I want to make two observations about Foyzur's intervention in the lesson. First, what he says – the way in which he talks about Richard and about the play – is, within the context of the first 20 minutes of this lesson, unprecedented. If the whole-class conversation has provided impressive evidence of the students' knowledge of the play, of Richard's actions and of plausible interpretations of his character, no attention had been paid to the play *as a play*. Monica's questions had not encouraged such a perspective: they were focused, as I have suggested earlier, on unproblematised notions of character and of character study. What Foyzur does is to open up a new field of inquiry. He directs attention to the ways in which meanings are made, to the relationship between actor and audience, to the techniques whereby perspectives are established and privileged.

Foyzur's comment reveals a remarkable understanding of the complexity of theatrical/dramatic relationships – the actor to the role, the character to other characters within the world of the play, the actor/character to the audience – and the specific and very powerful ways in which these relationships are established in the early part of *Richard III*. What Foyzur gestures at here is not merely a more elaborate version of Kemi's 'He wanted to be noticed': in place of character analysis, he offers an account of Richard that pays attention to the artifice of the play, to its constructed nature – and to the theatrical nature of Richard's power.

I want to say more about Foyzur's reading of Richard. Before I do, though, I want to make a second point about his intervention. Although it is, quite clearly, *a propos* – it is a direct (and brilliant) answer to Monica's third question ('How far has Richard got?') – it appears to come from nowhere. Not building on other contributions to the lesson, not developed from the earlier group discussion, it emanates from a student who has shown no sign of interest in the lesson up to this moment (and many outward and visible signs of interest in a series of other events that might constitute a recalcitrant counterscript to the lesson, as Gutierrez *et al.* might see it).

The pre-history of an idea, or who did the work?

If we ask where Foyzur's insight comes from, we have to start with a recognition that we do not know. There is no definitive answer, no sure means of establishing the genesis of his idea. And it is worth making a point about the elusiveness of learning: we may recognise evidence of learning happening (or, to introduce another aspect to the conundrum, having happened), but we cannot trace the thread of learning back to its source. What I want to suggest in the rest of this chapter is that it is possible to reconstruct a history of Foyzur's idea in the work that had been done in previous lessons. What this reconstruction provides is evidence of the inadequacy of the 'Robinson Crusoe model of epistemology' (Ilyenkov [1960] 2008: 40) and of the need for a conception of learning that takes account of the social and historical nature of consciousness (see Chapter 2).

Before I do so, though, I want to offer an explanation for Foyzur's intervention in the lesson. We don't know what was going on in Foyzur's head. The digital video footage does provide data, however, that may be interpreted as evidence for what triggered Foyzur's apparently sudden engagement. Less than two minutes before he speaks, his friend and neighbour, Mutib, has been addressed directly by Monica. I have already suggested that Mutib is dissatisfied with his contribution to the lesson, and that he sought to enlist Foyzur's help in producing a more impressive answer: tone of voice, gaze, posture and expression all support this interpretation of the event and of the significance of this moment for both students. Whether to deflect censure from Mutib or himself, or to (re-)assert his own intellectual credentials after he has appeared tongue-tied, it seems to me that the immediate trigger for Foyzur's speech is provided by Mutib's earlier failure to produce a satisfactory answer (and Foyzur's failure to rescue the situation).

The significance of this is that what moves Foyzur to speak is not, in any simple sense, the sudden appearance of an idea but rather the minutely complex social interactions of the classroom, in which may simultaneously be implicated feelings of awkwardness, solidarity, embarrassment and pride, relationships with peers and with the teacher, relationships that have developed over time, and are still developing. Thus, even in a lesson segment that might seem, up to the moment of Foyzur's intervention, to support a reading of what is happening as script (constructed by Monica and some of the students) coexisting alongside a separate and oppositional counterscript (produced by Perry, Foyzur, Mutib, Jo and others), the students' relations to the script – the work of the lesson – are much more complex than such a reading would suggest.

In an attempt to uncover the process that led to Foyzur's intervention in this lesson, I want to explore some episodes in English lessons observed by me in the preceding fortnight. I should make it clear that I am not proposing a causal chain: what I am suggesting is that Foyzur's intervention might helpfully be seen within a context larger than the single lesson, and as a contribution to a longer conversation.

On 15 November, Monica had asked the students, working in pairs, to look at a selection of images of Richard III, images that she had found through an internet search. Each pair of students was given a single image mounted in the centre of a blank sheet of A3 paper. The first part of the task was to talk about, and then record, what the students could see in the image. Monica then explained the second part:

[18:16]
TEACHER: The second thing I want you to think about is what can you infer, Helen, what do I mean by that, asking what can you infer?

HELEN: What you think's happening.

TEACHER: OK, what you think's happening.

ALI: Um, I was about to say something else.

TEACHER: Tell me what you were about to say.

ALI: Like between, um, *[3 seconds]* I was going to say, reading, reading between the lines.

TEACHER: Reading between the lines, OK, good, would you like to say a little bit about what that means, reading between the lines?

CHRIS: Make a guess.

TEACHER: Making a guess about . . .

CHRIS: Something, like the . . .

NAZRUL: {Predictions . . .

CHRIS: {First picture you showed, he's got a crown on so we infer that he's a king.

TEACHER: OK, good, excellent, so making an educated, making a guess, if you like, about what's happening, using some information that's already there.

KEMI: Miss.

TEACHER: Kemi.

KEMI: Are you making your own interpretation of it?

(15 November 2005)

I'm not sure how tenable in practice or theory is the distinction between the first and second parts of the task. Is it possible, in other words, to engage in a meaningful conversation about a text without interpreting it? Can one describe what one sees without interpretation? Chris's point about the crown is a good one – but to name the thing sitting on the person's head as a crown is also, inevitably, an act of interpretation. But what happens in this part of the lesson is that students begin to explore what might be involved in the task – and they do so in a way that foregrounds their interpretive role. Prompted by Monica, Kemi and Ali take this further:

[19:08]

TEACHER: Very good, making your own interpretation, can you give me an example, say {a little bit . . .

KEMI: {Say if you saw the picture, like one person could think that he could be, er, posing as the king or something like that, and other people could think that he's actually the proper king.

TEACHER: OK, yeah.

ALI: Like writing your own opinions and writing what kind of a perspective do you get of that character.

TEACHER: OK, good, I want you think about as well, there are sort of three things, about these, because when you think about the play . . . so these people are all actors, so they're people, a person who takes a part, because you all play parts in, you all do role-play, and you all think, and sometimes we do the same scene and different people do it in different ways, don't they, it's what the actor thinks about that part, it's what, how the actor interprets the part of Richard, so there's the person, yeah.

(15 November 2005)

Richard III exists in the lesson in multiple forms. Lurking somewhere in the background, there may be the idea of the play as a canonical text, the text on which these students will be examined six months later in their Key Stage 3 tests. But Richard is more obviously present in different incarnations, in the form of the production-based images which have been distributed to each pair: because of the plurality of images, as Monica insists, there is space for students to perceive each image as an interpretation. Already, too, Monica is inviting students to make the move that Foyzur makes two weeks later: to see the play as a performance, to consider the interpretive possibilities, to make links between the actor's adoption of the role of Richard and the role-plays that are a prominent – and much-relished – feature of the class's experience of English.

Six days later, in a lesson on 21 November, the sense of *Richard III* as a performance text was reinforced when the class watched the openings of two film versions, one from 1995, directed by Richard Loncraine and starring Ian McKellen, the other the 1955 production, starring and directed by Laurence Olivier. In the last 10 minutes or so of the lesson, Monica invited students to compare the two beginnings. Mutib, holding the two DVD cases and referring to the images of the title role on each front cover, began to describe the mood of the two actors playing Richard. Caroline expressed a preference for the McKellen version and, pressed by Monica, explained why:

[47:46]
CAROLINE: I dunno because when you look at his face, when he's round his friends and that it looks like he wouldn't do that, but when you see him before when he shot them men and that, then you can think he looks like a person who would do that.
TEACHER: OK, good, so he's able to change the way that he looks depending on the people that he's with, yep, OK, excellent.

(21 November 2005)

Immediately, then, Caroline has opened up a consideration of the character as a dissembler – the character as, in other words, a consummate actor; more than this, though, she is able to acknowledge the ways in which our reading of the character is framed and shaped by the opening sequence, with its representation of Richard's killing of Edward and Henry at the Battle of Tewkesbury. This sense of the film as constructed, as the product of directorial choices, also informs

Ali's reflection on his uncertainty about the kind of film – the genre – that he was watching:

[49·53]

ALI: Yeah, a man looks like Hitler, yeah, and I thought the film was going to be like drama without the man like actually facing the camera, then I found out that it was something else other than drama.

TEACHER: Can I ask you about those bits when he's actually speaking to the camera, what's happening in those bits? Lucy?

LUCY: He's like saying what's on his mind.

TEACHER: He's saying what's on his mind, so he's saying to the audience what's on his mind.

(21 November 2005)

For Ali, it would seem that a (film) drama is defined by its adherence to naturalist conventions: thus, when McKellen (who 'looks like Hitler') speaks to camera, these conventions are broken – so Ali concludes that what he is watching is 'something else other than drama'. This provides an opportunity for Monica, assisted by Lucy, to explore the function of the soliloquy, providing access to Richard's thoughts and thereby establishing the relationship between the central character and the audience. And, of course, Foyzur's intervention more than a week later is based on an understanding of the force of the soliloquy as a theatrical device – an understanding that might be construed as a development from this moment.

In the course of this discussion, it becomes clear that there is a difference among the students as to which version they prefer. Helen advances the opinion that the Olivier is a more authentic production, because it was closer to what she had imagined, to her sense of historicity: '[the] one that we just watched was more like the Richard III that I think about . . . I think about the olden like kings and queens and dukes'.

Foyzur takes a contrary view:

[51:07]

I think, the first one was more nicer because it was like 1930s and I don't know, the films are really nice, yeah, with the settings, but when it's set in like mediaeval times, yeah, it's kind of boring like Robin Hood and stuff, so it's like, and when the man, the second one, *[Olivier]* was saying the words, it wasn't that interesting because, like, we know what happens and it's exactly like the play, the Shakespeare play, but the other one *[the McKellen version]* was a completely different setting, different characters . . . yeah, and you don't know what's going to happen, like it's going to be something different to Shakespeare.

(21 November 2005)

The difference, then, is an aesthetic one; but more is at stake here than a personal preference for (or aversion to) men in tights. Foyzur accepts that the Olivier is authentic ('it's exactly like the play'), but what for Helen was a confirmation of her prior expectations makes the whole thing just too familiar for Foyzur. What he values in the McKellen interpretation is its novelty – 'different setting, different characters' – and hence its unpredictability. Is Foyzur's appreciation of the uncertainty of McKellen's performance as Richard – his enjoyment of the fact that he doesn't quite know how the play is going to be realised in this production – a contributory factor in his developing sense of the dramatic power of McKellen-as-Richard, the grip that he has over the attention of Foyzur as his audience?

The following day, the class has another English lesson. It starts with the short period of private reading that is departmental policy for all Key Stage 3 classes. Then, after about eight minutes, Monica introduces the first activity. She has printed off still images from the two films watched the previous day, and mounted them on pieces of A3 paper. She wants students, working in pairs, to analyse the images. Before the activity starts, she works with the whole class to assemble the questions that they will use to structure their analysis of the images:

[8:16]

TEACHER: OK, the first thing that we're going to do today is that you're going to look at some still pictures from the video that we looked at, the two videos that we watched yester— not videos, two DVDs, two productions of *Richard III* and I want you just to, first of all, to think about who's in that picture, who do you think these people are. *[3 seconds]* OK, so the first thing is, who's who's there *[writes on the board – out of shot]* secondly, what do you think they are saying? *[writes on board]* OK, that's the second thing, what do you think the third thing might be?

[4 seconds]

ALI: Setting.

SUBHAN: Plot.

TEACHER: OK. *[writes]* That's a good one, erm . . .

[Speaker unidentified]: What time is it in?

TEACHER: Let me just take Ali's, I think 'where do you think . . .

ALI: {It's set.

TEACHER: { . . . they are?', that's the setting.

SUBHAN: What about the plot?

TEACHER: Um, what's happening. Yeah? Good, *[writes]* 'what is happening?'

SUBHAN: What has happened.

TEACHER: Or 'what has hap- just happened?'

BILLY: Or what's going to happen.

TEACHER: *[laughs]* OK.

[10:08]

ALI: What we infer from that?

TEACHER: *[4 seconds – teacher is writing Billy's question]* OK . . . OK, excellent, 'What can you infer?' *[writing Ali's question on the board]* Who can remind me what that means?

CAROLINE: Like, what can you get from that picture, like what can you guess.

TEACHER: Right, good, what can you guess, reading between the lines.

(22 November 2005)

The activity is similar to the one that students were participating in seven days earlier. Now, however, their reading of the images is inflected by their knowledge of the cinematic texts from which the stills are derived. So, right from the start, Ali and Subhan volunteer 'setting' and 'plot' as foci for investigation, thereby placing it within the analytic frame of work on (dramatic/cinematic) narrative.

The move that the teacher makes in response to the boys' suggestions is an interesting one. In phrasing the questions on the board, she omits the technical, subject-specific lexis that the students have offered, opting rather for 'Where do you think they are?' and 'What is happening?' I do not know what prompted Monica to formulate the questions in this way. What it achieves, I think, is three effects. Firstly, it renders the line of inquiry maximally accessible to everyone in the class. Secondly, it tends to direct attention towards the image itself, rather than to the film from which it had been extracted, so encouraging students to pay close attention to the meanings of the image in front of them. Thirdly, the reformulation of Subhan's 'plot' as 'What is happening?' enables Billy, simply by changing the tense of the question, to make an important leap towards interpretation and hypothesis; and Ali builds on this intervention by introducing the concept of inference.

The sequence is one that reveals a great deal about Monica's pedagogy: rather than being presented with a list of questions by the teacher, students are invited to become active participants, collaborating with the teacher in the construction of the activity. They are able to do so because this is familiar territory for them – they are used to taking part in this way. It is also worth considering the teacher's handling of the introduction of inference. Once again, as she had done a week earlier (see above), she ensures that the concept – a vital one in the reading practices that she is encouraging – is explained and explored; later in the same lesson, the value of this recursive approach becomes clear.

Students spend just over 10 minutes talking with their partners about the image that they have been given. Towards the end of this time, Kirsty asks Monica, 'Miss, what does infer mean again?' Rather than construing this as an indication that a student was not paying attention when the term was defined, 10 minutes or one week earlier, I want to suggest that this is evidence of learning happening. Kirsty and her partner have been busy making inferences from the image in front of them; what is going on at this stage of the activity is, I think, that she is rehearsing what she is going to say when she reports back on her findings. She wants to check, before venturing to use the word in so public a forum, that her understanding of its meaning accords with the way Monica and the other students use it. The significance of this does not rest in the question of vocabulary alone, but rather in the conjunction of the word and the activity: Kirsty's understanding of 'infer' comes both from the definitions that are offered in her class and from her involvement in acts of inference: the sign 'inference' is becoming populated with Kirsty's intentions, and 'concepts and word meanings evolve, and . . . this is a complex and delicate process' (Vygotsky 1987, quoted in Chapter 2).

Four minutes later, when it is Kirsty and Nazrul's turn to share their findings with the class, this is what happens:

[24:35]
NAZRUL: OK *[holds up picture and shows it round]* this is our picture.
TEACHER: OK, thank you.
NAZRUL: This picture shows that they're both brothers and the other brother is going to jail and that they the other brother is showing that they're going to miss each other, stuff like that.
TEACHER: So it looks like they are going to miss each other, OK, anything else?
KIRSTY: We infer that Richard's *[inaudible]* being too nice.
TEACHER: Yes, so why do you, what makes you think about the fact that he's planning something and he's being so nice, what came before, do you remember? *[3 seconds]* Can't remember? OK.

(22 November 2005)

Kirsty's attempt to share her inference is not entirely successful, even when Monica tries to help her to refer to the prior knowledge that she has of Richard that might provide an explanation for her inference that his apparent solicitude for Clarence is not to be taken at face value. Here she is working, I think, at the very limits of her powers of expression: that she is able to make this intervention at all, to contribute to the class's developing sense of Richard as an actor, is evidence of the way that the ZPD is socially constructed within the class.

Billy had been looking at the same image as Kirsty and Nazrul. When he gets his turn to report back to the class, his contribution builds on theirs:

[27:16]
TEACHER: Billy . . .
BILLY: Right, this is our picture. *[shows it]*
TEACHER: Yeah, good.
BILLY: And er it looks like he's being two-faced, he's waved his brother off who's going off to jail, he set him up, it looks like a place during the 1940s during

World War II, and he's a murderer, it's Richard the third, he wants to be king, he looks like Hitler, he looks angry, yeah, he's just come out of the parliament . . . he don't look trustworthy . . .

(22 November 2005)

There is a fluency – and an urgency – to Billy's delivery here: he has a lot of things to say, and he knows that this is his opportunity to say them. What he produces, though, is a list, in which items that can be read off from the image ('he looks like Hitler') and items that depend on knowledge of the play ('he set him up') are not distinguished from each other or from inferences that he is making: 'it looks like he's being two-faced', for example, is presented in a way that obscures Billy's position as the author of this judgement. Perhaps, then, Billy's contribution might enable us to gain a sharper sense of the difficulty – and the achievement – of Kirsty's 'we infer that Richard's . . . being too nice'. In particular, her use of the first person plural, though it can be construed (merely) as an acknowledgement that she is speaking for Nazrul as well as for herself, marks the beginning of an explicitness about the audience's perspective – and the audience's relationship with Richard.

In her contribution to the feedback, Caroline talks about the isolation of Richard in the Olivier version:

[25:46]

CAROLINE: It's the part where he's saying the speech and he looks like he might be planning to do to kill or capture someone and it looks like he could be in a church or a chapel and it looks like it's a place where not a lot of people go and it looks like there's just been a crowning and everyone's outside and in the picture he looks like he's evil and might be plotting something, and we writ questions as well, um . . .

TEACHER: Go on.

CAROLINE: Where exactly is he, what is he planning to do, why is he by himself and how did he get in there, who let him in?

TEACHER: Excellent, that's, I asked that question as well, I was just asking that question yesterday about why he was by himself, why he was in that . . . and why they bring the camera back to show you.

(22 November 2005)

It is not entirely clear whether Caroline intends her questions to have an orientation towards the directorial decisions of setting and camerawork. The very fact, though, that she has problematised the way in which Olivier is framed at this point in the film enables Monica to make explicit that these aspects of the image can be analysed as choices made by the film-maker, and not only as ingredients in the story of Richard. That point was not lost on Foyzur.

Towards the end of this part of the lesson, there is a discussion about the darkness of the stills taken from the 1995 (Loncraine/McKellen) film. Ali and

Foyzur start from a position that this aspect of the film is not, in effect, semiotically significant. Ali, confusing the time at which the film is set with the time of its production (and also showing a limited knowledge of cinematic history), suggests that 'they probably never had the cameras that could take pictures of the dark', while Foyzur offers the mundane explanation, 'probably because it was set in the night'. These ideas are quickly challenged by Billy and Subhan, who propose a much more sophisticated theory:

[33:15]
BILLY: Because it's like dark and there's a dark evil man that says like . . .
SUBHAN: I agree with Billy, yeah, but I think it's to show the evilness and, er, the personality of the man and what he's up to and everything . . . the darkness is trying to show the evilness.

(22 November 2005)

Their suggestion that the lighting carries a symbolic load convinces Foyzur – and makes him think more about the representation of Richard in both the films he has watched:

[34:44]
FOYZUR: You know when he's alone, yeah, in the second film we watched, yeah, that's like, and everybody's celebrating outside, that's like representing inside his head what's his view of everything, yeah, and he's saying a really long speech but, like everyone's celebrating outside and you can hear the noise in the background, that's like what's going on in the real world, and you know in the, I think it was the first film, that's like set in the 1930s, and it's kind of dark because they are trying to create like a similar . . .
NAZRUL: . . . atmosphere.
FOYZUR: A similar way of representing like what he's what he's trying to say.

(22 November 2005)

This is a remarkable contribution. It synthesises what emerged from Caroline's questions about setting and camerawork with Billy and Subhan's understanding of the symbolic significance of lighting. Simultaneously, it reaches back to Lucy's characterisation of the soliloquy in the previous lesson, when she described it as Richard 'saying what's on his mind.'

The argument that I am making, then, in relation to this sequence of lessons, is that there is a history to Foyzur's intervention in the lesson on 1 December: this history is Foyzur's, but it is also a collective history, the history of the class's readings of the multiple texts that constitute their experience of *Richard III*. An adequate account of this reading has to be attentive to the complexity of the social construction of meaning, to the social semiotic work that is being accomplished, to the struggle that is involved in the appropriation and remaking of signs (see Chapter 2).

I want to emphasise that this work matters – that it constitutes an intellectual accomplishment – and also that it is hard to spot. The work that Foyzur and his peers are engaged in is easy to miss in the hurly-burly of the classroom – and it leaves no monument behind. What counts, though, what merits our attention, is the fleeting, evanescent evidence of dialogic learning.

Notes

1 On the Vygotskian distinction between sense and meaning, see Chapter 2.
2 For approaches that problematise this understanding of character, see, for example, Cloud (1991).

Chapter 10

Agency, interest and multimodal design as evidence of reading

In this chapter, I continue to interrogate the ways in which reading is conceptualised in policy and to question whether the account that policy provides is adequate as a description of the literacy practices that are to be found in the secondary English classroom.[1] The data at the heart of this chapter are PowerPoint slides produced by two students in Monica's class (at the start of the year or so that I spent with them). The claim that I will make is that these data provide evidence of the productivity of school students, and in particular of their capacity to operate as sophisticated, multimodal sign-makers, using the resources of digital technologies in ways that are not acknowledged within the domain of schooled literacy (Gee 2004; Street 1984, 1995; Street *et al.* 2007).

Efferent and aesthetic reading in policy and practice

In the English National Curriculum programmes of study that were in force at the time these data were collected (DfEE 1999a), reading was categorised according to two broad kinds of text, literary and non-literary. Each of these categories was then further subdivided, literature into texts belonging to the 'English literary heritage' and 'Texts from different cultures and traditions' (DfEE 1999a: 49), non-literary texts into 'Printed and ICT-based information texts' and 'Media and moving image texts' (DfEE 1999a: 50). Two main purposes of reading were also identified: 'Reading for meaning' and 'Understanding the author's craft' (DfEE 1999a: 49): the latter purpose was defined in ways that imply that what was envisaged was an approach to literary texts; the former would seem to be applicable to all kinds of text (though the relationship between purposes and kinds of text was not made explicit).

The taxonomies that are at work here may well seem common-sensical: they bear a family resemblance to the binaries of fiction and non-fiction which are fundamental to the spatial organisation of (most) libraries and bookshops.

They are also closely related to Rosenblatt's well-known distinction between aesthetic and efferent reading orientations:

> the difference between reading a literary work of art and reading for some practical purpose. Our attention is primarily focused on selecting out and analytically abstracting the information or ideas or directions for action that will remain when the reading is over.
>
> (Rosenblatt [1938] 1995: 32)

And yet, as Carol Fox (2007) has argued in relation to comic books, the binary opposition of efferent and aesthetic reading is simply inadequate to deal with the layered richness of meanings that texts such as Anderson's *King* (2005) or Spiegelman's *Maus* (1987, 1992) have to offer. It may be that the affordances of multimodal texts, and the complexities of contemporary textual practice, pose particular difficulties for the rigid categories of text and reading practice that policy presents. On the other hand, it may be that new texts simply reveal more sharply the simultaneous presence of aesthetic and efferent orientations in textual practices across time. 'Reading for meaning' is not always and everywhere neatly separable from aesthetic engagement, and aesthetic engagement may be a means of getting things done.

As part of their work on Shakespeare's *Julius Caesar*, Monica's class was asked to do some research on other famous assassinations. Pairs of students were given the name of a historical figure who had been assassinated (Malcolm X, Martin Luther King, Mahatma and Indira Gandhi, Salvador Allende, Anwar Sadat, Leon Trotsky, J. F. Kennedy, Abraham Lincoln, H. F. Verwoerd, John Lennon and Rosa Luxemburg). Using the resources of the school library and of the internet, they were to find out about their allocated figure and share their findings with the rest of the class. The activity ran over three one-hour lessons in May 2005. In the first, the class was taken to the school library, where students were expected to begin their research; in the second, each pair had access to laptop computers in their English classroom, and worked on their presentations; in the third, students presented their findings to the rest of the class. I observed the second of these lessons and interviewed the class teacher, Monica, after the lesson.

This was the students' brief, as outlined on a task guidance sheet:

Research task

You are working in a pair. You have been given the name of a person who has been assassinated. You have to find out the following:

1   What is (or was this) person famous for?
2   Do you know why this person was killed?
3   When and where was this person assassinated?
4   Three more facts or information you can tell us about this person.

Rules: You must use at least one book *and* the internet or a CD-ROM.

You MUST write your sources down (the title of the book, the Dewey number and the internet website's correct address).

The task had been devised a year earlier, by the English teacher who had first planned the scheme of work for *Julius Caesar*. In outlining, for the rest of the department, the aims that would inform the work on the play, she had envisaged this activity as one that would provide an 'opportunity . . . for doing background research using both books and the internet'. The orientation suggested here derives from the National Curriculum programme of study for reading, in particular the section headed 'Printed and ICT-based information texts':

To develop their reading of print and ICT-based information texts, pupils should be taught to:

1   select, compare and synthesize information from different texts
2   evaluate how information is presented
3   sift the relevant from the irrelevant, and distinguish between fact and opinion, bias and objectivity
4   identify the characteristic features, at word, sentence and text level, of different types of texts.

(DfEE 1999a: 50)

This emphasis on information – on texts as repositories of data, and on reading as the identification, ordering and evaluation of these data – is reflected in the way that the students' task is framed through a series of questions: there are facts to be established. The students' work on a Shakespeare play thus provides an opportunity to explore a relevant theme – assassinations – and through this exploration to develop their skill at retrieving, sifting and synthesising the information that books and ICT-based resources have to offer. In its original conception, then, the task reflects and embodies the categories of reading set forth in the National Curriculum. Embedded within a longer-term engagement with a literary text, the Shakespeare play – where students might be expected to begin to understand a thing or two about 'the author's craft' – the task encourages a different kind of reading: efferent, not aesthetic.

In adopting this task, Monica made only one obvious amendment. Whereas, in its original form, students were to demonstrate what they had learned through an oral presentation to the rest of the class, Monica decided that her students would produce PowerPoint presentations – a decision that arose out of her knowledge of the class, of students' interests and expertise, knowledge that is itself the product of a long-term engagement with the class:

That class in particular has always been very good [with ICT] . . . and they've got a couple of people in there who are REALLY good – Paul and Helen, so if there's ever a problem we can call on Paul or Helen because they always know, and they share. Last year we did a big advertising project . . . and they did PowerPoint presentations there, and they [the two students] taught them, because they knew things I didn't know, about how to do slide transitions, about how to add sound, about how to superimpose things – they found images of bottles of drink and they wanted to superimpose their own labels on them, and Helen and Paul could show them how to do this – so they were rushing around the class inducting all the groups . . . so they're all quite good now.

(Interview, 12 May 2005)

Already, in Monica's awareness of what the students brought to the lesson and to their work on assassinations, there is a perspective on teaching and learning that is irreducibly social and dialogic, a perspective that acknowledges the agency, interests and expertise of the learners. This approach contrasts sharply with the pedagogic assumptions that inform policy, assumptions that are reflected in the frequency with which the sentence stem, 'pupils should be taught . . .', precedes the specification of an area of knowledge. The language of policy, positioning students as passive recipients of education, suggests a transmission model of teaching – what Freire termed the 'banking concept' (1972).

Making sense of Allende: shaping the material

I want to look at one of the presentations produced by two students, Jo and Paul, who were asked to research the death of Salvador Allende. I am interested in what can be established by an analysis of the two PowerPoint slides that they produced – what do they know about Allende and what do they know about ICT-based information texts?

Before considering the students' work, I should make it clear that what follows is my interpretation of the sign(s) that they produced. I cannot triangulate this interpretation by adducing in evidence the students' commentary on their work. I do not have access to such data – but I would also want to suggest that my analysis is no less plausible for the absence of such extrinsic correlation. As Kress and Jewitt (2003: 12) argue, semiotic work – sign-making – always involves making a selection, based on the interests of the sign-maker, from the material that is available to them:

If the sign in all its (formal and material) aspects represents the interests of its maker, we can make inferences, hypothetically, from the shape of the sign to the interests of its maker. The sign is evidence of the interests of its maker in the moment of representation, the sign-maker's engagement with the world to be represented. The sign is also evidence of its maker's interests in communication, their engagement with the social world in which the sign is a (part of a) message.

I turn, then, to the students' work, as evidence of their interests and of their learning. Let's start with the words. The first slide, entitled 'Salvador Allende', contains the following account of his life and death:

> Salvador Allende was the president of Chilean 1970 to 1973 and he was a founder of the Chilean socialist party. Salvador Allende died as he was overthrown, he died in a military coup led by general Augusto Pinochet. The nature of his death is unclear: His personal doctor said that he committed suicide with a machine gun given to him by Fidel Castro, while others say that he was *murderer* by Pinochet's military forces while defending the palace. He was born in Valparaiso. He was a president for three years.

The second slide, entitled 'Assassinators of Salvador Allende,' continues thus:

> Henry Kissinger and the CIA, directly responsible for his death, and view him as a victim of 'American Imperialism'. Members of the political right, however, tend to view Allende much less favourably.
>   To find out more go to: www.brainyencyclopedia.com

The students acknowledge their source, as their briefing notes had instructed them to. In its turn, the website they reference acknowledges that the article on Allende 'uses material from the Wikipedia article "Salvador Allende"'. And thus, by consulting the Wikipedia website, it is possible to reconstruct the editorial processes whereby Jo and Paul produced the text of their presentation.[2]

The article from which they derived their information runs to about 1,800 words; their version, not including headings and the reference to their source, is 122 words long. There is no evidence, I think, that they were synthesising information from more than one source. If they had consulted any library books in their library lesson, there is no trace of this in the work they produced. This is, perhaps, not surprising: web-based material, for their purposes in producing a PowerPoint presentation, is both more accessible and more easily re-worked, re-fashioned, than print-based sources. Moreover, as I show in the analysis that follows, what is involved in the production of such a presentation from web-based material is, in itself, a highly complex activity.

The text on the first page of their slide provides answers to the questions posed on the task guidance sheet (see above). They explain who Allende was, why he was famous, and then they focus on the circumstances of the assassination. Nearly half of the text is copied and pasted from the section of the original article that deals with the coup:

> On September 11, the Chilean military, led by General Augusto Pinochet, staged the Chilean coup of 1973 against Allende. During the capture of the La Moneda Presidential Palace, Allende died. *The nature of his death is unclear: His personal doctor said that he committed suicide with a machine gun*

given to him by Fidel Castro, while others say that he was murdered by Pinochet's
military forces while defending the palace.

(<http://en.wikipedia.org/w/index.php?title=Salvador_
Allende&oldid=6176578>, accessed 10 May 2007)

So is this mere 'copying out' – evidence of the dangers posed by the affordances of new technology, of the too-easy availability of information via the internet? On the contrary, what Paul and Jo have done is to identify the 40 words from their source (italicised in the quotation above) that answer their central research questions. At the very least, then, they have made a selection of what is relevant for their purposes.

More than this, though, has been going on in the construction of Paul and Jo's text, the first part of which is a carefully crafted synthesis of the information on Allende provided by the website.There are only two small errors here. One is where 'murdered' is mis-copied as 'murderer'. The other occurs in the opening sentence, where the adjective 'Chilean' is used in place of the noun, 'Chile'. I can find no evidence that this error was a product of copying text from the source: it may be that the students were confused about the adjectival status of 'Chilean' or it may be the product of eye-slip from the following line, where the adjective is used correctly in the phrase 'the Chilean socialist party'. In the source, the information about Allende's part in the formation of the Socialist Party is presented, in a subsequent section headed 'Background', as 'Allende co-founded Chile's socialist party'. The students have combined this with the statement about the dates of Allende's presidency, derived from the introductory section on the website, to produce a well-formed, fluent and succinct sentence, in which the form of the nominalisation, preceded by an indefinite article – '*a* founder' – suggests an awareness of the force of the prefix (*co-*) used in the source:

> Salvador Allende was the president of Chilean 1970 to 1973 and he was a founder of the Chilean socialist party.

From the same ('Background') section in their source, the students have copied the information about Allende's place of birth. What they have done with this, though, is to move it to near the end of the block of text on the first slide, after the sentence that deals with Allende's death. It is hard not to read this as a deliberate editorial decision, reflecting their sense of the relative unimportance of this fact. What I am proposing, then, is that the material from the website was carefully selected and shaped by the students in ways that reflected their interests. They were exploring Allende as someone who, like Julius Caesar, had been assassinated, and so it is this fact – albeit a disputed fact, as their text acknowledges – which assumes prominence in the version of events that they produce. The order that they have chosen is a journalistic one. They start with the main facts, provide more detail about the most important event, and then, down-page as it were, furnish the reader with a little background.

When we turn to the second of the two slides, however, it might seem that the claims being made for the students' control over their material become more tendentious. Under the heading 'Assassinators of Salvador Allende', the words included in the body of the text are copied verbatim from their source. Here are the two paragraphs from within which the words were copied, with the students' selection italicised:

> Allende is seen as a hero to many on the political left. Some view him as a martyr who died for the cause of socialism. His face has even been stylized and reproduced as a symbol of Marxism, similar to the famous images of Che Guevara. Members of the political left tend to hold the United States, specifically *Henry Kissinger and the CIA, directly responsible for his death, and view him as a victim of 'American Imperialism'*.
>
> *Members of the political right, however, tend to view Allende much less favorably.* His close relationship with Fidel Castro has led many to accuse him of being a communist who was destined to eventually transform Chile into a Castro-style dictatorship. They also argue that the socialist reforms he implemented while in power were the cause of the country's economic woes in 1973.

The students' version, extracting text from the middle of a sentence, pays no attention to the grammar of the original, so that the verb 'view' is left without a subject (originally the 'Members of the political left') and the pronoun 'him' sits uneasily, detached as it is syntactically from the 'Allende' that begins the paragraph in the original. If the first sentence doesn't quite hold together in this reduced form, the second suffers from even more fundamental problems of incoherence. The force of 'however' depends on the binary opposition of political left and right and their different perspectives on Allende. Because 'Henry Kissinger and the CIA' has, in effect, replaced 'Members of the political left' as the subject of the first sentence, the original's balanced presentation of contrary judgements collapses entirely. The violence that Jo and Paul have done to the grammatical coherence and political poise of their source might indicate, then, evidence of the failure of this activity if it is to be construed as a contribution to teaching students to 'sift the relevant from the irrelevant, and distinguish between fact and opinion, bias and objectivity', as the National Curriculum has it.

Talking after the lesson in which students were working on their presentations, Monica revealed that Jo and Paul's second slide might have been prompted by her intervention:

> In going round [the class] the things that I'm picking out, that's the key thing I want them to look at – the history that surrounds these individuals, 'so and so is responsible' – but are they really responsible, what other factors and forces lay behind these things – I want them to be aware of those – the whole idea of conspiracies . . . in lots and lots of cases it mentions . . . I was

talking to Jo and Paul about Allende and they said 'He wasn't killed, he died in the coup' and I said 'Look at what it says' and they had found stuff on Henry Kissinger, so I was asking them 'How is Henry Kissinger connected to it?' And that's a big idea for them to grasp, and I don't know what they will come up with tomorrow [when the presentations are made to the rest of the class].

(Interview, 12 May 2005)

The students' PowerPoint presentations, however, were not monomodal productions. The words that they used, borrowing and adapting from articles they found on the internet, constituted one element among many. What I want to do now is to turn to the PowerPoint slides themselves.

Design as evidence of learning

The first and most striking thing about the slide shown in Figure 10.1 this is that it has been designed. The affordances of PowerPoint are such, of course, that it would be difficult for the user not to think about design: the software is constructed in such a way that design choices are presented to the user. There are obvious constraints, such as the dimensions of the screen and the fairly

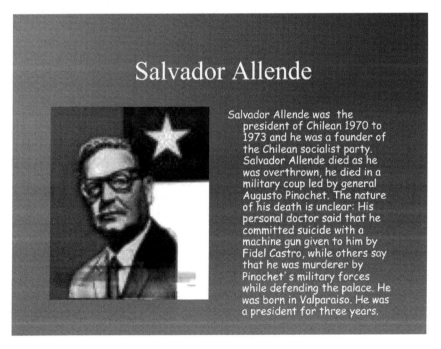

Figure 10.1 Jo and Paul's first slide

prescriptive ways in which the user is encouraged to organise the content. Here, the three elements – title, image and printed text – derive from a stock PowerPoint template, a template that enforces a particular spatial disposition of the three elements. What I want to suggest, though, is that the constraints and affordances of the software (and of this template in particular) have been adapted to serve the interests of the students creating the presentation. (Almost as an aside, I would also like to venture that the binary of aesthetic and efferent orientations becomes untenable, meaningless even, in the context of the students' multimodal design.)

The website that the students had consulted contains no images, so they found an image of Allende elsewhere on the internet.[3] What then seems to have happened is that Paul and Jo, with ingenuity and considerable skill, created a background to the slide that is an extrapolation from the design of the image of Allende that they had pasted into the slide. In the image, a photograph of Allende's head and shoulders is superimposed on a background of the Chilean flag, with the flag represented as if hanging from a horizontal pole, so that the left side is red, and in the top right-hand corner is the white star on a deep blue background, below which falls the white rectangle. The background of the slide picks up the red of the flag, which becomes the dominant colour of the whole slide. The blue of the flag's upper right corner is echoed in the top right-hand corner of the slide, where the red background fades through purple to blue. The white of the flag is echoed in the headline and in the body of the text.

Even if viewed in isolation, the dominant mode of the slide is colour (Kress and van Leeuwen 2001): it carries a weighty semiotic load and it frames, literally and figuratively, both the words and the image. So what does red mean here, in this context? Any doubt about this is dispelled by the second slide (Figure 10.2).

The layout of the second slide parallels the first, with the disposition of title, image and written text the same on each. The image of Kissinger[4] may well have been chosen because it, too, mirrors the image of Allende. Both men are presented with their bespectacled faces and their besuited torsos angled very slightly to the left of the viewer. One again, though, the dominant mode is colour, and the most prominent sign on the slide is blue. The sentence grammar of the writing on the second slide may be unclear, confused and incoherent; the grammatical organisation of the two slides as a single multimodal text is exemplary in its coherence. Central to the students' design is the opposition of red and blue, signifying political affiliations and orientations. (There might also be a subsidiary meaning in the sequence of the slides, which represents a chronological movement: the triumph of the blue forces is thus prefigured in the blue corner of the first slide, its placing on the right an indication, within western reading conventions, of futurity – Kress and van Leeuwen 1996.)

I want to return now to the issue of the grammatical coherence of the writing on the second slide. In my earlier analysis, I treated it as a piece of continuous discursive prose – as if it were the same kind of text as the source from which it was derived. I am not at all sure that this assumption is warranted. The words are the same, but they have been differently framed.

Figure 10.2 Jo and Paul's second slide

The website where the words originated presents information much as it might be presented in a print-medium encyclopaedia: perhaps the only significant difference is that the use of hyperlinks allows the reader to navigate between entries with greater facility. The article on Allende starts with a short summary, which is followed by a number of sections, organised more or less chronologically, each of which provides more detail on aspects of Allende's life and times; it then concludes with a list of references. Despite the complicating presence of hyperlinks, then, the organisation of the article is predominantly linear and temporal.

In contrast, the students' PowerPoint presentation is organised spatially. Within each slide, the different elements stand in apposition to each other: that is the meaning of their presence on the same slide. Thus, on the first slide, Allende is represented by the title, the image and the written text – and also by the red background that infuses all the separate blocks of semiotically significant material. On the second slide, the same set of relationships exists. The presence of the image of Kissinger identifies him as one of the 'Assassinators of Salvador Allende', as the title has it. What, then, of the written text on this slide? In PowerPoint, written text tends to be organised not in continuous prose but in bullet points, with each bullet point standing in parallel to the others on the same slide: the internal organisation of writing thus mirrors in detail the appositional relationships of the larger blocks of semiotic material within a single slide. If we apply these organising principles to the words that Jo and Paul pasted into the text box on their second slide, the issue of their (in)coherence begins to look rather different. What they have done is to identify two categories of people who can be labelled as 'Assassinators of Salvador Allende':

- Henry Kissinger and the CIA, and
- members of the political right.

What looked like carelessness or a lack of understanding of the sentence grammar and textual coherence of the source might better be understood as motivated selection of appropriate material. There is an additional piece of evidence that suggests that what the students did was to choose two sections from the article, and that is the absence of the inverted commas after 'imperialism'. The most plausible explanation for this omission is that the text was imported in two sections, each section standing in an appositional relationship to the title: in the blue corner we have these forces, as it were.

One of my starting points for the analysis of the students' work was the question of what it reveals about their knowledge of ICT-based information texts. What the analysis suggests is the inadequacy of the way such knowledge is framed within the discursive world of policy. Within the version of the National Curriculum in force at the time, the separation of 'Printed and ICT-based information texts' from 'Media and moving image texts' seems, at best, somewhat arbitrary, and carries with it the implication that questions of design can somehow be relegated to a special category of text, safely insulated from the business of retrieving, sifting and synthesising information from the written (printed) word. In a more recent revision to the National Curriculum, there is the suggestion that 'Pupils should be able to . . . understand how meaning is created through the combination of words, images and sounds in multi-modal texts' (QCDA 2008). Even here, though, it is only when school students are positioned as readers that multimodality is mentioned. As far as the productive capacity of school students is concerned, there is nothing more adventurous than the injunction that they should be able to 'present material clearly, using appropriate layout, illustrations and organisation': what the gloss on this reveals is that what is envisaged is that this 'could include headings, subheadings, bullet points, captions, font style and size, and the use of bold or italics when presenting work on screen' (QCDA 2008.). For students as writers, then, all that the new technologies can provide is scope for some presentational embellishment, typographical aids to ensure that the meaning of the words gets through.

The problem with this is, firstly, that it does not begin to describe what Jo and Paul know about ICT-based texts, and, secondly, that the perspective of policy encourages the kind of misreading of students' work that was exemplified by my initial (monomodal) approach to what Jo and Paul had produced. The meaning of their PowerPoint presentation does not reside in the words, with the images and the background supplying a little decorative curlicue or two: it resides in the multimodal ensemble, in the totality of the presentation. The meaning of any element within this design is relational and contingent, no more reducible to its parts than any other complex text – *Julius Caesar*, say.

(Mention of the Shakespeare play prompts me to raise a further layer of complexity involved in the PowerPoint presentation, to which I have not attended at all. I have treated the two slides as if they were the presentation, as if the students' semiotic work was all on screen, rather in the manner of those Shakespearean critics who treat the script as if it were the play itself, as if performance were merely the shadows in Plato's cave. I have little choice in the matter: I did not observe the subsequent lesson, and have no data on the presentation that Jo and Paul gave to the rest of their class. But I must at least register my awareness of this lack. The affordances of PowerPoint consist of the means whereby the software encourages and constrains the disposition of elements on the screen, but also involve the ways in which it functions as a mediational tool, as something between a script and an *aide memoire* as well as a backdrop to the live presentation. How did Paul and Jo present their research? Where and how did they stand? What did they say? And how did the audience of their peers respond? I don't know.)

Allende and *Julius Caesar*: reading the word and the world

Consideration of the meaning of the students' PowerPoint presentation takes me back to the other question with which I started: what do they know about Allende? One way of answering this question would be to look at the content of the first of their two slides, to identify the pieces of information that Jo and Paul have extracted from their source. They know, too, that there is a debate about whether Allende was assassinated: this is clear from the words that they have included to describe the different interpretations of the circumstances of Allende's death – words that gesture at the controversy that has rumbled on for years within the Wikipedia site, as well as more widely. They have learned, with specific reference to Allende's death, something of the difficulty of distinguishing, as the National Curriculum demands, 'between fact and opinion, bias and objectivity'.

But the second slide reflects a different kind of learning. As I have suggested above, its creation would seem to owe something to the teacher's intervention, her suggestion that Jo and Paul should go on thinking about what the website had to say about the role of Henry Kissinger, among others. The intellectual step that she encouraged them to take, to move from a conception of assassination as bounded by the immediate physical circumstances of the death (did Allende shoot himself or was he shot by Pinochet's troops?) to a broader, more contextualised and more political understanding, is, as Monica acknowledges, a big one. And it is possible to construe linguistic features of the second slide as evidence that the students are operating at the limits of their conceptual reach. The collapse of sentence structure might indicate this; so might the heading that they have used. 'Assassinators' is an intriguing choice. Is it that neither Jo nor Paul had come across 'assassin'? This seems unlikely, partly because the word has currency within the lexis of video-gaming: for example, *Hitman 2: Silent Assassin* was a popular game, available on a variety of platforms (and first released in October 2002). It might be more plausible, then, to speculate that the students did not quite connect the word 'assassin' with Allende's assassination and the way that Monica was inviting them to think about wider issues of agency, power and responsibility. The students' solution is to coin a new word – and it is an apt coinage. Effectively a back-derivation from 'assassination', its Latin suffix suggests power and impersonality (a bit like Terminator). If the assassin is the individual who fires the bullet, the assassinator is the one whose word makes the death happen.

What makes this interpretation of the heading as the product of motivated decisions by the students rather less fanciful is the fact that the heading exists, and has meaning, within the multimodal semiotic ensemble of the slide presentation as a whole. For what the second slide, with its carefully constructed mirror image of the first, does is to move the students' presentation of Allende beyond the death in the Presidential Palace of La Moneda and out into the arena of world politics.

This shift has implications for more than the focus of the students' research project. As it had been conceived by the teacher within the English department who had originally devised the scheme of work for *Julius Caesar*, the opportunity for students to find out about other assassinations was tangential to the exploration of Shakespeare's play. The activity, thematically linked to the play, involved a different kind of text – information, not literary – and different kinds of reading: reading that was oriented towards the retrieval of specific bits of information. In its original conception, then, the activity did not disturb the taxonomies of the National Curriculum. Monica's approach to the activity is significantly different:

> That's the key thing I want them to look at – the history that surrounds these individuals, 'so and so is responsible' – but are they really responsible, what other factors and forces lay behind these things.
>
> (Interview, 12 May 2005)

The presentation on Allende that Jo and Paul produce demonstrates their understanding that the events of 1973 can be differently framed, differently interpreted. This conceptual development has huge implications for their understanding of *Julius Caesar*. More than this, though, it opens the possibility that their reading of *Julius Caesar* will inform and be informed by their understanding of the world. The questions that Monica poses here bring the research project and the study of *Julius Caesar* into a different alignment. The distinction between literary and information text becomes much less important, since both kinds of text become tools for thinking with. This conception of the text, and hence of what reading is for, is central to Monica's pedagogy.

It is, perhaps, worth making the point that the presentation is a collaborative production: it is the work of Jo and Paul, as it were. It is not just that we have no means of assigning particular contributions to either individual student, but also that to attempt to do so would be in some sense to miss the point of the activity. The PowerPoint presentation is, in a very specific sense, a sign that is 'a construct between socially organized persons in the process of their interaction' (Vološinov [1929] 1986: 21, quoted in Chapter 2 of this volume). What I have sought to demonstrate in this chapter is a particular instance of the process whereby the two students make the words of a website their own, populating them with their own intentions (Bakhtin [1975] 1981: 293, and see Chapter 2 of this volume). And the semiotic work that the students do is both powerful evidence of their cognitive development – their learning – and, simultaneously, the means by which this learning is accomplished.

Notes

1 An earlier version of this chapter appeared as Yandell (2011).
2 The website consulted by the students, www.brainyencyclopedia.com, republishes almost verbatim the text from the Wikipedia article (<http://en.wikipedia.org/wiki/Salvador_Allende>). Wikipedia articles undergo a continual process of collaborative – and contested – amendment. The version that the students consulted would seem closest to the version that was posted on the Wikipedia website at 23:44, 26 September 2004. It can be found in the Wikipedia archive at http://en.wikipedia.org/w/index.php?title=Salvador_Allende&oldid=6176578, accessed 10 May 2007. There is no equivalent archive for the www.brainyencyclopedia.com site.
3 The image of Allende was probably imported from www.yorku.ca/cerlac/recent03–04.html, the website of the Centre for Research on Latin America and the Caribbean, York University, Canada, where it was used to advertise a two-day conference entitled 'CHILE: Civil Democracy in Neoliberal Times' (Friday, November 28 and Saturday, November 29 2003).
4 The Kissinger image comes from www.wtv-zone.com/Mary/NEWWORLD ORDER.HTML, an American Christian website, with quotations from a variety of public figures on the idea of a New World Order. The evidence that this is the source is the file size: the size of the image in the students' PowerPoint is the same as that of the image from this site (224.9 kb). The same image of Kissinger, in different file sizes, is available on a number of different websites.

Chapter 11

Mind the gap

Investigating test literacy and classroom literacy

In Chapter 3, I quoted George W. Bush on the importance of literacy: 'You teach a child to read, and he or her will be able to pass a literacy test' (*Times Educational Supplement*, 24 August 2001). As I suggested in Chapter 3, there are significant points of correspondence between George W. Bush's model – that learning to read is important because one is thereby enabled to pass a literacy test – and the neck-verse literacy that saved the lives of (some) functionally literate felons. Neck-verse literacy shares three key features with George W. Bush's literacy: it assumes a simple binary opposition of literacy and illiteracy (pass/fail or hanged/not hanged); it can easily be tested; it is the property of the individual (Bush's 'he or her'). Modern literacy tests, of course, are more sophisticated, the assessments more finely calibrated, the outcomes more nuanced; but the underlying assumptions about literacy have more in common with the neck verse than might be imagined.

Test literacy: the case of *Richard III*

I want to explore in some detail one such test, the 2006 Key Stage 3 English examination paper on Shakespeare's *Richard III* (QCA 2006a).[1] I will look at how reading and the reader are constructed by the test, before considering one candidate's response to the paper. Using evidence provided by classroom observation of the same student and by his writing outside the exam, I will compare his performance in the test with his reading of *Richard III* in the classroom. What emerges from this comparison is not, however, a story of differential performance in the same kind of literacy so much as a recognition of the chasm that separates test literacy from the literacy practices of the urban English classroom, the literacy practices that have been described in the preceding chapters. Jane Coles has argued persuasively that the effect of 'the system of national tests [with] Shakespeare at their heart . . . will be to support and uphold hegemonic practices' (Coles 2004: 57). While I agree with this analysis of the impact of such tests, what my research data suggest is the continuing possibility of counter-hegemonic practices, the continuing 'opportunities to create classrooms where new forms of cultural discourse can be opened up and explored' (Coles 2004: 57).

As part of the assessment regime designed to ensure the accountability of the education service and intended to raise standards, almost all 14-year-olds within the English state education sector sat an examination paper on Shakespeare.[2] The Qualifications and Curriculum Authority (QCA), the government body with responsibility for overseeing the National Curriculum and its assessment at the time, selected three plays from within the canon: in 2006, *Richard III* was, for the first time, one of the three. Within the examination, candidates were presented with two extracts from the play. They had 45 minutes to answer a question. As the cover to the examination paper explained, 'This booklet contains one task which assesses your reading and understanding of *Richard III*' (QCA 2006a: 1). Where, one might wonder, did reading end and understanding begin? Were reading and understanding envisaged as separate activities? Where and when did they take place – in the classroom, over time, or in the examination hall?

There was, nonetheless, a clear commitment to a model of literacy that went beyond the recitation of the neck verse. The inside cover presented candidates with the task:

Richard III

Act 1 Scene 1, lines 32 to 96

Act 3 Scene 7, lines 110 to 172

In these extracts, how does Richard use language to deceive others and to hide his plans to become king?

Support your ideas by referring to both of the extracts which are printed on the following pages.

(QCA 2006a)

The claim on the front cover is that the task would assess the candidate's 'reading and understanding of *Richard III*' – that is, the whole play – but what the task insists on, twice, is a focus on two extracts from the play. At best, then, an assumption is made that candidates' 'reading and understanding' of a part of the play will be an accurate proxy indicator of their 'reading and understanding' of the whole.

In reality, though, because the scenes which were to be the focus of the examination question were published in advance, many candidates had an entirely different reading experience of the 'SATs scenes', as they were known, than they had of the rest the play. In many of the schools where I visited my PGCE students, school students were presented with photocopies of the SATs scenes, and no other part of the play. At worst, their preparation for the exam consisted solely of exercises relating to the set scenes, exercises that were designed to enable the candidate to regurgitate the required gobbets in response to the examination question (see also Barker 2003; Coles 2003). The version of literacy that was being promulgated in such contexts bears a striking resemblance to neck-verse literacy.

According to the italicised rubric, the candidate was meant to have 'ideas' – though, to be sure, ones that were rooted in, and hence might have been adequately supported by, the extracts. This might suggest scope for personal response, as outlined in the National Curriculum attainment targets for reading:

Level 7
Pupils show understanding of the ways in which meaning and information are conveyed in a range of texts. *They articulate personal and critical responses to poems, plays and novels*, showing awareness of their thematic, structural and linguistic features.

(DfEE 1999c: 5, emphasis added)

The concept of personal response has a long history, with roots in the Wordsworthian tradition explored in Chapter 3 and also in I. A. Richards' *Practical Criticism* (1929) as much as in reader-response criticism (Rosenblatt [1938] 1995, 1978), and it is a concept that, given the nexus of power relationships that shape all encounters between students and canonical texts, has tended to promise more liberality, more openness, than it has delivered. If this is the case in all contexts where texts and readers meet, the scope for personal response in the (literature) examination room is far more circumscribed. As Tony Davies observed in relation to literature examinations in higher education more than a quarter of a century ago:

The required 'discussion', seemingly no more than an extension in writing of the friendly open-ended dialogue of the tutorial, is in fact a monologue in which the student, to 'cover the question', is obliged both to reply 'in his or her own words' and to assume the position ('*we* find . . .') of the absent but watchful questioner. Given the complex intertextualities that have gone to produce a student's 'own words', the writing of a simple examination essay becomes a feat of multiple and simultaneous impersonation beside which *The Waste Land* looks like the performance of an amateur impressionist.

(Davies 1982: 39)

As Davies also notes, 'most examination questions are in fact assertions or commands'.

The question on the *Richard III* paper enforces a series of assumptions about the play and about the candidates' reading(s) of the play. It asserts that 'Richard use[s] language to deceive others and to hide his plans to become king'. The student's task, then, is merely to explain *how* this happens. The play arrives pre-packaged, the task of understanding what is enacted already accomplished by the examiner. The student is invited to focus on a single character, but even here most of the interpretive work has already been done. Richard is presented as both knowable and known: his motives, his intentions, his ambitions and his methods are all presented as facts. All that remains for the student is to explore language as one of the methods that the character, so we are informed, uses. The focus on language here may be linked to the emphasis on 'understanding the author's craft' in the National Curriculum (DfEE 1999a: 49) and in the Literacy Strategy (DfEE 2001b). If so, what is really quite bizarre is that the question transfers attention from the author's craft to the *character's*. Richard, rather than being seen as a product of the author, a character created, at least in part, through and in language, has somehow become an autonomous user of language. There is, thus, no room in the exam question for interrogating the conception of 'dramatic characters as recognizably 'real' people, where . . . characters are not an effect of text but autonomous entities' (Shepherd 1991: 91); no room, either, for a recognition that even the issue of Richard's name is problematic (in the early quarto editions, he appears as 'Gloster'; see also Cloud 1991).

The test is, thus, predicated on the assumption that the student's 'reading and understanding' of the play can be assessed through a task that concentrates on two short extracts from the script, that treats character as stable, unproblematic and known, and that treats the language of these extracts as the property of the character, the means whereby the character achieves planned goals (deceiving others and hiding his plans to become king).

On the remaining pages of the test booklet are printed the two extracts, each of which is prefaced by a piece of explanatory text, contained within a shaded box. The first extract is introduced thus:

> In this extract, Richard tells the audience his plans. He then talks to his brother, Clarence, who is being taken by Brakenbury to be imprisoned in the Tower.
>
> (QCA 2006a: 3)

The candidate who reads this is entitled to feel somewhat confused. The task question asserts that 'Richard use[s] language to deceive others and to hide his plans', yet the very next page announces that 'Richard tells the audience his plans'. Perhaps one is meant to infer that the audience is not included in the 'others' to whom the question refers. If so, this is not made explicit; moreover, such an inference seems to imply that what Richard says to the audience provides transparent access to his soul. It is hard to maintain this, though, when the speaker reveals that he is 'subtle, false and treacherous'. Richard's opening soliloquy, the last part of which is included in the extract, sets up a relationship with the audience which does not seem to be characterised by simple plain-dealing. It begins with a statement that simultaneously locates the historical moment (after the battle of Tewkesbury) and announces the speaker's allegiance to the victorious faction: 'Now is the winter of our discontent/Made glorious summer by this son of York'. Or does it? The first line, seeming to be a semantically and syntactically complete statement, misleads the audience: what it means is utterly transformed by the introduction of the (unexpected) main verb at the start of the second line: the season that is 'now' is not winter but summer, brought on by the sun/son of York. The surface meaning, then, is sunny enough. But the reason that the first line of the play is often quoted in isolation is not through ignorance of the second line: it is because the first line allows Richard to reveal his (present) discontent before swiftly concealing it behind the punning mask, the correction offered by the second line. So language is both showing and hiding, and Richard is both telling the truth and lying. Even in his soliloquies – especially in his soliloquies – transparency is not on offer. He is as playful (and as unreliable) as his theatrical ancestor, the Vice of the morality plays. (And here I, too, am entering into the spirit of the exam paper, playing the literary critical game, offering up an interpretation of Richard, a dash of close reading with just a hint of theatrical-historical context. But my words are not an exam rubric and do not have the same power to constrain others' readings.) What I am suggesting, however, is that, even within the discursive confines of traditional literary criticism, the examination task is constructed of so crass a series of oversimplifications as to encourage an utterly banal (mis)reading of the text.

The contradiction between the task question and the introduction to the first extract is troubling for a much more fundamental reason than its oversimplification of Richard's character. As I have indicated above, the easiest way of resolving this contradiction is to assume that the question is directing the candidate to consider only the ways in which Richard uses language in relation to other 'characters' within the play. So it is not just that Richard, for the purposes of this examination, is to be treated less as a character in a play and more as a (real) person; it is that the kind of play that *Richard III* is has been redefined by the exam paper. To encourage students to write about Richard's use of language while ignoring the ways in which the actor playing Richard uses language to develop a relationship with the audience is to transform the Renaissance drama into a different kind of theatrical animal altogether – less Shakespeare than Shaw, maybe. It puts the play behind a proscenium arch – and it does so because this is the only way that Richard can become domesticated, turned into a realist character, and the whole edgy business of his tricky, unreliable, mediating relationship with the audience ignored.[3]

Matters don't become much more straightforward when we reach the second extract. Its explanatory gloss informs us that:

> In this extract, Buckingham and Richard carry out their plan to trick the Mayor into believing that Richard deserves to be king. The Mayor and citizens are on the stage watching and listening.

> (QCA 2006a: 5)

Again, one might want to ask, what about the other audience? How does this audience-on-stage alter the way that the wider audience reads what is being enacted? The mention of the stage is, nonetheless, the most explicit acknowledgement in the examination paper that *Richard III* is a play. The problem is that this gesture sits uneasily, particularly in this scene, with the instruction to focus on language. Words, in *Richard III*, are part of embodied action. Richard's act, here, does not start when he opens his mouth; it starts when he appears:

> *Enter RICHARD aloft, between two Bishops*
> Mayor. See where his Grace stands,'tween two clergymen;
> Buck. Two props of virtue for a Christian Prince,
>   To stay him from the fall of vanity;
>   And see, a book of prayer in his hand.
>
> (Shakespeare 1981: III.vii.93ff)

The decision not to start the extract from this point but from 15 lines later in the scene would seem perverse if the intention were to enable students to write about Richard's performance, about the act that he and Buckingham put on for the benefit of the Mayor and citizens. The scene has been stage-managed: where Richard stands (between two bishops) and the prop he holds (the prayerbook) are as much a part of the designed effect as are the words he speaks. When, a few lines into the extract, Richard asks 'Else wherefore breathe I in a Christian land?' the impact of the rhetorical question depends on the iconography of his appearance. The insistence of the examination paper that students write about Richard's use of language amounts to a denial of the multimodal semiotic resources of drama. There is a kind of absurd Platonism at work here. Examiners tend to complain grumpily about candidates who write about Shakespeare plays as if they were films – about *Romeo and Juliet* as if Tybalt shot Mercutio on Verona Beach and the lovers' eyes met across a crowded fishtank, and so on. But at least such candidates approach the plays as *drama*, as texts instantiated in performance. Might this not be preferable to an approach that neglects entirely the materiality of the drama?

Those responsible for the examination paper are quite explicit about their approach to task-setting:

> The reading task on the Shakespeare paper is a test of prepared reading via a single task. It tests the same set of skills as are assessed on the unseen texts on the Reading paper. The emphasis is on pupils' ability to orchestrate those skills and demonstrate their understanding of, and response to, the Shakespeare text they have studied, and so the assessment focuses are not separately identified.
>
> Each task targets one of the following areas related to the study of a Shakespeare play:
>
> - character and motivation;
> - ideas, themes and issues;
> - the language of the text;
> - the text in performance.

In 2006, the areas targeted for assessment are:
Macbeth character and motivation;

Much Ado About Nothing ideas, themes and issues;
Richard III the language of the text.

(QCA 2006b: 29)

The assumption, then, is that it is both possible and desirable to target separate areas for assessment – that to set a single task on the play will enable all candidates to demonstrate 'their understanding of, and response to, the Shakespeare text they have studied'. There is, I think, a further assumption in the use of the word 'text' here. It is that the object of study is, in effect, the words on the page. The script is seen as primary, its instantiation in performance as merely secondary. The 'text in performance' thus becomes one of four possible areas of assessment – the one area that was not assessed in any of the tasks set in 2006. Shouldn't all students be encouraged – expected, even – to make sense of any Shakespeare play primarily as a text in performance?

I want to turn now to consider how the examination question was answered by one candidate. This is what Billy, a student in Monica's Year 9 class, wrote:

> In the opening Richard mention how he going to set his two brothers Clarence and King Edward in deadly hate one against the other. But then Clarence enters guarded by Brakenbry, soon to be sent to the tower. When then Richard ask the question 'Brother good day what means this armed gard that waits upon your grace' when he knows why those guard are there and where his going to. Richard know this because Clarence was not the one that was going to kill the king. It was Richard York or GLOUCESTER.
>
>   In Act 3 scene 7 Buckingham say to Richard that you should take the trone that It in his blood to becom King But Richard dicives [deceives] the mayor by re[fu]sing and it is his fault. This makes the mayor think that Richard shold have the throne and Richard being King will not bee a bad thing but a good thing

The script was awarded two out of a possible eighteen marks. This placed it in the middle of the lowest band, which the published mark scheme characterises in this way:

> A few simple facts and opinions about what Richard says or does in these extracts, eg in the first, *he tells lies*, and in the second, *he is acting*, though some misunderstanding may be evident. Parts of the extracts are retold or copied and answers may be only partly relevant.

(QCA 2006b: 56)

It is not my intention here to mount a defence of Billy's examination script. It may well be that the marker was correct to judge his answer as a Band 1 response. What is it, though, about Billy's answer that is deficient? Is it his reading and understanding of the play? Or is it his ability to write a literary critical essay in examination conditions? When, for example, he quotes Richard's faux-naif question to Clarence, he is doing considerably more than mentioning a 'few simple facts about what Richard says or does'; but what he cannot yet do is to achieve a level of explicitness about what is going on in this exchange. Likewise, when he capitalises 'Gloucester' in the final sentence of his first paragraph, he is, I think, attempting to draw attention to the layers of irony in the trap that Richard has set: King Edward, as both Richard and the audience know, is imprisoning the wrong 'G'. But the way that Billy has attempted to communicate this – through typography – will not do in an essay where the expectation is that knowledge will be rendered explicit in well-formed sentences. He both knows a great deal more than he says, and also has problems finding an appropriate way of saying what he knows within the discursive constraints of the examination essay.

Classroom literacy: Billy's reading of Shakespeare

I make these claims partly on the internal evidence of Billy's examination essay, but chiefly on the basis of what I observed of Billy in the year preceding his *Richard III* exam. I want to move on now to some of the data collected during the year leading up to the SATs exams. Using these data, I want to make two linked but nonetheless separable arguments: first, that what Billy wrote in his exam essay cannot be taken as an accurate gauge of his 'understanding of, and response to, the Shakespeare text [he had] studied', as was proposed in the QCA's *English Test: Mark scheme* (QCA 2006b); second, that an adequate account of Billy's reading and understanding of the play must attend to the different literacy practices of the urban English classroom, where he and his peers had explored (and enjoyed) *Richard III*.

In January 2006, as Billy's class was nearing the end of their work on the play, students were asked to write a series of entries in Richard's diary. The assignment was intended to provide students with the opportunity to reflect on the main events of the play and on how these events might be represented in Richard's consciousness. Billy made the decision to word-process his 'Richard III Diary', as he called it, choosing a font that looked more like cursive handwriting. His second entry covers the wooing of Anne:

> **Dear Diary**
> Arr I love you I feel so sorry for you blah de blah de blah, whatever. At last my persuasive words have got Anne in the deep palms of my hands. I feel great everything is going just as I planned. Will I keep her? . . . For the moment I will because she helps me become more powerful more powerful than I fought.

What Billy wrote in his exam essay might have appeared to be not much more than narrative, a not very skilful retelling of what happens in the extracts; what Billy writes here reveals much more of his reading of the play. He understands that the simple dichotomy of war and peace, battle and courtship, which Richard presented in the soliloquy with which the play begins, is an illusion: both offer paths to power. He remembers the cool cynicism of Richard's 'I will have her but I will not keep her long', echoed here in his question, 'Will I keep her?' He has a sense of Richard's ability to manipulate others, largely through his 'persuasive words'. And the diary form enables Billy to communicate something of Richard's self-awareness, his relishing of his own bravura performance. But it is the first sentence of this entry that I find compelling. Billy's use of direct speech, as his Richard records his wooing voice, dissolves in the mockery of 'blah de blah de blah, whatever'. The effect, the jolting, shocking transition in mid-sentence, mirrors Richard's 'Was ever woman in this humour woo'd?/Was ever woman in this humour won?' (I.ii.233–234): as soon as Anne has left the stage, he steps outside his role as lover, revelling in his power, inviting the audience to join him in admiring his performance and in the calculating misogyny of his attitude to Anne.

Behind the words of Billy's diary entry lies a history of his – and his class's – engagement with this moment in the play. Two months earlier, as preparation for their first reading of the scene between Richard and Anne (Act 1, Scene 2), students were asked to participate in group improvisations. The activity, involving rehearsal time and group presentations, occupied the final 20 minutes or so of the lesson. I have described the activity in some detail in Chapter 8. As break-time neared, Billy volunteered, with a little prompting from Jo, to perform a second improvisation:

[53:38]

JO: Billy, come on, do your other one then.

BILLY: Come on, then. We need some glue, or sellotape.

TEACHER: No, no, I think that sounds too complicated.

KEMI: It's about drugs, it's about drugs.

[Billy is already moving around the room, as is Jo, who is moving chairs to establish the set. Billy is using a piece of file paper to construct a gigantic spliff as he moves]

BILLY: It's about persuading someone to take it . . . miss, we got blu-tak.

TEACHER: OK. Come on then hurry up.

[Lucy gets out of her seat and joins Billy]

TEACHER: We've only got four minutes and I'm on duty and we have to put the tables back.

BILLY: *[throwing the spliff to Lucy]* You can persuade me to.

[Billy and Lucy take up their positions, sitting at right angles to one another, Lucy holding the spliff]

ALI: 3, 2, 1

TEACHER: Go!

LUCY: *[thrusting the spliff towards Billy]* You wanna take it?

BILLY: Nah, nah, look, no.

LUCY: Just take it.

BILLY: No.

LUCY: It's not gonna kill you, just take it.

BILLY: No, man.
LUCY: Take it.
BILLY: What, what will my par—
LUCY: Your parents!
BILLY: What would they think if—
LUCY: Your parents are on holiday.
[As the conversation continues, Lucy turns to face Billy more directly. Her eye-contact is hard to evade]
BILLY: Yeah . . .
LUCY: They're in another country, just take it.
[Billy shakes his head]
LUCY: Take it.
[Billy shakes his head, but his hand is reaching out towards the spliff]
LUCY: Now!
[Billy takes the spliff]
BILLY: If I pass out or something . . .
LUCY: *[turns her head away, rolling her eyes upwards]* I'll run you to the hospital, la la la, whatever. Just take it.
[Billy draws on the spliff, coughs, stands up]
BILLY: Man, that shit's strong!
[General laughter]

(22 November 2005)

There is an unmistakeable playfulness about this moment. It is the end of the lesson, and the teacher allows the students to push boundaries. The focus of the improvisation – the consumption of illegal substances – is not the usual stuff of school learning; Billy and Lucy have grabbed the attention of their audience before they even begin, and they maintain it thereafter. At best, though, this belongs in a box labelled Citizenship, or Personal, Social and Health Education, doesn't it? What does it have to do with Shakespeare?

At the risk of stating the obvious, there is a fair amount of playfulness about *Richard III*, too. By this I mean more than the fact – largely ignored in the examination paper which confronted Billy later in the year – that it is a play, that language is embodied in action, that actors take on roles; I also want to draw attention to Richard's playfulness, to the way in which he adopts roles – the soldier, the lover, the reluctant king, the victim of disability – and presents these roles to us, the audience, demanding that we admire him for his skill as a performer and for the power of his performance, that is, for the power that is both demonstrated in and created through the performance. Like the Cat in the Hat (and the mediaeval Vice), Richard is constantly saying:

Look at me!
Look at me!
Look at me NOW!

It is fun to have fun
But you have to know how.

(Seuss 1957: 18)

Billy and Lucy are having fun, too. What licenses their improvisation is not merely the indulgence of the teacher at the end of the lesson but the fact of the role-play, the fact that they are thus enabled to play with other identities, to experience the power and the pleasure of being someone else. At the same time, they are learning about persuasion. They have understood, too, that the teacher's instruction to 'do it with words' meant simply that physical coercion is not allowed: Lucy's performance is one in which she draws on resources of language but also, simultaneously, on gesture, gaze, posture. What she achieves with language, too, is not merely through the words she chooses but also through tone and inflection. Thus, for example, she crushes Billy's final objection ('If I pass out or something') with the withering, casual superiority of 'I'll run you to the hospital, la la la, whatever.' It seems plausible to me that two months later, when Billy was thinking how to represent in diary form Richard's seduction of Anne, he was able to draw on Lucy's line to help him shape the sneering, searing mockery of 'I love you I feel so sorry for you blah de blah de blah, whatever.'

Test literacy, as George Bush acknowledged, is justified in functional terms. Quite different claims can be made for the literacy practices outlined above – claims that, I think, are central to the justification for English as a school subject. The act of improvisation, like the literary text they are reading, enables students to imagine and inhabit other possible selves, other possible worlds. Billy, Lucy and their peers are exploiting the doubleness of the fictive, of play, where simultaneously things are and are not, to engage in the serious work of cultural making, work that is semiotically rich and ethically important.

But did the improvisation help Billy to read (and understand) *Richard III*? The problem with the question is that it might depend on what one meant by reading, how one thought that understanding might be demonstrated, and what one understood by '*Richard III*'. The testing regime assumes that *Richard III* is, in essence, language-as-print, the words on the page; it treats performance as accidental. Moreover, it assumes that a student's reading (and understanding) can be assessed on the basis of the student's ability to produce a particular kind of written text. The good reader, the one who would be awarded full marks, would produce a piece of writing that looked like this:

> Coherent analysis of how Richard deceives others and hides his plans to become king, eg in the first extract, to make himself appear innocent, almost naïve, he pretends to really believe the king is having Clarence imprisoned because his name is George, and in the second, Richard gives the impression that being king would be a great hardship by using words like 'impose' and 'yoke'. Appreciation of the effects of features of language, eg in the first extract, he is sarcastic when he describes the Queen as 'fair, and not jealous'

as previously he had said the opposite, and in the second, Richard plays with words when he says 'I do suspect I have done some offence', because the audience are fully aware of his real offences, but he knows the mayor isn't and is going to offer him the throne. Comments and precisely selected references to the text integrated into well-developed argument.

(QCA 2006b: 56)

The description of a Band 6 answer certainly looks very different from the exam paper handed in by Billy. And there are – as indicated in this descriptor – things that Billy needs to learn about forms of discursive writing if he is to prosper within the education system, if he is to acquire the capital of qualifications. But to admit that what Billy lacks is skill in producing 'coherent analysis' and 'well-developed argument' is not at all the same as to concede that it is his *reading* that is deficient, nor that he has failed to grasp the *ideas* that are outlined above.

Whereas reading and writing in the examination are resolutely individual and monomodal pursuits, in Monica's classroom texts are explored collectively, over time, in and through an ensemble of multimodal resources. Something of this has already been suggested by the glimpse into the class's involvement in the production of improvised scenarios. Students talked about, analysed and annotated still images derived from a wide range of productions of the play; they watched, discussed and compared two film versions, starring Olivier (1955) and McKellen (1995); they recapped and predicted and argued and questioned; they read the script – and they talked about it. Their experience of reading *Richard III* involved the reading of still and moving images, DVDs and the Cambridge School Shakespeare edition of the play, unrehearsed readings and rehearsed improvisations.

Here they are, a little over a week after the lesson in which they had improvised the role-plays, reading Act 1, Scene 2. Anne's long opening speech is read by Jenny, and then Monica interrupts:

[40:31]
TEACHER: OK, who's she cursing? She's cursing several people – hands up . . . Billy?
BILLY: {Richard
KEMI: {His wife
TEACHER: Yes, why is she cursing him?
BILLY: Because he's the one that killed him her husband.
TEACHER: Right, good, so she starts off by cursing Richard, then who else does she curse?
BILLY: His wife.
TEACHER: She curses his wife and?
BILLY: His family – baby.
TEACHER: His child, yeah, she says that the child's going to be, she cursing the child . . .

BILLY: She says she'll make it be born early, so that it's deformed.

TEACHER: Yeah, she says the mother will take fright when she sees it, so she's cursing Richard and the wife that he's going to marry, which is interesting, because who's he planning to marry?

(1 December 2005)

Billy's eagerness to offer answers to Monica's questions, like his vocal enthusiasm for role-play in the earlier lesson, is entirely characteristic. Other students sometimes make more considered contributions, but Billy can be relied upon to keep the conversation going. Because of this, he has an important effect on the dynamic of the classroom, on the learning that happens in the group. But what should not be overlooked is the evidence that his responses provide for his understanding of the speech that Jenny has just read. There is a pause after Monica's last question; once again, it is Billy who responds, though what he has to say does not at first glance seem to be an answer:

[41:11]

BILLY: Shakespeare, Shakespeare's a good writer, isn't he?

TEACHER: He is good. *[laughs, then pauses]* Tell me why you think that?

BILLY: Because his play's *awesome*.

TEACHER: Awesome. *[pause]* When Anne says, 'If ever he have a wife', why does she put it like that?

BILLY: {Because she might be his wife.

KEMI: {Because he's bare butters.

BILLY: Because he's ugly, ugly {deformity

TEACHER: {So what does she think?

FOYZUR: Nobody's ever going to marry him.

TEACHER: Nobody's ever going to marry him – she curses his wife if he ever has one but he never will because he's so ugly . . . why's that significant in terms of what's about to happen?

KEMI: Because she falls in love with his personality.

TEACHER: Yeah . . .

KEMI: Even though the personality's butters as well.

TEACHER: Yeah.

BILLY: Butters, man.

TEACHER: Excellent, OK.

(1 December 2005)

Billy is, I think, in a fairly self-conscious way, playing the role of the good student here. He offers a scholarly translation of Kemi's description of Richard's appearance – so 'bare butters' is glossed by him first as 'ugly', then as 'deformity'. (Kemi, as I have indicated in earlier chapters, is the class's conspicuous high achiever: her use of urban slang is equally self-conscious, her way of asserting a 'street' identity at the same time as demonstrating her grasp of the play. One can see, too, in this exchange, how Kemi and Billy are both competing for the floor, for the right to speak, at the same time as supporting – and supplementing – each other's reading of the play.) But Billy's appraisal of Shakespeare as a good writer is not just part of his act; it is a touchingly direct, honest – and thoughtful – response to *Richard III*. It is also a deep answer to Monica's question, which, though ostensibly about Richard's intention to marry Anne, is encouraging her students to think about the construction of the scene, to consider how Shakespeare heightens the drama of the confrontation between Anne and Richard.

If we consider Billy's contributions to this lesson in the light of the National Curriculum attainment target for reading, quoted above, we might conclude that Billy 'show[s] understanding of the ways in which meaning and information are conveyed' in the play, and that he can 'articulate personal and critical responses' to it, 'showing awareness of [some of its] thematic, structural and linguistic features' (DfEE 1999c: 5).

The case of Billy poses a problem that is linked to the point raised at the end of the preceding chapter. The dominance of the assessment regime reinforces the assumption that learning, like reading, happens in the individual, the test subject. Is it, then, that Billy is able to achieve these things in the context of the activity, the literacy practices, of the English classroom? Or is it that these things are achieved by the class, in activities to which Billy has contributed? And what would be the consequences for our thinking about assessment if we were able to conceptualise learning as a fully social, distributed activity?

Notes

1 An earlier version of this chapter appeared as Yandell (2008a).
2 The Key Stage 3 tests were abandoned in late 2008, after spectacular mismanagement of the marking of the papers earlier that year (see e.g. http://news.bbc.co.uk/1/hi/education/7669254.stm).
3 This is, of course, the relationship that was explored by Foyzur and his peers in Chapter 9.

Chapter 12

Conclusion

Throughout this book, there has been an insistence on the value of a fully social model of the reading that takes place in the classroom. The description and theorisation of what was accomplished in Monica's and Neville's English lessons provide a challenge to dominant paradigms of reading and of pedagogy. The preceding chapters offer a version of English that does not sit easily with Buckingham and Sefton-Green's binary opposition between attitudes to textual work in English and Media Studies:

> Despite the current emphasis on the 'sense of audience' in English, and despite the growing influence of 'reader response' approaches . . . both the reader and the writer are typically perceived as isolated individuals. Reading and writing are abstracted from the social contexts in which they are performed and placed in a supposedly 'pure' personal space. By contrast, Media Studies goes beyond the individual student's own behaviour and responses to consider the different ways in which specific social audiences use and make sense of texts. If English is concerned with the individual reader's personal response to the individual writer's personal vision, Media Studies is concerned with the *social production of meaning*, both on the part of audiences and on the part of media institutions.
> (Buckingham and Sefton-Green 1994: 134, original emphasis)

In Wharfside, in the lessons that I observed, English was consistently and powerfully concerned with the 'social production of meaning'. This is what we have seen, even – or perhaps especially – in those chapters that have maintained a focus on the contributions of individual students – Foyzur (Chapter 9), Jo and Paul (Chapter 10), and Billy (Chapter 11).

This emphasis on the centrality of the social, on the dialogic and collaborative production and contestation of meaning, poses questions about the model of progression in reading competence as largely a matter of increasing degrees of independence (see Chapter 3). The ways of reading literary texts that I have tried to describe in Chapters 5 to 11 also stand in an uneasy relation to the assumptions about literacy and the reading of literature that are implicated in the regimes of assessment whereby secondary students' reading is measured and credentialised. This tension is the dominant concern in Chapter 11; it is also explored in Chapter 7, where it is manifested in Darren's rejection of the teacher's presentation of *A View from the Bridge*. If Neville's reading is informed by and mindful of the specifications of the examination syllabus, Darren draws on his sense of social class as he begins to articulate a different reading of the text and a different reading position.

The role of play – and students' agency

In Chapter 2, I spent some time examining the different constructions that have been put on Vygotsky's ZPD. I drew attention to Daniels' (2001) suggestion of 'the possibility of a dialectical conception of interaction within the ZPD', which I contrasted with the more limited dyadic version, increasingly associated with a version of 'scaffolding' and hence with teacher-initiated interventions in the learning of individual students. In 'The Problem of Play in Development,' an essay that was included as Chapter 7 of *Mind in Society* (1978), Vygotsky returns to the idea of the ZPD; this time, though, the idea appears in a context that does not seem to have much to do with questions of assessment or instruction. Instead, it appears in a remarkable passage where Vygotsky argues for play as a centrally important contributor to development:

> play creates a zone of proximal development of the child. In play a child always behaves beyond his average age, above his daily behaviour; in play it is as though he were a head taller than himself. As in the focus of a magnifying glass, play contains all developmental tendencies in a condensed form and is itself a major source of development.
>
> (Vygotsky 1978: 102)[1]

Throughout this book, I have been making the case for taking seriously the work that school students do; threaded through this argument, though, particularly in the analysis of the data from classroom observation, is an argument for the productive potential of students' play. I referred in Chapter 1 to my earlier exploration of the value of writing in role, in relation to Hong Hai's reading of *The Merchant of Venice* (Yandell 1997a). The empirical data that have been presented in this book are rich in examples of students making similarly productive use of role-play: the scenarios from *Julius Caesar* described in Chapter 5; the improvisations around *Richard III* that form an important element in the account presented in Chapters 8 and 11; Billy's writing in-role in Chapter 11; and the work that Neville's students did in imagining contexts for 'excuse me' as preparation for their reading of John Agard in Chapter 6.

Monica has a clear rationale for the use of role-play in the classroom – a rationale that suggests that play and pedagogy are much more closely aligned than they might at first sight appear to be:[2]

> Why do I do role-play? Partly I suppose because I think that it helps to access abstract concepts. It gives pupils the opportunity to explore ideas, characters and concepts; to put themselves into a story and make it into something that makes sense to them. It allows them to bring their own world knowledge, their own context to that story whether it is historical or fictional. I think that it is difficult to explain anything without narrative and the role-play lets the pupils bring their own narratives into their learning. It shifts the power from the teacher to the pupil and invites them to work with peers to construct their own interpretations.
>
> The process is as important as the finished piece for in the course of preparing a role-play they are talking, offering ideas, revising, contesting, incorporating, justifying, accepting . . . In presenting they are throwing their interpretation into the ring to be picked up and developed by others sometimes in subsequent presentations, sometimes in class discussion, sometimes in writing. This process of course happens in other collaborative activities, in exploring text or images, but in these activities the teacher usually gives the resources and the talk (and hence the outcome) can be more restricted.
>
> (MB to JY, 8 May 2008)

Empathetic engagement in lives and worlds different from the students' own is seen by Monica as an important part of the work of the classroom. Students are engaging with texts by drawing on their resources of culture and history, the 'funds of knowledge' (Moll 1994, 2000; Gonzalez *et al.* 2005) that they bring with them to the classroom.

This active and collaborative engagement is, simultaneously, serious and playful. Its relationship to the text is highly variable: sometimes, students incorporate lines, present recognisably Shakespearean characters; at other times, the activity will involve the exploration of a scenario, the relationship of which to the play that they are studying only becoming apparent in a subsequent lesson. Such work extends over time, and the effects are often not immediately discernible. Monica's emphasis on process rather than product, and on the unpredictability of the uses to which such interactions will subsequently be put, does not conform to the current fashion for measurable outcomes. Textual meaning is construed as irreducibly intertextual and social, arising out of the readers' experience of other texts, other subjectivities, other histories. Textual appreciation – the aesthetic dimension of the experience of Shakespeare – tends to emerge less from any obvious focus on language or form than, almost tangentially, from the juxtaposition of different versions, different performances, different texts.

Something else has occurred to me as I have reviewed the video footage of Monica's lessons. Even when her students are not engaged in improvisation as a discrete activity, her classroom seems to be an arena of serious play. As students offer interpretations and evaluations of the text, they inhabit ever so slightly exaggerated scholarly roles, not quite parodic yet not quite their everyday selves. In the literature classroom, the play really is (and is not) the thing.

Role-play in Monica's classroom needs to be seen through a Vygotskian lens. The relationship between cognitive development and semiotic activity is a complicated one: work in all semiotic modes, including language, enables the development of thought, gives learners access to resources beyond their immediate experience (Barrs 1987). Over time, signs are remade, filled with increasingly dense, rich meanings. In the process, a dialectical relationship is established between 'scientific' and 'everyday' concepts (Vygotsky 1987; and see Chapter 2 in this volume): the everyday knowledge that students bring with them has the capacity to transform and reorganise the curricularised, canonical knowledge of schooling.

This is central, in my view, to an understanding of the work that is done in these classrooms. When Foyzur or Billy, for example, adopt a self-consciously 'academic' voice or position, as we have seen them doing in the lessons described in Chapters 9 and 11, this is not just playing at being an intellectual; it is (playfully) claiming real expertise. When, in Neville's Year 10 class, Darren challenges the class basis of Alfieri's choric role in *A View from the Bridge* (Chapter 7), this is not some watered-down, encapsulated version of literary criticism: it is a reading that demands to be taken seriously. At the same time, what is being investigated is not simply Miller's text but the students' own class positioning and the social relations of the classroom. There is, in all these moments, a dialectical relationship between disciplinary and everyday knowledge: this dialectic is transformative, both of the participants (this is what learning looks like) and of the subject (this is what English becomes).

The starting-point for this view of reading in the classroom might, broadly speaking, be construed as within a tradition of reader-response theory (as outlined in Chapter 3); but what I am proposing is something more radical, more unsettling. My argument is that interpretive communities (Fish 1980) belong, and are constituted, not merely in the academy but in urban English classrooms. These are places where, as Kress *et al.* have argued, English is re-made, daily. But it is not only 'English teachers [who] actively construct their subject day by day, *differently*, in the settings of the different classrooms' (Kress *et al.* 2005: 117; quoted in Chapter 5); this work is also accomplished, differently, by school students, in dialogue with each other as well as with the teacher and with the texts that they read together. As the preceding chapters have shown, students act as sign-makers, not merely as sign-users (see Chapter 2), in their reading of literary texts.

The value of re-reading

I started by acknowledging that the category of literature was a contentious one. Literature, in this account, is valuable precisely as a site of contestation, a site where new cultures and new meanings are produced. In the account that I offer of the Wharfside students' encounters with *Julius Caesar* and *Richard III*, with *A View from the Bridge* and with twentieth-century poetry, what is salient is not the transmission of a cultural heritage, nor even of a handful of valorised texts, but the work that the students, with their teachers, have done.[3]

What should, I hope, have become clear in the preceding chapters is that the literacy practices of the classrooms I have been observing have much more in common with those of Shirley Brice Heath's Trackton than with those represented by the image of Jane Eyre with which I started. My argument is that the reading of literature that goes on in such classrooms is irreducibly social, collaborative, dialogic, and that these characteristics mean that it stands in tension with the dominant, policy-endorsed paradigm of reading. What I also want to suggest is that the practice that is evident in Monica's and Neville's classrooms is powerfully productive. It is productive of new meanings and of meaningful ways of reading the texts that students engage with; these meanings are produced in history and in culture, by students who draw on extensive repertoires of knowledge and experience, both of the world and of other texts.

Part of my argument, also, is that the forms of pedagogy represented in Monica and Neville's practice are significant – are worth attending to – precisely because of their concern to make space for, and to attend carefully to, the meanings that their students make of the texts that are studied in their classrooms. An anecdote illustrates that these qualities are not universal attributes. Monica remembered a conversation she had had with another teacher who had joined the English Department at Wharfside at the same time as Neville. Monica had been talking about her experiences of reading 'The Lady of Shalott' with the class with whom I observed her, experiences that Monica recalls in Turvey *et al.* (2006). When Monica told of Mutib's reading of an image of the Lady of Shalott as a woman in purdah, her colleague's reaction was, 'But that's wrong – that isn't what the image represents.' Behind this response lies a very different pedagogy, a very different assessment of school students and the work that they do: it is a pedagogy that is more attuned to the discourse of cultural transmission than to a view of school students as culturally active, as meaning-makers.

This anecdote notwithstanding, my argument is not that such productivity only happens in classrooms where the teacher is responsive to the meanings that students make. Not at all. As I sit in classrooms observing my student teachers, I never fail to be struck by school students' capacity to make sense of things (and texts) in their own terms, to bring their funds of knowledge to bear. The difference is not whether this activity goes on or not; it is the extent to which it becomes incorporated into a shared script, a collaborative making of meaning. So I would want to suggest that these forms of activity are present in all classrooms, and are worth attending to.

This leads into a methodological point. In Chapters 5–11, the readings of data, the data of classroom observation and of school students' work in different modes and media, are my readings, my interpretations of particular moments, particular interactions. The selection of these moments is not, of course, arbitrary: it reflects my interests. And I am conscious that there were many other moments, in these and other lessons that I observed and filmed, equally worthy of analysis, equally revelatory of students' engagement. The claim that I am making, therefore, is that the moments on which I have focused attention are representative of what went on in the classrooms where Neville and Monica taught. The analyses of these moments that I have offered are readings, situated in history and culture – in *my* history and culture: they are a product of my positioning as a teacher and a teacher educator and of my experience of working in inner London schools over the past three decades. Like all readings, they are motivated, reflecting my interests and my beliefs. To recognise this, however, is not to suggest that these readings have interest or validity only for me. My argument is that close and interested observation is necessary if we are to gain a sense of what is going on in literature classrooms: it is an argument for attending to the significance (the sign-making) of the everyday, to borrow the contested term from Gavin and Martin in Neville's Year 10 class. It is an attempt to take seriously, in the context of contemporary urban classrooms, the ordinariness of culture (Williams 1958) and the cultural productivity of ordinary school students.

This reading – my reading – is, like the students' reading of the texts that they share, both intertextual and recursive. It is informed by my readings of other classrooms, other students, as much as it is by my reading of other texts – of theory (Vološinov, Bakhtin, Vygotsky and so on) and of literature (including those texts that the students read). Such reading tends to be recursive, to involve a process of re-reading. In Chapter 4, my disagreement with Doecke *et al.* (2007) was, *inter alia*, an argument for the value of re-reading, and hence for the benefits of digital video data. But equally formative, for me, has been the re-reading of theory and of literature, where each re-reading is the production of a different text, produced in different circumstances by a 'me' who is not quite the same as earlier versions: Vygotsky, just as much as *A View from the Bridge*, carries different meanings for me now than when I started haunting the classrooms in Wharfside (and I am not the same I that I was then).

My argument, therefore, is an argument about how literature is read, or can be read, in secondary urban English classrooms. It is an argument for forms of pedagogy that allow room for playing with texts and with identities. It is an argument for taking seriously the learning that happens in such contexts and such activities. And it is an argument for ways of reading, and re-reading, classrooms and the work that is done in them, an argument for reading that remains attentive to the specificity and complexity, to the magnificent ordinariness of classrooms in which culture is continually being remade.

Notes

1 Vygotsky is addressing the development of much younger (pre-school) children here, but what he has to say about the role of play seems to me to be applicable to the students at Wharfside.

2 An earlier version of the following discussion of Monica's use of role-play appeared in Turvey and Yandell (2011: 164–165).

3 The fact that the majority of the lessons that I observed in Wharfside were devoted to the exploration of plays was, to some extent, an accident of timing. Had I been able to observe at different moments during the school year, I would have seen Monica's Year 9 class reading *Stone Cold* (Swindells 1997) or Neville's Year 10 class reading *Of Mice and Men* (Steinbeck [1937] 2000). But the prominence of Shakespeare in my data is also a fairly accurate reflection of the prominence of Shakespeare in the secondary English curriculum. In any case, I would want to suggest that my argument about how literature is read in these classrooms is not dependent on the characteristics of particular literary genres.

Bibliography

Aarsleff, H. (1982) *From Locke to Saussure: essays on the study of language and intellectual history*. Minneapolis, MN: University of Minnesota Press.

Aarsleff, H. (1983/1967) *The Study of Language in England, 1780–1860*. Minneapolis, MN: University of Minnesota Press.

Anderson, H. C. (2005) *King: A Comic Biography of Martin Luther King Jnr*. Seattle, WA: Fantagraphic Books

Anderson, P. M. and Summerfield, J. P. (2004) Why is urban education different from suburban and rural education? In Steinberg, S. R. and Kincheloe, J. L. (eds) *19 Urban Questions*. New York: Peter Lang, pp. 29–39.

Apple, M. W. (1996) *Cultural Politics and Education*. Buckingham: Open University Press.

Apple, M. W. (2001) Markets, standards, teaching, and teacher education, *Journal of Teacher Education*, 52(3): 182–196.

Apple, M. W. (2004) *Ideology and Curriculum* (3rd edn, original work published 1978). New York: RoutledgeFalmer.

AQA (Assessment and Qualifications Alliance) (2002) *Anthology (GCSE English/ English Literature, Specification A)*. Oxford: AQA/Oxford University Press.

AQA (2005a) *General Certificate of Secondary Education: English Literature 2007, Specification A*. Manchester: AQA.

AQA (2005b) *General Certificate of Secondary Education, English 3702/3712, Specification A: Examiners' Report, 2005 examination – June series*. Manchester: AQA.

Ashton, P. and Simons, M. (eds) (1979) *Our Lives: young people's autobiographies*. London: ILEA English Centre.

Bakhtin, M. M. ([1975] 1981) *The Dialogic Imagination* (trans. C. Emerson and M. Holquist). Austin, TX: University of Texas Press.

Bakhtin, M. M. and Medvedev, P. N. ([1928] 1991) *The Formal Method in Literary Scholarship: a critical introduction to sociological poetics* (trans. A. J. Wehrle). London: Johns Hopkins University Press.

Bakhurst, D. (1990) Social memory in Soviet thought. In Middleton, D. and Edwards, D. (eds) *Collective Remembering*. London: Sage, pp. 203–226.

Bakhurst, D. (1991) *Consciousness and Revolution in Soviet Philosophy: from the Bolsheviks to Evald Ilyenkov*. Cambridge: Cambridge University Press.

Barber, M. (1996) *The Learning Game: arguments for an education revolution*. London: Gollancz.

Barker, A. (2003) Bottom: a case study comparing teaching low ability and mixed ability Year 9 English classes, *English in Education*, 37(1): 4–14.

Baron, N. S. (2000) *Alphabet to Email: how written English evolved and where it's heading*. London: Routledge.

Barrs, M. (1987) Voice and role in reading and writing, *Language Arts*, 64: 207–218.

Barthes, R. ([1973] 1990). *S/Z*. Oxford: Blackwell.

Barton, D. and Hamilton, M. (1998) *Local LIteracies: reading and writing in one community*. London: Routledge.

Barton, D., Hamilton, M. and Ivanic, R. (eds) (2000) *Situated Literacies: reading and writing in context*. London: Routledge.

Baynham, M. (1995) *Literacy Practices: investigating literacy in social contexts*. Harlow: Longman.

Beard, R. (1998) *National Literacy Strategy: review of research and other related evidence*. London: DfEE.

Bewick, T. ([1797] 1847) *A History of British Birds*, vol. I. Newcastle, Blackwell. Available at: www.google.co.uk/books?id=PjUtAAAAYAAJ, accessed 22 April 2012.

Board of Studies, New South Wales (2007) *English K-6 Syllabus*. Available at: http://k6.boardofstudies.nsw.edu.au/files/english/k6_english_syl.pdf, accessed 11 April 2012.

Boston, K. (2007) Speech at the launch of the new National Curriculum. Available at: http://www.qca.org.uk/qca_12423.aspx, accessed 1 September 2007.

Bottoms, J. (2000) Familiar Shakespeare. In Bearne, E. and Watson, V. (eds) *Where Texts and Children Meet*. London: Routledge, pp. 11–25.

Bourdieu, P. and Passeron, J.-C. (1977) *Reproduction in Education, Society and Culture* (trans. R. Nice). London: Sage.

Boyarin, D. (1993) Placing reading: ancient Israel and medieval Europe. In Boyarin, J. (ed.) *The Ethnography of Reading*. Berkeley, CA: University of California Press, pp. 10–37.

Boyarin, J. (ed.) (1993) *The Ethnography of Reading*. Berkeley, CA: University of California Press.

Boyne, J. (2006) *The Boy in the Striped Pyjamas*. Oxford: David Fickling Books.

Brady, M. (1989) Whose history? *Socialist Teacher*, 42: 11.

Brandist, C. (2002) *The Bakhtin Circle: philosophy, culture and politics*. London: Pluto Press.

Brice Heath, S. (1983) *Ways with Words: language, life and work in communities and classrooms*. Cambridge: Cambridge University Press.

Brice Heath, S. (1996) *Ways with Words: language, life and work in communities and classrooms* (2nd edn). Cambridge: Cambridge University Press

Britton, J. (1987) Vygotsky's contribution to pedagogical theory, *English in Education*, 21(3): 22–26.

Brontë, C. ([1847] 1948) *Jane Eyre*. London: Blackie & Son.

Brown, A., and Dowling, P. (1998) *Doing Research/Reading Research: a mode of interrogation for education*. London: RoutledgeFalmer.

Bruner, J. (1975) The ontogenesis of speech acts, *Journal of Child Language*, 2(1): 1–19.

Buckingham, D. and Sefton-Green, J. (1994) *Cultural Studies Goes to School: reading and teaching popular media*. London: Taylor & Francis.

Burgess, T. (1984) Diverse melodies: a first-year class in a secondary school. In Miller, J. (ed.) *Eccentric Propositions: essays on literature and the curriculum*. London: Routledge & Kegan Paul, pp. 56–69.

Burgess, T. (1988) On difference: cultural and linguistic diversity and english teaching. In Lightfoot, M. and Martin, N. (eds) *The Word for Teaching is Learning: essays for James Britton*. London: Heinemann, pp. 155–168.

Burgess, T. and Hardcastle, J. (1991) A tale of three learners: the cultural dimension of classroom language learning. In Gordon, P. (ed.) *Teaching the Humanities*. London: Woburn Press, pp. 36–49.

Butler, M. (1984) *Theatre and Crisis, 1632–1642*. Cambridge: Cambridge University Press.

Clandinin, D. J. and Connelly, F. M. (2000) *Narrative Inquiry: experience and story in qualitative research*. San Francisco: Jossey-Bass.

Cloud, R. R. M. (1991) 'The very names of the Persons': editing and the invention of dramatick character. In Kastan, D. S. and Stallybrass, P. (eds) *Staging the Renaissance: reinterpretations of Elizabethan and Jacobean drama*. New York: Routledge, pp. 88–96.

Cole, M. and Scribner, S. (1974) *Culture and Thought: a psychological introduction*. New York: John Wiley & Sons.

Coles, J. (2003) Alas, poor Shakespeare: teaching and testing at Key Stage 3, *English in Education*, 37(3): 3–12.

Coles, J. (2004) Much ado about nationhood and culture: Shakespeare and the search for an 'English' identity, *Changing English*, 11(1): 47–58.

Collins, J. and Blot, R. K. (2003) *Literacy and Literacies: texts, power and identity*. Cambridge: Cambridge University Press.

de Condillac, E. B. ([1998] 2001) *Essay on the Origin of Human Knowledge* (trans. H. Aarsleff). Cambridge: Cambridge University Press.

Cope, B. and Kalantzis, M. (eds) (2000) *Multiliteracies: Literacy Learning and the Design of Social Futures*. London: Routledge.

Coupland, J. and Gwyn, R. (2003) Introduction. In Coupland, J. and Gwyn, R. (eds) *Discourse, the Body, and Identity*. London: Palgrave Macmillan, pp. 1–16.

Daniels. H. (ed.) (1996) *An Introduction to* Vygotsky. London: Routledge.

Daniels, H. (2001) *Vygotsky and Pedagogy*. New York: RoutledgeFalmer.

Darling-Hammond, L. (2004) Standards, accountability, and school reform, *Teachers College Record*, 106(6): 1047–1085.

Darnton, R. ([1991] 2001) History of reading. In Burke, P. (ed.) *New Perspectives on Historical Writing*. Cambridge: Polity, pp. 157–186.

Davies, T. (1982) Common sense and critical practice: teaching literature. In Widdowson, P. (ed.) *Re-Reading English*. London: Methuen, pp. 32–43.

Denscombe, M. (1998) *The Good Research Guide for Small-scale Social Research Projects*. Buckingham: Open University Press.

DES (Department of Education and Science) (1975) *A Language for Life* (The Bullock Report). London: HMSO.

DES (1984) *Curriculum Matters*. London: HMSO.

DES (1987) *The National Curriculum 5–16: a consultation document*. London: HMSO.

DES/Welsh Office (1990) *English in the National Curriculum*. London: HMSO.

DfE (Department for Education)/Welsh Office (1995) *English in the National Curriculum*. London: HMSO.

DfE (2011) *The National Curriculum: English*. London, DfE. Available at: www. education.gov.uk/schools/teachingandlearning/curriculum/primary/b00198874/ english/, accessed 11 April 2012.

DfEE (Department for Education and Employment) (1999a) *The National Curriculum: handbook for secondary teachers in England*. London: DfEE.

DfEE (1999b) *The National Curriculum: handbook for primary teachers in England*. London: DfEE.

DfEE (1999c) *The National Curriculum: attainment targets*. London: DfEE.

DfEE (2001a) *Key Stage 3 National Strategy: English department training*. London: DfEE.

DfEE (2001b) *Key Stage 3 National Strategy: framework for teaching English – Years 7, 8 and 9: management summary*. London: DfEE.

DfEE (2001c) *Key Stage 3 National Strategy: literacy across the curriculum*. London: DfEE.

DfEE (2001d) *Key Stage 3 National Strategy: literacy progress unit: writing organisation*. London: DfEE.

Doecke, B., Green, B., Kostogris, A., Reid, J.-A. and Sawyer, W. (2007) Knowing practice in English teaching? Research challenges in representing the professional practice of English teachers, *English Teaching: Practice and Critique*, 6(3): 4–12.

Dyson, A. H. (1997) *Writing Superheroes: contemporary childhood, popular culture, and classroom literacy*. New York: Teachers College Press.

Dyson, A. H. (2003) *The Brothers and Sisters Learn to Write: popular literacies in childhood and school cultures*. New York: Teachers College Press.

Eagleton, T. (1996) *Literary Theory: an Introduction*. Oxford: Blackwell.

Eagleton, T. (2003) *After Theory*. London: Penguin.

Early, M. and Ericson, B. O. (1988) The act of reading. In Nelms, B. F. (ed.) *Literature in the Classroom: readers, texts and contexts*. New York: NCTE, pp. 31–44.

Edelsky, C. (1996) *With Justice and Literacy for All: rethinking the social in language and education*. London: Taylor & Francis.

Eisenstein, E. L. (1983) *The Printing Revolution in Early Modern Europe*. Cambridge: Cambridge University Press.

Engeström, Y. (1996) *Non scolae sed vitae discimus*: towards overcoming the encapsulation of school learning. In Daniels, H. (ed.) *An Introduction to Vygotsky*. London: Routledge, pp. 151–170.

Fish, S. (1967) *Surprised by Sin: the reader in Paradise Lost*. Basingstoke: Macmillan.

Fish, S. (1972) *Self-consuming Artifacts: the experience of seventeenth-century literature*. Berkeley, CA: University of California Press.

Fish, S. (1980) *Is There a Text in This Class? The authority of interpretive communities*. Cambridge, MA: Harvard University Press.

Fish, S. (1995) *Professional Correctness: literary studies and political change*. Oxford: Clarendon.

Fox, C. (2007) History, war and politics: taking 'comix' seriously. In Ellis, V. *et al.* (eds) *Rethinking English in Schools: towards a new and constructive stage*. London: Continuum, pp. 88–101.

Flower, L. (1994) *The Construction of Negotiated Meaning: a social cognitive theory of writing*. Carbondale and Edwardsville, IL: Southern Illinois University Press.

Forster, E. M. ([1927] 1962) *Aspects of the Novel*. Harmondsworth: Penguin.

Franks, A. (1996) Drama education, the body and representation (or, the mystery of the missing bodies), *Research in Drama Education,* 1(1): 105–119.

Franks, A. (2003) Palmers' kiss: Shakespeare, school drama and semiotics. In Jewitt, C. and Kress, G. (eds) *Multimodal Literacy.* New York: Peter Lang, pp. 155–172.

Franks, A. and Jewitt, C. (2001) The meaning of action in learning and teaching, *British Educational Research Journal,* 27(2): 201–218.

Freedman, S. W. (1995) Crossing the bridge to practice: rethinking the theories of Vygotsky and Bakhtin, *Written Communication,* 12: 74–92.

Freire, P. (1972) *Pedagogy of the Oppressed.* Harmondsworth: Penguin.

Freire, P. and Macedo, D. (1987) *Literacy: reading the word and the world.* London: Routledge & Kegan Paul.

Fuller, A., Hodkinson, H., Hodkinson, P. and Unwin, L. (2005) Learning as peripheral participation in communities of practice: a reassessment of key concepts in workplace learning, *British Educational Research Journal,* 31: 49–68.

Gallego, M. A. and Hollingsworth, S. (2000) Introduction: the idea of multiple literacies. In Gallego, M. A. and Hollingsworth, S. (eds) *What Counts as Literacy: challenging the school standard.* New York: Teachers College Press, pp. 1–23.

Gee, J. P. (2003) *What Video Games Have to Teach Us About Learning and Literacy.* New York: Palgrave Macmillan.

Gee, J. P. (2004) *Situated Language and Learning: a critique of traditional schooling.* New York: Routledge.

Gee, J. P., Hull, G. and Lankshear, C. (1996) *The New Work Order: behind the language of the new capitalism.* St Leonards, NSW: Allen & Unwin.

Geertz, C. (1973) *The Interpretation of Cultures: selected essays.* New York: Basic Books.

Gillan, A. (2000) Life for farmer who shot burglar. *The Guardian,* 20 April.

Gillen, J. (2000) Versions of Vygotsky, *British Journal of Educational Studies,* 48(2): 183–198.

Gonzalez, N., Moll, L. C. and Amanti, C. (eds) (2005) *Funds of Knowledge: theorizing practices in households, communities, and classrooms.* Mahwah, NJ: Lawrence Erlbaum.

Goodwin, C. (2001) Practices of seeing visual analysis: an ethnomethodological approach. In van Leeuwen, T. and Jewitt, C. (eds) *Handbook of Visual Analysis.* London: Sage, pp. 157–182.

Goody, J. (1987) *The Interface between the Written and the Oral.* Cambridge: Cambridge University Press.

Goody, J. (2000) *The Power of the Written Tradition.* Washington: Smithsonian Institute.

Gove, M. (2010) All children will learn our island story, available at: www.conservatives.com/News/Speeches/2010/10/Michael_Gove_All_pupils_will_learn_our_island_story.aspx accessed 11 October 2010.

Graff, H. J. (1979) *The Literacy Myth: literacy and social structure in the nineteenth-century city.* New York: Academic Press.

Gregory, E. (1996) *Making Sense of a New World: learning to read in a second language.* London: Paul Chapman.

Gregory, E. (2004) 'Invisible' teachers of literacy: collusion between siblings and teachers in creating classroom cultures, *Literacy,* 97–105.

Gregory, E. and Williams, A. (2000a) *City Literacies: learning to read across generations and cultures.* London: Routledge.

Gregory, E. and Williams, A. (2000b) Work or play? 'Unofficial' literacies in the lives of two East London communities. In Martin-Jones, M. and Jones, K. (eds) *Multilingual Literacies*. Amsterdam: John Benjamins, pp. 37–54.

Greig, D. (2000) Making sense of the world: language and learning in Geography. In Lewis, M. and Wray, D. (eds) *Literacy in the Secondary School*. London: David Fulton, pp. 69–90.

Gruber, H. E. and Voneche, J. J. (eds) (1977) *The Essential Piaget*. London: Routledge & Kegan Paul, pp. 65–88.

Gurr, A. (1987) *Playgoing in Shakespeare's London*. Cambridge: Cambridge University Press.

Gutierrez, K., Rimes, B. and Larson, J. (1995) Script, counterscript, and underlife in the classroom: James Brown versus Brown v. Board of Education, *Harvard Educational Review*, 65: 445–471.

Halliday, M. A. K. (1978) *Language as Social Semiotic: the social interpretation of language and meaning*. London: Edward Arnold.

Hammersley, M. and Atkinson, P. (1983), *Ethnography: principles in practice*. London: Tavistock.

Hardcastle, J. (2009) Vygotsky's enlightenment precursors, *Educational Review*, 61(2): 181–195.

Harris, R. (2006) *Integrationist Notes and Papers, 2003–2005*. Threshers Crediton: Tree Tongue.

Harrison, C. (2002) *The National Strategy for English at Key Stage 3: roots and research*. London: DfES.

Hasan, R. (2005) *Language, Society, Consciousness*. London: Equinox.

Hatcher, R. and Jones, K. (eds) (1996) *Education After the Conservatives: the response to the new agenda of reform*. Stoke-on-Trent: Trentham.

Hazlitt, W. (1825) *The Spirit of the Age*, available at: http://en.wikisource.org/wiki/The_Spirit_of_the_Age/, accessed 12 April 2012.

Heider, K. (1976) *Ethnographic Film*. Austin, TX: University of Texas Press.

Heinemann, M. (1980) *Puritanism and Theatre: Thomas Middleton and opposition drama under the early Stuarts*. Cambridge: Cambridge University Press.

Higgins, J. (1999) *Raymond Williams: literature, Marxism and cultural materialism*. Abingdon: Routledge.

Hill, J. (2004) What is urban education in an age of standardization and scripted learning? In Steinberg, S. R. and Kincheloe, J. L. (eds) *19 Urban Questions*. New York: Peter Lang, pp. 119–126.

Hobson, P. (2002) *The Cradle of Thought: exploring the origins of thinking*. London: Macmillan.

Hobson, R. P., Chidambi, G., Lee, A. and Meyer, J. (2006) *Foundations for Self-awareness: an exploration through autism*. Boston, MA: Blackwell.

Hodge, R. and Kress, G. (1988) *Social Semiotics*. Ithaca, NY: Cornell University Press.

Holquist, M. (2002) *Dialogism*. London: Routledge.

Howe, N. (1993) The cultural construction of reading in Anglo-Saxon England. In Boyarin, J. (ed.) *The Ethnography of Reading*. Berkeley, CA: University of California Press, pp. 58–79.

Ilyenkov, E. V. ([1960] 2008) *The Dialectics of the Abstract and the Concrete in Marx's Capital* (trans. S. Syrovatkin). Delhi: Aakar.

Iser, W. (1978) *The Act of Reading: a theory of aesthetic response.* Baltimore, MD: Johns Hopkins University Press.

Jackson, B. and Marsden, D. (1966) *Education and the Working Class.* London: Penguin.

Jauss, H. R. (1982) *Towards an Aesthetic of Reception* (trans. T. Bahti). Minneapolis, MN: University of Minnesota Press.

Jewitt, C. and Kress, G. (2003) A multimodal approach to research in education. In Goodman, S. *et al.* (eds) *Language, Literacy and Education: a reader.* Stoke-on-Trent: Trentham/Open University, pp. 277–292.

Johns, A. (1998) *The Nature of the Book: print and knowledge in the making.* Chicago: University of Chicago Press.

Jones, K. (1989) *Right Turn: the conservative revolution in education.* London: Hutchinson.

Jones, K. (2003) *Education in Britain: 1944 to the present.* Cambridge: Polity.

Jones, S. (2004) Shaping identities: the reading of young bilinguals, *Literacy*, 38(1): 40–45.

Kellogg, D. (2009) Classic book review: [V.N. Volosinov, 1929/1973, *Marxism and the Philosophy of Language* and L.S. Vygotsky, 1934/1987, *Thinking and Speech*], *International Journal of Applied Linguistics*, 19(1): 84–96.

Kelly, C., Gregory, E. and Williams, A. (2001) Home to school and school to home: syncretised literacies in linguistic minority communities, *Language, Culture and Curriculum*, 14(1): 9–25.

Kemmis, S. (2005) Knowing practice: searching for saliences, *Pedagogy, Culture and Society*, 13(3): 391–426.

Kendon, A. (2000) Language and gesture: unity or duality? In McNeill, D. (ed.) *Language and Gesture.* Cambridge: Cambridge University Press, pp. 47–63.

Kozulin, A. (1998) *Psychological Tools: a sociocultural approach to education.* Cambridge, MA: Harvard University Press.

Kozulin, A., Gindis, B., Ageyev, V. S. and Miller, S. M. (eds) (2003) *Vygotsky's Educational Theory in Cultural Context.* Cambridge: Cambridge University Press.

Kress, G. (1997) *Before Writing: rethinking the paths to literacy.* London: Routledge.

Kress, G. (2001) You've just got to learn how to see: curriculum subjects, young people and schooled engagement with the world, *Linguistics and Education*, 11(4): 401–415.

Kress, G. (2003) *Literacy in the New Media Age.* London: Routledge.

Kress, G. (2010) *Multimodality: a social semiotic approach to contemporary communication.* London: Routledge.

Kress, G. and Jewitt, C. (2003) Introduction. In Jewitt, C. and Kress, G. (eds) *Multimodal Literacy.* New York: Peter Lang, pp. 1–18.

Kress, G. and van Leeuwen, T. (1996) *Reading Images: the grammar of visual design.* London: Routledge.

Kress, G. and Van Leeuwen, T. (2001) *Multimodal Discourse: the modes and media of contemporary communication.* London: Arnold.

Kress, G., Jewitt, C., Ogborn, J. and Tsatsarelis, C. (2001) *Multimodal Teaching and Learning: the rhetorics of the science classroom.* London: Continuum.

Kress, G., Jewitt, C., Bourne, J., Franks, A., Hardcastle, J., Jones, K. and Reid, E. (2005) *English in Urban Classrooms: a multimodal perspective on teaching and learning.* London: RoutledgeFalmer.

Kristeva, J. (1980) *Desire in Language: a semiotic approach to literature and art* (trans. T. Gora, A. Jardine and L. S. Roudiez). New York: Columbia University Press.

Laird, E. and Nimr, S. (2003) *A Little Piece of Ground*. London: Macmillan.

Lave, J., and Wenger, E. (1991) *Situated Learning: legitimate peripheral participation*. Cambridge: Cambridge University Press.

Lawton, D. and Chitty, C. (eds) (1988) *The National Curriculum*. London: Institute of Education.

LeBaron, C. and Streeck, J. (2000) Gestures, knowledge, and the world. In McNeill, D. (ed.) *Language and Gesture*. Cambridge: Cambridge University Press, pp. 118–138.

Lecercle, J.-J. (2005) *A Marxist Philosophy of Language* (trans. G. Elliott). Chicago: Haymarket.

Lee, C. D. (2001) Is October Brown Chinese? A cultural modeling activity system for underachieving students, *American Educational Research Journal*, 38(1): 97–141.

Lee, H. (1960) *To Kill a Mockingbird*. London: Heinemann.

Levin, R. (1979) *New Readings vs. Old Plays: recent trends in the reinterpretation of English Renaissance drama*. Chicago: University of Chicago Press.

Li, G. (2008) *Culturally Contested Literacies: America's 'rainbow underclass' and urban schools*. London: Routledge.

Locke, J. ([1690] 2004) *An Essay Concerning Human Understanding*. Harmondsworth: Penguin.

Lomax, H. and Casey, N. (1998) Recording social life: reflexivity and video methodology, *Sociological Research Online*, 3(2), available at: www.socresonline. org.uk/socresonline/3/2/1.html, accessed 26 July 2006.

Loncraine, R. (dir.) (1995) *Richard III*. DVD. USA/UK: Pathé.

Lunenberg, M., Ponte, P. and Van De Ven, P.-H. (2007) Why shouldn't teachers and teacher educators conduct research on their own practices? An epistemological exploration, *European Educational Research Journal*, 6(1): 13–24.

Marx, K. ([1867] 1976) *Capital: a critique of political economy* (vol. 1) (trans. B. Fowkes). Harmondsworth: Penguin.

Marx, K. (1973) *Economic and Philosophical Manuscripts of 1844* (trans. M. Milligan). London: Lawrence & Wishart

Marx, K., and Engels, F. (1970) *The German Ideology* (ed. C. J. Arthur). London: Lawrence & Wishart.

Massachusetts Department of Education (2001) *Massachusetts English Language Arts Curriculum Framework*, available at: www.doe.mass.edu/frameworks/ela/0601. doc, accessed 11 April 2012.

Miller, A. ([1955] 1995) *A View from the Bridge*. London: Heinemann.

Miller, A. ([1987] 1990) *Timebends: a life*. London: Mandarin.

Miller, J. (1983) *Many Voices: bilingualism, culture, and education*. London: Routledge & Kegan Paul.

Miller, J. (1995) Trick or treat? The autobiography of the question, *English Quarterly*, 27 (3): 22–26.

Miller, S. M. (2003) How literature discussion shapes thinking: ZPDs for teaching/learning habits of the heart and mind. In Kozulin, A. *et al.* (eds) *Vygotsky's Educational Theory in Cultural Context*. Cambridge: Cambridge University Press, pp. 289–316.

Milton, J. ([1674] 1971) *Paradise Lost*. London: Longman.

Ministry of Education (1994) *English in the New Zealand Curriculum*, available at: www.minedu.govt.nz/~/media/MinEdu/Files/EducationSectors/Schools/EnglishInTheNewZealandCurriculum.pdf, accessed 11 April 2012.

Ministry of Education, Singapore (2001) *English Language Syllabus*, available at: www.moe.gov.sg/education/syllabuses/languages-and-literature/files/english-primary-secondary.pdf, accessed 11 April 2012.

Moger, R. and Richmond, J. (eds) (1985) *Say What You Think: argument and discussion writing by London school students*. London: ILEA English Centre.

Moll, L. C. (1994) Mediating knowledge between homes and classrooms. In Keller-Cohen, D. (ed.) *Literacy: interdisciplinary conversations*. Cresskill, NJ: Hampton Press, pp 385–410.

Moll, L. C. (2000) Inspired by Vygotsky: ethnographic experiments in education. In Lee, C. D. and Smagorinsky, P. (eds) *Vygotskian Perspectives on Literacy Research*. Cambridge: Cambridge University Press, pp. 256–268.

Moll, L. C. and Whitmore, K. F. (1993) Vygotsky in classroom practice: moving from individual transmission to social transaction. In Forman, E. A. *et al.* (eds) *Contexts for Learning: sociocultural dynamics in children's development*. New York: Oxford University Press, pp. 19–42.

Moore, A. (1999) *Teaching Multicultured Students: culturism and anti-culturism in school classrooms*. London: Falmer.

Moss, G. (2007) *Literacy and Gender: researching texts, contexts and readers*. London: Routledge.

Moss, G., Jewitt, C., Levačić, R., Armstrong, V., Cardini, A. and Castle, F. (2007) *The Interactive Whiteboards, Pedagogy and Pupil Performance Evaluation: an evaluation of the schools whiteboard expansion (SWE) project, London challenge*. London: DfES.

Naidoo, B. (1985) *Journey to Jo'burg: a South African Story*. London: Longman.

NCC (National Curriculum Council) (1990) *Non-statutory Guidance: English*. York: NCC.

NEAB (Northern Examinations and Assessment Board) (1996) *Anthology (GCSE English/English Literature)*. Oxford: NEAB/Heinemann Educational.

NEAB/AQA (1998) *Anthology (GCSE English/English Literature)*. Oxford: AQA/Heinemann Educational.

Nelms, B. F. (1988) Sewing the dragon's teeth: an introduction in the first person. In Nelms, B. F. (ed.) *Literature in the Classroom: readers, texts and contexts*. Urbana, IL: National Council of Teachers of English, pp 1–16.

Nystrand, M. *et al.* (2003) Questions in time: investigating the structure and dynamics of unfolding classroom discourse, *Discourse Processes*, 35(2): 135–198.

Obied, V. (2007) 'Why did I do nothing?' Poetry and the experiences of bilingual pupils in a mainstream inner-city secondary school, *English in Education*, 41(3): 37–52.

Olivier, L. (dir.) (1955) *Richard III*. DVD. UK: Wienerworld.

Olson, D. R. (1994) *The World on Paper: the conceptual and cognitive implications of writing and reading*. Cambridge: Cambridge University Press.

Ong, W. J. (1982) *Orality and Literacy*. London: Methuen.

Pallister, D. and Jones, S. (2005) Mother stabbed on walk with young son: teacher may be paralysed after daytime attack in quiet village. *The Guardian*, 22 April.

Plaskow, M. (2004) The process curriculum. In Benn, M. and Chitty, C. (eds) *A Tribute to Caroline Benn: education and democracy.* London: Continuum, pp. 111–118.

Porter, R. (2000) *Enlightenment: Britain and the creation of the modern world.* London: Allen Lane.

Prinsloo, M. and Breier, M. (eds) (1996) *The Social Uses of Literacy: theory and practice in contemporary South Africa.* Bertsham: SACHED Books and John Benjamins.

QCA (Qualifications and Curriculum Authority) (2006a) *Key Stage 3 English test: Shakespeare paper: Richard III.* London: QCA.

QCA (2006b) *Key Stage 3 English Test: mark scheme – reading.* London: QCA.

QCDA (Qualifications and Curriculum Development Authority) (2008) *National Curriculum*, available at: http://curriculum.qcda.gov.uk/key-stages-3-and-4/subjects/key-stage-4/english/programme-of-study/index.aspx?tab=1, accessed 6 January 2010.

Reid, I. (2004) *Wordsworth and the Formation of English Studies.* Aldershot: Ashgate.

Reid, V. S. (1967) *Young Warriors.* Harlow: Longman.

Resnick, L. B. (2000) Literacy in school and out. In Gallego, M. A. and Hollingsworth, S. (eds) *What Counts as Literacy: challenging the school standard.* New York: Teachers College Press, pp. 27–41.

Rey, F. G. (2011) A re-examination of defining moments in Vygotsky's work and their implications for his continuing legacy, *Mind, Culture and Activity,* 18: 257–275.

Richards, I. A. (1929) *Practical Criticism: a study of literary judgment.* London: Routledge & Kegan Paul.

Richardson, E. (2003) *African American Literacies.* London: Routledge.

Richter, H. P. ([1961] 1971) *Friedrich.* London: Heinemann.

Robson, C. (2002) *Real World Research.* Oxford: Blackwell.

Rogoff, B., Turkanis, C. G. and Bartlett, L. (2001) *Learning Together: children and adults in a school community.* Oxford: Oxford University Press.

Rogoff, B. (2003) *The Cultural Nature of Human Development.* Oxford: Oxford University Press.

Rosenblatt, L. M. ([1938] 1995) *Literature as Exploration.* New York: The Modern Language Association of America.

Rosenblatt, L. M. (1978) *The Reader, the Text, the Poem: the transactional theory of the literary work.* Carbondale, IL: Southern Illinois University Press.

Said, E. W. (1978) *Orientalism.* New York: Pantheon.

Said, E. W. (1983) *Culture and Imperialism.* London: Chatto & Windus.

Sanchez-Jankowski, M. (2002) Representation, responsibility and reliability in participant-observation. In May, T. (ed.) *Qualitative Research in Action.* London: Sage, pp. 144–160.

Saussure, F. de ([1915] 1986) *Course in General Linguistics* (trans. R. Harris). Chicago: Open Court.

Searle, C. (ed.) (1971) *Stepney Words.* London: Reality Press (reprinted 1973 by Centerprise Press).

Searle, D. (1984) Scaffolding: who's building whose building? *Language Arts,* 61: 480–483.

Service, R. (1979) *More Collected Verse.* London: Ernest Benn.

Seuss, Dr (1957) *The Cat in the Hat.* New York: Random House.

Shakespeare, W. (1981) *King Richard III* (ed. A. Hammond) (Arden edition). London: Methuen.

Shakespeare, W. (2000) *King Richard III* (ed. P. Baldwin and T. Baldwin) (Cambidge School Shakespeare edition). Cambridge: Cambridge University Press.

Sharpe, K. (2000) *Reading Revolutions: the politics of reading in early modern England.* New Haven, CT: Yale University Press.

Shepherd, S. (1991) Acting against bardom: some utopian thoughts on workshops. In Aers, L. and Wheale, N. (eds) *Shakespeare in the Changing Curriculum.* London: Routedge.

Simons, M., Raleigh, M. and Ashton, P. (eds) (1982) *City Lines: poems by London school students.* London: ILEA English Centre.

Solsken, J. W. (1993) *Literacy, Gender and Work in Families and in School.* Norwood, NJ: Ablex.

Spiegelman, A. ([1987] 1992) *Maus: A Survivor's Tale* (2 vols) London: Penguin.

Spivak, G. C. (1988) Can the subaltern speak? In Nelson, C. and Grossberg, L. (eds) *Marxism and the Interpretation of Culture.* Urbana, IL: University of Illinois Press, pp. 271–313.

Stalin, J. V. (1954) *Marxism and Problems of Linguistics.* Unknown: Wildside Press.

Steinbeck, J. ([1937] 2000) *Of Mice and Men.* Harlow: Longman.

Stock, B. (1983) *The Implications of Literacy: written language and models of interpretation in the eleventh and twelfth centuries.* Princeton, NJ: Princeton University Press.

Stock, B. (1990) *Listening for the Text: on the uses of the past.* Philadelphia, PA: Pennsylvania University Press.

Stone, C. A. (1998) The metaphor of scaffolding: its utility for the field of learning disabilities, *Journal of Learning Disabilities,* 31: 344–366.

Street, B. (1984) *Literacy in Theory and Practice.* Cambridge: Cambridge University Press.

Street, B. (1995) *Social Literacies: critical approaches to literacy in development, ethnography and education.* London: Longman.

Street, B. (ed.) (2001) *Literacy and Development: ethnographic perspectives.* London: Routledge.

Street, B. (2009) Multiple literacies and multi-literacies. In Beard, R., Myhill, D., Riley, J. and Nystrand, M. (eds) *The Sage Handbook of Writing Development.* Los Angeles: Sage, pp. 137–150.

Street, B., Lefstein, A. and Pahl, K. (2007) The National Literacy Strategy in England: contradictions of control and creativity. In Larson, J. (ed.) *Literacy as Snake Oil: beyond the quick fix* (2nd edn). New York: Peter Lang, pp. 123–154.

Swindells, R. E. (1997) *Stone Cold.* Oxford: Heinemann.

Szwed, J. F. (1981) The ethnography of literacy. In Whiteman, M. F. (ed.) *Writing: the nature, development and teaching of written communication.* Mahwah, NJ Lawrence Erlbaum, pp. 13–23.

Todorov, T. (1984) *Mikhail Bakhtin: the dialogical principle.* Minneapolis, MN: University of Minnesota Press.

Tolman, C. W. (1999) Society versus context in individual development: does theory make a difference? In Engeström, Y. *et al.* (eds) *Perspectives on Activity Theory.* New York: Cambridge University Press, pp. 70–86.

Tomasello, M. (1999) *The Cultural Origins of Human Cognition.* Cambridge, MA: Harvard University Press.

Turvey, A., Brady, M., Carpenter, A. and Yandell, J. (2006) The many voices of the English classroom, *English in Education,* 40(1): 51–63.

Turvey, A. and Yandell, J. (2011) Difference in the classroom: whose reading counts? In van de Ven, P.-H. and Doecke, B. (eds) *Literary Praxis: a conversational inquiry into the teaching of literature*. Rotterdam: Sense.

Uglow, J. (2006) *Nature's Engraver: a life of Thomas Bewick*. London: Faber & Faber.

van de Ven, P.-H. and Doecke, B. (eds) (2011) *Literary Praxis: a conversational inquiry into the teaching of literature*. Rotterdam: Sense.

van der Veer, R. and Valsiner, J. (1991) *Understanding Vygotsky: a quest for synthesis*. Oxford: Blackwell.

van der Veer, R. and Valsiner, J. (eds) (1994) *The Vygotsky Reader*. Oxford: Blackwell.

van Leeuwen, T. and Jewitt, C. (eds) (2001) *Handbook of Visual Analysis*. London: Sage.

Vološinov, V. N. ([1927] 1976) *Freudianism: a critical sketch (Freudianism: A Marxist critique)* (trans. I.R. Titunik). Bloomington, IN: Indiana University Press.

Vološinov, V. N. ([1929] 1986) *Marxism and the Philosophy of Language* (trans. L. Matejka and I. R. Titunik). Cambridge, MA: Harvard University Press.

Vygotsky, L. S. (1962) *Thought and Language* (trans. E. Haufmann and G. Vakar). Cambridge, MA: Massachusetts Insitute of Technology Press.

Vygotsky, L. S. (1978) *Mind in Society: the development of higher psychological processes* (ed. M. Cole). Cambridge, MA: Harvard University Press.

Vygotsky, L. S. (1987) *Problems of General Psychology, including the Volume Thinking and Speech* (trans. N. Minick). New York: Plenum.

Vygotsky, L. S. (1994) Imagination and creativity of the adolescent. In van der Veer, R. and Valsiner, J. (eds) *The Vygotsky Reader*. Oxford: Blackwell, pp. 266–288.

Vygotsky, L. S. (2004) Imagination and creativity in childhood, *Journal of Russian and East European Psychology*, 42(1), 7–97.

Watt, I. ([1957] 1979) *The Rise of the Novel: studies in Defoe, Richardson and Fielding*. London: Chatto & Windus.

Wegerif, R. (2008) Dialogic or dialectic? The significance of ontological assumptions in research on educational dialogue, *British Educational Research Journal*, 34(3): 347–361.

Weis, L. and Fine, M. (2004) *Working Method: research and social justice*. New York: Routedge.

Wells, G. (1999) *Dialogic Inquiry: towards a sociocultural practice and theory of education*. Cambridge: Cambridge University Press.

Wells, G. (2000) Dialogic inquiry in education: building on the legacy of Vygotsky. In Lee, C. D. and Smagorinsky, P. (eds) *Vygotskian Perspectives on Literacy Research*. Cambridge: Cambridge University Press, pp. 51–85.

Wenger, E. (1998) *Communities of Practice*. Cambridge: Cambridge University Press.

Wertsch, J. V., Tulviste, P. and Hagstrom, F. (1993) A sociocultural approach to agency. In Forman, E. A. *et al.* (eds) *Contexts for Learning: sociocultural dynamics in children's development*. New York: Oxford University Press, pp. 336–356.

Williams, R. (1958) Culture is ordinary. In Mackenzie, N. (ed.) *Conviction*. London: MacGibbon & Kee, pp. 74–92.

Williams, R. ([1961] 1965) *The Long Revolution*. Harmondsworth: Penguin.

Williams, R. (1973) *The Country and the City*. London: Chatto & Windus.

Williams, R. (1977) *Marxism and Literature*. Oxford: Oxford University Press.

Wood, D., Bruner, J. S. and Ross, G. (1976) The role of tutoring in problem solving, *Journal of Child Psychology and Psychiatry*, 17: 89–100.

Woolf, V. (1925) *The Common Reader*. Harmondsworth: Penguin.

Wordsworth, W. and Coleridge, S. T. (1800) *Lyrical Ballads with Other Poems* (2nd edn). London: publisher unknown.

Wray, D. and Lewis, M. (1997) *Extending Literacy: children reading and writing non-fiction*. London: Routledge.

Wray, D. and Lewis, M. (2000) Extending literacy: learning and teaching. In Lewis, M. and Wray, D. (eds) *Literacy in the Secondary School.* London: David Fulton, pp. 15–28.

Yandell, J. (1994) Really useless knowledge, *Changing English*, 2(1): 2–15.

Yandell, J. (1995) Ways into the secret garden. *Guardian*, 12 September.

Yandell, J. (1997a) 'Sir Oracle': *The Merchant of Venice* in the classroom, *Changing English*, 4(1): 105–122.

Yandell, J. (1997b) Reading Shakespeare, or ways with Will, *Changing English*, 4(2): 277–294.

Yandell, J. (1999) White coats and two dogs a week: teachers and research, *Education and Social Justice*, 1(3): 38–43.

Yandell, J. (2000) Measure for measure, or inspecting the inspectors, *Changing English*, 7(2): 119–128.

Yandell, J. (2001) What's in a name, or electric cars for all, *Changing English*, 8(2): 145–154.

Yandell, J. (2005) Turning others' leaves: snapshots of literacy in London classrooms, *Changing English*, 12(2): 219–226.

Yandell, J. (2006) Class readers: exploring a different view from the bridge, *Changing English*, 13(3): 319–334.

Yandell, J. (2007) Investigating literacy practices within the secondary English classroom, or where is the text in this class? *Cambridge Journal of Education*, 37(2): 249–262.

Yandell, J. (2008a) Mind the gap: investigating test literacy and classroom literacy, *English in Education*, 42(1): 70–87.

Yandell, J. (2008b) Exploring multicultural literature: the text, the classroom and the world outside, *Changing English*, 15(1): 25–40.

Yandell, J. (2008c) Embodied readings: exploring the multimodal social semiotic resources of the English classroom, *English Teaching: Practice and Critique*, 7(1): 36–56.

Yandell, J. (2010) 'New Labour, old school tie': what is education for? *Changing English*, 17(2): 113–127.

Yandell, J. (2011) Reading in a secondary English classroom: agency, interest and multimodal design, *Visual Communication*, 10(1): 1–14.

Yin, R. K. (2003) *Case Study Research: design and methods* (3rd edn). Thousand Oaks, CA: Sage.

Young, M. F. D. (2008) *Bringing Knowledge Back In: from social constructivism to social realism in the sociology of education*. London: Routledge.

Index